ON THE EDGE OF INFINITY

Clemens Cavallin

On the Edge of Infinity

A Biography of Michael D. O'Brien

IGNATIUS PRESS   SAN FRANCISCO

Cover photograph: Anton R. Casta

Cover design by John Herreid

© 2017 by Justin Press, Inc., Ottawa, Ontario.
This edition published by agreement with Justin Press, Inc., Canada
All rights reserved
ISBN 978-1-62164-260-2
Library of Congress Control Number 2018949820
Printed in the United States of America ∞

Super muros tuos Hierusalem constitui custodes
tota die et tota nocte perpetuo non tacebunt.
(Upon your walls, O Jerusalem, I have set watchmen;
all the day and all the night they shall never be silent.)

—Isaiah 62:6

CONTENTS

PROLOGUE

In the Beginning

I retrieved my luggage from the carousel and rolled the bag with its small, squeaking plastic wheels into the arrivals hall of Ottawa International Airport. Jetlagged, but relieved to have passed immigration, I saw my host, the artist and novelist Michael O'Brien—a rather tall, lean man in his sixties with silvery, curling hair—standing at the exit. In his right hand, he held a little, red wooden horse from Dalarna, Sweden: it was a tribute to my home country, but also the agreed sign of recognition. After introduction and greetings, he smilingly beckoned me with a deep voice to follow him to his car, or not quite his car, but a vehicle belonging to one of his children.

Driving away from the airport, we entered almost instantaneously into a vigorous conversation on topics close to both our hearts; the flow of dialogue drifted from religion to art and modern society, and then back to religion again. The car was slightly unreliable as a vital part of the automatic gear—a small, red ball—kept falling down on the floor, making it impossible to put in the reverse gear; three times during the trip we had to search for the little thing that rolled away unnoticed. On a visit two years later, I think I saw the same vehicle in a rather terminal condition parked outside his house.

We had a whole weekend to ourselves in the silent, almost lonely house, as his wife was away visiting one of their children. Outside the boundary of the garden, a seemingly limitless Canadian forest began, interrupted here and there by clear lakes. The weather was of the chilly November type before the arrival of snow. Warmed by the roaring fire in the living room, we spoke about literature, his life story, God, the calling of a Christian artist, and so on. The discourse was more structured when I recorded it and stuck to the questions that I had sent to him in advance regarding his novel writing. But it was obvious to me that this was more than merely collecting

13

information for writing a piece of pure, disinterested scholarship—I felt included in a grace-filled moment of friendship, in a personal conversation on the Church, sacred art, and Catholicism.

This turn from my initial intention of focusing on a literary analysis of Michael O'Brien's novels, toward his personality and life story, became stronger the next time I arrived in Canada for fieldwork in 2013. Then I interviewed him in his studio, surrounded by his colourful paintings and energized by a mixture of intense heat emanating from the small iron stove and fresh crisp air let in through an open window. I also met his wife, Sheila, for the first time and some of their children and grandchildren.

During one of our interview sessions, he told me that his Canadian publisher had urged him to write his autobiography, but that he felt reluctant to do so—indeed, he had declined. Through the interviews, I had at that point collected a significant amount of material on his life, which I deemed to be important in itself, so to focus on his life story seemed like a natural development of my project. Therefore, during this second round of interviews, we agreed that I could expand my original study into a biography. In that sense, this is an authorized biography, and I have enjoyed full support and vital encouragement from him during the whole work process.

As Michael O'Brien is very much alive, assiduously writing and painting, it is not possible to summarize his life as a whole, analyzing events with the clear eye of hindsight. Every year that he continues to work, his life expands and changes, and with it the meaning of individual events, even those of his childhood. Instead, the aim of this biography is to give the essentials of his life story and to present succinctly the major themes of his writing and painting. One can say it is an introduction to Michael O'Brien's life and art, not the definitive work on it.

The Mystery of Life

To write a life story is in many ways a demanding task. Despite the extensive amount of work in collecting the material, organizing it, and, finally, the actual process of writing, a life is always more than what has been captured. So much has to remain untold, and one can always ask: Has the story and the analysis, really, managed to dive beneath the surface of a unique human personality? In his biography of the painter William Kurelek, Michael O'Brien admonishes those tempted to embark on such a project:

> A great mystery lies at the heart of every life. Biography, as it approaches the mystery in search of understanding, should go carefully and reverently. At best, it can offer intuitions, flashes of insight. The writer is, after all, describing a geography of the soul, an entire universe, equipped only with the crude instruments that come to hand.
> Biography fails when the researcher, blithely unaware of his own prejudices, sets forth in pursuit of knowledge of his subject.[1]

The task of the biographer is here made both difficult and humbling. For to what extent can we become aware of our prejudices? And, even when seeing them, how can we understand a life without them?

I have tried to go carefully about my task, but I have no illusion of having captured the totality of a life or fathomed the depth of a man's soul. This book is the story of a life seen through a particular temperament—mine. The mystery remains. Even Jesus needed four biographers, despite providing them with divine inspiration. Accordingly, this account is written from the perspective of a Swedish religious studies scholar sharing with Michael O'Brien a Catholic background, the experience of working with both writing and painting, having six children (both of us have three boys and three girls), and a weakness for things Croatian.

Material

I have used many different types of material in writing Michael O'Brien's life story. One important backbone is the interviews with him and Sheila that I have recorded from 2011 to 2016—mostly in Combermere and Barry's Bay, Canada. In addition, we met one time at a Christian festival in Krk, Croatia. We have also used Skype on some occasions and have had continuous contact through email.

Moreover, I have done interviews and had email correspondence with Michael and Sheila's six children and with a number of

Michael's friends and co-workers, such as the translators of his books and his publishers.

Another important source that I have consulted extensively is his handwritten diary stretching from 1970 until the first decade of the twenty-first century. It chronicles predominately his interior thoughts and spiritual experiences, but contains, as well, important information on major events and decisions.

As Michael O'Brien made his personal archive available to me, I have been able to consult his unpublished texts, collected newspaper clippings, and family photos. In the archive is also the typewritten story of his paternal grandfather's experiences during the First World War, a tape recording of his father the year he died, and two recordings of Michael and his family in the 1980s.

I have had access to some of his correspondence, of which I would like to mention especially the correspondence with Professor Peter Kreeft from 1998 onward, which Kreeft graciously agreed that I could access and use.

Michael O'Brien's website StudiOBrien.com contains essays, information on published books, and a collection of his paintings. To access earlier incarnations of the website, I used the site Internet Archive Wayback Machine (archive.org/web), which scans and saves the content of websites.

On the Internet, I found, unsurprisingly, an abundance of material, such as video recordings of interviews with him on YouTube, reviews of his books in different languages, and so on. Especially, I would like to mention the Amazon and Goodreads websites that provide reader responses and ratings of published books.

The True Story

My personal meetings with Michael O'Brien have been crucial for writing this biography. To a great extent, the writing process has been a reflection on our first meeting and its continuation during the past five years. This means that the story is different from a pure reconstruction of a life through long hours spent in an archive. In the latter case, biography is like necromancy; the dead, great man is made to live again. When writing about Michael O'Brien's childhood, adolescence, and struggles through middle age, I, of course, had to reconstruct something no longer with us. At the same time, as the writing moved chronologically closer to our first meeting, the reconstruction and the living presence began to coalesce, like a picture coming into focus. The story, therefore, at least temporarily, ends where this project began, in the personal meeting, and experience of a life being lived—with the end not decided yet.

A critique could be made that this personal connection has led me to abstain from revealing the "true" story. In his book *How to Do Biography*, Nigel Hamilton writes:

> The search for the truth behind the mask, then, is the challenge that faces every biographer in today's post-Freudian age—the X-ray machine through which you must slowly pass your subject's profile, before you can make your own work into a work of true art.[2]

Though I have not used a Freudian X-ray machine on Michael O'Brien, I have endeavoured to the utmost of my capacity to be truthful in handling the material at my disposal, with all the limitations that are inevitably connected to such work. He has been extremely generous with letting me access all his material without any filtering on his part—I think that this act proceeded from his distaste for flattery and his desire for spiritual purity and poverty. Nevertheless, he was somewhat taken aback when he realized what an impression the emotional roller coaster depicted in his diary made in a more condensed format. To some extent this is because he had chosen mainly to use his diaries—notebooks stretching across forty-five years—to reflect on his struggles and to remember intense religious experiences, while numerous joyful and mundane day-to-day events went unrecorded. Even so, it is difficult to come to terms with one's own personality, as we all know.

My main concern has been in relation to Michael O'Brien's wife and children, who have not chosen to be public persons. I have tried to tread carefully, and I appreciate that Sheila agreed to share so much of her own life story, though publicity is the last thing she desires. I am very grateful for her cooperation, as Michael's life without Sheila would have been merely half the story. As regards their children, in the biography they mostly figure in their youth, and less as they grow up. This is a conscious choice; they will have to decide how to tell their own stories, at a time when they are ready to do so.

The Larger Story

Another question is what kind of biography this is. Michael O'Brien is a man of many talents. Is it a literary biography, a biography of an artist, or of a Catholic intellectual, or even the life story of a modern type of prophet? As you will see, it is none and all of these at the same time. The foundation of his creativity is his intense, mystical relation to God. His spirituality, family life, art, and imagination do not constitute different spheres; they spring from and rely on the same source. This biography is, thus, not merely an attempt to link the literary works of an author to his life, to see how they interconnect and explain each other; and the same applies to his art. Probably the best categorization is to call this a religious biography.

The larger story is that of the new roles opened up for Catholic laypeople by the Second Vatican Council, and the intense difficulties encountered when they were to be realized in the Western world. The infrastructure of the preconciliar Church was gone or in a state of decay; new structures had to be built, but now in a social climate where the Christian message seemingly had lost its relevance for most individuals and the nation. The Western societies were, at an accelerating pace, developing according to secular and liberal values, putting emphasis on personal autonomy and material satisfaction. And all of this was sustained and animated by an increasingly powerful entertainment industry.

This is more particularly a Canadian story of how during the pontificate of John Paul II, in the 1980s and 1990s, a new lay "orthodox" Catholic subculture was built and how it solidified into institutions.

The smaller story is that of a person struggling with his inadequacies, failures, and lack of material resources and recognition, facing temptations to despair and hopelessness, while, at the same time, having deep human relations and spiritual experiences of overwhelming peace and joy, channelled into a flood of creative work.

The combined story is about how this personal struggle and creativity went from the local to the Canadian and North American scene to the global level in the twenty-first century. In a sense, the creations of Michael O'Brien now live their own lives, in many different languages and cultures.

I hope that after reading this biography you will see the works of Michael O'Brien in a new light, but also that you will gain some fresh perspectives on the post–Vatican II Catholic Church, the situation for Christian sacred art, and the courage and persistence that a sincere religious life demands in late modern times.

Acknowledgments

I must here express my gratitude to STINT (the Swedish Foundation for International Cooperation in Research and Higher Education), which made it possible for me to spend a semester at Haverford College in 2013, where I could begin writing the biography.

Also, my alma mater, the University of Gothenburg, and more specifically the Department of Literature, History of Ideas, and Religion, deserves to be mentioned, as it provided me with a research sabbatical during the fall of 2015.

Furthermore, I would like to express a special note of thanks to Our Lady Seat of Wisdom College (formerly Our Lady Seat of Wisdom Academy) in Barry's Bay, Ontario, and its president, Dr. Keith Cassidy, and his wife, Elizabeth, for their hospitality and support.

To all the members of the O'Brien family who contributed to the work by letting me interview them, I want to express my sincere gratitude. Foremost of them, of course, is Sheila O'Brien, whose cooking sustained me during my weeks in Combermere and Barry's Bay, and whose secret brew, though an acquired taste, cures any cold. Then, the siblings of Michael—Terry and Patti—and the six children of Sheila and Michael; this is also partly their story.

Moreover, I am grateful to the friends of Michael O'Brien who provided me with vital information and perspectives: Dr. David Beresford, whose wonderful story about pigs in sneakers I will never forget; Professor Peter Kreeft for giving me access to his letters; Posie McPhee for her help with telling the story of the Nazareth Retreat Centre; also Leonardo Defilippis; Carine Rabier-Poutous; Edoardo Rialti; Mate Krajina; Father Robert Wild; Father Joseph Hattie;

Professor Mark Miravalle; Tony Časta; Gregory Bourassa; Father Joseph Fessio; John-Henry Westen; and, finally, Dr. John and Barbara Gay.

Then, of course, I must thank Michael, for his generosity toward a Swedish scholar whom he did not know, and for in no way restricting my work. If there were indulgences connected to works of biography, Michael O'Brien most definitely would have received a complete one.

Lastly, my wife and parents deserve a special recognition for patiently reading drafts and ever-new versions of the chapters with a sharp judgment that definitely helped improve their quality and readability.

Nevertheless, I am, of course, responsible for whatever errors and infelicitous passages remain.

1. Dire Straits

The Recession

In 1959, a year after the O'Brien family had returned to Ottawa from their two-year stay in Los Angeles, their situation was precarious. Due to the ongoing recession, the father of the family, David, then thirty-four years old, had to take any odd job that he could find: he had been a taxi driver, but also vended washing machines, vacuum cleaners, and encyclopaedias.[1] His wife, Elaine, of the same age as her husband, was a nurse and worked part-time whenever she could be hired for a few hours at the hospital, but was mostly unemployed.[2]

They had sold more or less all their belongings, even the camera, an expensive 35 mm, a parting that was tough for David, as he found great joy in photography and had his own little dark room where he developed black-and-white negatives and photos. Also, Elaine's sewing machine had to be given up, which made it hard for her to repair the clothes of the four children, besides Michael, then eleven years old, Terrence (Terry) ten, Patricia (Patti) nine, and Daniel (Dan) seven years old—as buying new clothes was of course at this point even more difficult.

It was a stressful situation for David, and he became more and more discouraged, going from one odd job to another. During some periods, Michael recalls that the family ate a lot of porridge, even to the point of three meals a day—while, according to Patti, pasta was the staple food.

During that year, David hardly ever smiled or laughed, turning inward more than usual. He was not a practising Christian, but had, according to Michael, a marked moral character characterized by a strong sense of justice and fair play, combined with a particularly wry and whimsical sense of humour. His present downcast appearance was thus all the more ominous for the children.

21

Wars

During the Second World War, when he was eighteen years old, David enlisted in the Royal Canadian Air Force and served as a bomber pilot, patrolling the Canadian coast, searching for German submarines. His experience of war was mostly connected to the flying of airplanes—something that he clearly loved.[3] In his photo albums from this period, almost all of the black-and-white photos are of planes, and some are of his pilot comrades. The thought that struck me, as I glanced through the albums, was that David and his fellow pilots looked so young: only boys. I could not help thinking of my own two boys who are of the same age; how unprepared for war they are.

David's father, Stephen O'Brien, of Irish descent, enlisted at an even earlier age. He was only fourteen years old (and thus had to lie about his age) when he joined the Canadian forces in 1915 to fight an abhorrent and brutal war in France: the First World War. He even forged a letter from his mother consenting to his enlistment. In contrast to David, Stephen had to endure the full gamut and force of industrial warfare. As a result, he had to live with shrapnel and pain in his body for the rest of his life and developed alcoholism and a morphine addiction. In Stephen O'Brien, one can sense the capacity for doing great things—he was wounded, captured, and put into various German prisoner camps, escaping with some ingenuity three times—but also a recklessness, a seeking out of danger, like a moth attracted to the light.[4]

True to form, Stephen eloped in 1919 with Hilda Brown, the beautiful daughter of a wealthy Ottawa architect of English origin. She was seventeen years old at the time, and they were married secretly in a civil marriage. Her parents were Anglicans, who, not surprisingly, were horrified that she had run away and married an impoverished lower-class boy; but worst of all in their eyes was the fact that he was Catholic and Irish. She was not reconciled to her family until years afterwards, when one of her brothers arranged a meeting with their parents. The turning point had been the birth of David in 1925, when Hilda's mother considered it was time to bring about a reconciliation.

During the Second World War, David's parents separated after twenty-six years of marriage. According to Hilda, Stephen had never wanted a child and had said when she became pregnant, "That child is going to be trouble." Her interpretation, as told to her son, was that he wanted her for himself. The final straw was when Stephen came home one night drunk, and in a rage accused her of being unfaithful. Afterwards, Hilda described to David how his father had tried to strangle her. Stephen went to jail for domestic violence, but probably only for a few weeks.

Wearing his pilot uniform, David went to visit Stephen in jail. As he came up to his father's cell, he told him with stern determination, "I'm going to kill you when you get out." Fortunately, he did not put his words into action. But from that day, David and Hilda shut out Stephen from their lives, and they portrayed him to Michael and his siblings as a thoroughly bad man, prone to drinking and gambling. This seems to have been at least part of the truth, but Michael wondered later in life what Stephen's version of the story had been—whether he and his siblings had been deprived of a part of their history.

David was baptized and attended Catholic parish schools and high school before the war; but the faith life in the home was minimal, and he never practised the Catholic faith after childhood. However, Terry told me that in 1968, when he had asked his father about his views on religion, David had answered with a question: "Have you ever wondered why I never went to a church?" Terry, somewhat surprised, replied, "No"; and David continued, "Because in the Bible, it says you should honour your father, and I could not do that. If I went to church, I would be a hypocrite." Terry then asked if he believed in what the Catholic Church taught, to which David replied, "Yes." Terry had a hard time to believe it and asked, "All of it?" and David answered again, "Yes." David thus had a religious ethos, evidenced in his sense of justice, and even beliefs, but no religious practice.[5]

Family and Planes

David and Elaine met and got to know each other as they were part of a group of young people living and working in downtown Ottawa after the war. They married in 1947, and, as David remained with the air force, their first home was on an air force base in Centralia,

Ontario. Michael was born a year later; followed by Terry and Patti, who were only a year and a half apart; and, finally, two years later, Daniel saw the light of day, in 1952.

In 1953, a year after their fourth child had been born, David began to work for civil aviation companies, and the family moved to Ottawa. He flew old World War II bombers equipped with cameras over parts of North and South America, making high-altitude survey photomaps for various governments. Being a so-called bush pilot, he often had to land and take off in wild regions, usually in dangerous conditions, on hastily built gravel runways or on rivers and lakes, using skis in winter and pontoons in summer.

In 1956, the O'Brien family was preparing to move to Los Angeles, California, as David was to fly in South America. In this way, the family could be together, they thought; nevertheless, David would be away during his flying missions. Before leaving for California, Michael recalls that Elaine took the children to visit her mother, Jane. At that time, she was living in the Brockville Psychiatric Hospital. She was Irish, like David's father, Stephen, and like him, she had succumbed to the "Irish sickness"—that is, alcoholism. Addiction together with depression led to separation from her husband, Roland, and, eventually, to the stay at the asylum. As Jane sank deeper into her sickness, Elaine was sent to the Hochelaga convent school in Montreal, to be raised and taught by the Sisters of the Holy Names of Jesus and Mary. Elaine was then only six years old.

At the time of the visit to his grandmother, Michael was eight years old. He remembers that Jane gave him a pen, which he treasured, and that she was "a quiet person who said little, and was very kind to us children, but we did not really know her".[6] This was the last time they saw her, as she died that same year, when they were in California.

Living in the United States had its advantages as Elaine and the children were now closer to David, but the itinerant life with no stable place on earth was becoming hard for her. According to Michael, she had a reflective, gentle spirituality, which helped her through these long separations, sometimes lasting months, but it was still a demanding situation.

In 1958, they therefore returned to Ottawa with the intention of settling down, but also so that David could be more at home, as the long absences had become too burdensome for the family. He was looking for another kind of job that did not require so much travel. However, the return to Ottawa did not turn out as they had expected. Due to the recession, David had very little success in finding work. At that time, they lived in the house of David's mother, Hilda, who after a few months moved out. Still, the house was too small for a family of six persons.

An Unexpected Turn of Events

At Christmas 1959, there was no money for presents in the O'Brien family, so they made gifts for each other. Despite this lack of material abundance, Michael and his siblings remember it as their happiest Christmas. This ideal of simplicity has continued to be a strong theme in his life. Perhaps it would have been otherwise if David then had secured an office job in Ottawa. But another turn of events uprooted the family and provided the children with a new home, far away from urban life.

Toward the end of 1960, David got a job with the federal government in Coppermine (now named Kugluktuk), a small village in the Canadian Arctic. In this way, the family escaped poverty, and something new and exciting opened up; the settled middle-class life in Ottawa had to be postponed. They had moved south to sunny California, then back to Ottawa, and now they moved to the cold, far North. Within a period of a few years, the children had gained a very broad North American horizon. In a sense, the move to the Arctic was the logical conclusion of an itinerant life: a temporary home at the last outpost of civilization on the shore of the immense and ice-cold Arctic Ocean—a place truly on the edge of infinity.

2. The Arctic

Coppermine

In January 1961, the O'Brien family travelled all the way to Yellow-knife, the capital of the Northwest Territories, almost five thousand kilometres from Ottawa. To proceed farther north with their few suitcases and some boxes to their final destination, they had to board the Otter, a single-engine propeller plane on skis. As they flew, they could see spreading out beneath them nothing but a white, endless, flat expanse of Arctic snow.

After several hours, when they at last came to the coastline of the Arctic Ocean, they looked down upon their new home, Coppermine, which consisted of a few dozen buildings, shacks, and igloos. As they landed on the sea ice in front of the village, and the plane slowly skied toward the shore, about a hundred Inuit people in traditional parkas and mukluks (fur boots) came to greet them, smiling broadly and chatting happily.

The welcome party led them to their new home, a small government residence built upon stilts that prevented the heat of the building from melting the permafrost, and making their new home tilt and sink. It was heated by an oil burner with fuel shipped during the summer, when the ocean was clear of ice for two months. Their water for drinking and cooking (and washing) came from melting ice blocks, which were cut from a nearby river and put in a big metal barrel inside the house. The ice melted slowly, so they had to be careful about how they used water during the winter months.

At that time, the population of Coppermine was about two hundred Inuit people, most of them living in very primitive dwellings, and about twenty white people who lived in small houses without plumbing and with only minimal electricity from a village generator. There was no television, no radio, and only antique hand-crank telephones between the houses of the white people. The main communication with the outer world, besides Morse code radio, was the Otter that arrived every two weeks from the south, landing on skis or pontoons, bringing mail and some supplies.

The whites were the government presence in that region of the Arctic: David, a police officer, a government meteorological station staff, a nurse, and the Hudson Bay Company outpost manager, who sold some canned food and traded for the furs the native people trapped. There were also a Catholic missionary priest and a tiny church (with room for about twenty people), and an Anglican minister and church (with room for maybe forty), and a school with two teachers (grades one to eight).

The closest village was also Inuit and hundreds of kilometres away. David O'Brien was the "Area Administrator", dealing with government affairs for a vast region of thousands of square kilometres containing fewer than a thousand people. Looking back fifty years later, Michael described his attitude toward his father as one of admiration. He considered him a hero, as did his siblings. "He was, first and foremost, a pilot, which was an exotic and brave thing. He never bragged about himself. He was tall (six feet, three inches) and strong and very handsome. He had much courage in defending truth and dealing with difficult people. He had authority without harshness. He loved puns and witty sayings, and made ironic jokes—never unkind, always thoughtful whimsical humour."[1]

After the former rootlessness, the O'Brien family found a home here, on the shore of the Arctic Ocean, where they lived until 1964. It was a brief period, but it created a deep sense of belonging. Michael and Terry describe it as a happy and dramatic period in their lives, creating strong impressions. This is not surprising as they went north during the end of their childhood and the beginning of their teenage years, when openness to the fantastic and adventurous combines with a growing understanding.[2]

The Inuit and their humble life provided Michael with insights into an alternate civilization to Western modernity. He left the world of North American city life of the late 1950s and stepped into an entirely different culture. As the Inuit children spoke little English, and, even after some time, Michael spoke little or nothing of their language, he learned to communicate in a language that was not dependent upon spoken vocabulary.[3]

The barren, but beautiful, Arctic nature, the warm communication of the heart with the Inuit, and their well-developed art and storytelling free from the distractions of modern life formed Michael in a profound way. Since the time in the Arctic, he has felt a longing for a materially scaled-down life, which at the same time is full of humanity and art flowing naturally from the closeness to nature. And he has never been able to reconcile himself with high-paced technological city life.

Residential School

After their first summer in Coppermine, the experience of a beautiful, unbounded, new world was shattered when Michael and Terry were sent to a residential school in Inuvik, a newly created administrative centre, located a three-hour flight west of Coppermine. This experience of leaving home, just after finding one, became an acute source of alienation and dislocation for Michael. He was only thirteen years old at the time, and during ten months of the year, the children did not see their parents: they were allowed to return home for only two months during the summer. Since there was no telephone service to Coppermine, the sole line of communication for the two older brothers O'Brien was letter writing, and that was hampered by a sporadic mail service. The letters were also read and censored by the supervisor at school, making it difficult to send a cry for help if that included any criticism of the situation, and especially of the supervisor himself. When Michael once tried to do so, he was angrily ordered to rewrite the letter.

During the first year, Michael and Terry were lodged at Grollier Hall, a hostel for Catholic students. Michael was staying on the first floor with the senior boys, and was the only nonnative child, while Terry was on the second floor with the junior boys. The Anglicans and those from other Protestant denominations stayed in another hostel.[4] The brothers almost never saw each other and were only permitted contact during the afternoon of Christmas Day. This unhappy situation was aggravated by one dormitory supervisor, Martin Houston, who used his position of power over the senior boys to institute a regime of terror and sexual abuse.[5]

From the outside, it was difficult to grasp the destructive nature of the situation, because the boys appeared disciplined, if somewhat subdued. Michael recalls that Houston could be charming during inspections and fawning toward the bishop, who came for yearly inspections. The supervisor also followed the outer rituals of religion, and he could even be kind to the boys who formed part of his inner circle.

In this, the central mechanism of all oppressive regimes was manifest—the combination of violent persecution of those who dare to oppose authority, with favours lavished on those who are willing to be complicit in the abuse. It is a very effective means of governing and especially suited for those with no scruples who are driven by a violent desire for power and unrestrained lust. For Michael, this totalitarian mechanism, which leaves no part of the personality untouched, and where the human person is reduced to a mere function, later became a central topic of his fiction and essays.

Despite having argued with his mother before departure about the purpose of praying the Rosary and going to Mass, during the cruel regime of the supervisor, Michael felt an interior, mysterious urge to attend daily Mass. He rose every morning at six o'clock, while the other boys were soundly asleep, and walked to the chapel where he usually was the only one present in the pews. He also began to feel a desire to pray the Rosary, despite having denounced it as utterly boring and useless to his crying mother in Coppermine.

The "privileged" circle of senior boys met in the supervisor's room after the lights-out each night; the other boys could not even imagine what was happening. Michael says he never suspected the sexual nature of these rendezvous, which was later revealed when the boys testified in court the following year.

In the middle of one night, Michael was awakened by the favourite boy of the supervisor, who commanded him, "Get up! Mr. Houston *wants* you!" To his own astonishment, Michael answered firmly, in what he recalls as a state of inner peace, "No." Even to himself, this no was something of a surprise. Since he had refused to join the nocturnal party, the anger and malice of the supervisor was directed toward Michael the next day. The other boys were explicitly forbidden to address him using his name and were only allowed to call him "White Boy". Anyone who disobeyed was slapped or strapped. Michael was thus effectively made into a pariah and had to do the dirtiest jobs, like cleaning the toilets. Days and months went by, but Houston did not relent in his persecution of Michael, and most of the boys were silent. It proved to be a real spiritual and psychological dark night for Michael.

Weeks passed and the man's malice never abated. The winter was endless, dark, the sun shining only a few hours each day. That I might at some time in the future, return home was a meaningless abstraction. My total reality was a lonely, hopeless, and apparently eternal suffering. I spent a lot of time crying privately and praying, still rising before dawn to attend Mass. I could not understand the man's hatred, nor did I suspect the sexual roots of his relentless persecution. It did not occur to me that I had done nothing wrong, or that I might mention the state of things to the hostel administration. I merely assumed that I had no rights, and that any adult authority was beyond questioning.[6]

In the midst of all this darkness, however, there was one person who withstood the manipulation and conspiracy to crush Michael, a native boy named Gordon. He came from a family of trappers, and Michael sensed in him a natural dignity. Although he did not speak much, Gordon was not as affected by the terror as the rest of the boys. He did not oppose it in an explicit way, but his lack of fear gained respect, even from the supervisor; Gordon was the only boy who ever accompanied Michael to Mass.

Sometimes when I was bullied or harangued by the supervisor, the other students staring at the floor in frozen silence, Gordon would glance my way, and merely look into my eyes. Never in those ten months did he utter a word of sympathy, but when things were at their worst he was always there with the look. The look puzzled me. Raised in a family where verbal communication was dominant, I knew that his look was an expression of solidarity, but I could not then understand that a good deal more was being said through those eyes. I did not understand that love is primarily a language of presence. And that the nature of any form of love is revealed in its acts more than its words.[7]

In a postscript to the narrative above, Michael wrote that after his first year in school, the abusive supervisor was convicted and sentenced to ten years in prison, but released after nine years. What was worse, he then sought admission to a seminary; after several rejections, he was admitted by the archbishop of the Saint Boniface, Manitoba, diocese and in 1990 ordained a priest in the Catholic Church.[8] The bishop seems to have been aware of the history of the man, which makes it almost inconceivable that he did not halt this process.[9]

Thus, at a young age, Michael entered into one of the deepest wounds of the Catholic Church of the twentieth century, shared with governments using systems of residential schools. To separate children from their parents and hand them over to "professionals"—with little or no control of how things were managed and without any means for those being "educated" to send out a cry for help—was thought-less, but to do nothing when the situation was obvious, was cruel. Throughout Canada, this situation was aggravated by the fact that the overwhelming majority of the children in these schools were aboriginal peoples (Indian, Métis, and Inuit), making the pain of their separation and vulnerability even more severe.

Later, the Canadian government became increasingly aware of the different kinds of abuse that the whole system of residential schools for native children had brought with them. In 2008, it established the Truth and Reconciliation Commission of Canada to gather evidence and hear the victims with the goal of writing a complete historical record.[10] At a conference, the Northern National Event, arranged in Inuvik in June 2011, Michael gave a talk on his experiences at the residential school. The testimonies given to the commission are heart-rending, bearing witness to a systematic destruction of culture and in-dividuals.[11] In videos on the website of the commission, one can see how grown-up, even old, people break down and cry when they describe how they were separated from their parents and systemati-cally mistreated. After Michael's talk, some native men came to him one by one and told him of their experiences as victims of sexual abuse. They had never spoken about it to anyone, and he encouraged them to speak to the commissioners and to the Catholic bishops of the North, who were attending the conference, in an effort to bring healing and reconciliation. Michael was struck by the fact that, for the most part, they believed in Christ and prayed, though they retained a deep bitterness against the Church. Even so, Michael thought, the process of forgiveness had begun.

In the novel *A Cry of Stone*, Michael used his experience from residence school, but the story was resituated in Northern Ontario with all names changed. In the novel, the Métis boy Binemin Edzo, called Tchibi, is portrayed as suffering what Michael himself had experienced.

During the second year, 1962, the situation in Inuvik was better.[12] The supervisor had been removed after he had been investigated by the RCMP (Royal Canadian Mounted Police) on the suspicion of having sexual relationships with teenage boys. Michael and Terry were now both in senior boys, while Patti joined them at senior girls. The boys gained some new freedoms such as going to town for a few hours during the weekend. However, it came with the strict admonition that anyone attending the cinema would have his freedoms removed.[13]

Cambridge Bay

In early 1963, the O'Brien family moved to Cambridge Bay on the south shore of Victoria Island, as David had been appointed to the position of area administrator there.[14] From September 1963 to January 1964, Michael therefore attended an Indian residential school in Yellowknife, the capital of the Northwest Territories. Sir John Franklin School and Akaitcho Hall, the residence, was more like an ordinary high school: students could go to dances and were free to visit the town. Standard residential rules were in place, but not enforced with the oppressiveness and strict segregation that Michael and Terry had experienced in Inuvik.

When the children returned home for Christmas, their parents surprised them with the news that David had obtained a job at the Department of Northern Affairs in Ottawa, and that they were moving south the following month. Michael's feelings were mixed: on the one hand, he had loved the free life in the North, while, on the other hand, he was relieved to be out of residential school and able to live with his family once again.

3. Back to Civilization

Reverse Culture Shock

In January 1964, the O'Brien family returned to Ottawa from their three-year stay in the Canadian Arctic. They lived the next two years on the ground floor of an old house in the middle of the city at Gilmour and Elgin Streets. David had a mere fifteen-minute walk to his office at the Department of Northern Affairs. His work was to promote tourism in the Arctic, and later to market Inuit art in North America and Europe. At that time, German art collectors, together with certain galleries in the United States, were especially fascinated by Inuit art.

Soon after their return to Ottawa, Elaine began to work part-time as a nurse, while she had been a housewife in the Arctic. Their youngest child, Dan, was now twelve years old, Patti fourteen, and Terry fifteen. Michael, the oldest, was sixteen years old and had a special room in the basement, a sort of teenage hideaway, where he did some drawings, read, and relaxed. This incipient artistic interest, most probably inspired by his father, who was an amateur painter, however, faded away during the years that followed.

When they returned to Ottawa, Canada was living through the fast-paced transformation that had begun after the Second World War. The four-year recession at the end of the 1950s, which impelled the O'Briens to move north, had been preceded by a decade of intense urban growth fuelled by a booming economy, renewed European immigration, and increased fertility.[1] Since Michael and his family left in 1961, these growth and modernization processes had taken new steps, and David and Elaine finally achieved a steady middle-class life in Ottawa, after moving around the continent.

However, for the two adolescent boys the return to civilization was bewildering and disorienting. Terry, as well as Michael, struggled with loneliness and a sense of existential emptiness. The life on the

33

edge of civilization, with its experiences of nature and a low level of technology, had deeply affected them. Michael had worn moccasins and fur boots for so long in the North that shoes and rubber boots were now uncomfortable; he had not used a telephone or got onto a bus for several years and thus felt intensely the increasing speed and noise of the modern world. Dan, on the other hand, who never went to residential school, but had stayed at home with his parents in Coppermine, did not experience the culture shock in the same way as his two older brothers.

David and Elaine's decision to move back to city life was primarily based on the opportunity for better education in Ottawa, compared with the North. Elaine enrolled the two older sons at St. Patrick's High School, a boy's school that David had attended, while Patti went to a Catholic girl's school and Dan to a local elementary school. The description of St. Patrick's in Terry's autobiography paints a picture of unruly adolescents and slightly eccentric teachers unable to tame them.

In 1964, as a newly ordained priest, Father Joseph Hattie, O.M.I. (Oblates of Mary Immaculate), was one of the teachers at St. Patrick's. He remembers the boys at the school as "good, healthy, young men", but that it was necessary to establish a framework of discipline early on in the year, to curb their inclination for practical jokes and getting into difficulties; otherwise, things could easily get out of hand. According to Father Hattie, Michael was a lanky, quiet, shy person, "always questioning in his mind what was going on".[2] Michael became involved in a program that Father Hattie was developing in the Ottawa area called the Challenge Movement; it was aimed at helping high school students get a better understanding of their faith while encouraging them to become leaders. Michael took part in a course and joined a team arranging retreats, but he was wrestling with his faith—when he was with Father Hattie it was strong, while at other times he drifted. His heart was divided.

The Dying Grandfathers

In 1965, a year after David and Elaine had moved to Ottawa, both of Michael's grandfathers, Stephen and Roland, lay dying in a hospital in Ottawa; they were only a few rooms away from each other, but never met. Both had fought in the Great War (World War I). Stephen, David's father, came from a poor Irish background while Roland, Elaine's father, was from a more affluent Protestant-English family. They had both separated from their wives, and both of them were at this point Catholic, as Roland had converted to Catholicism to marry Jane. Both men had left the Catholic faith during their years of marital tribulations, but they received the sacraments at the end. This parallelism of two similar life trajectories, though reversed as in a mirror in certain respects, Irish–English, poor–rich, Catholic–Protestant, is, in this scene of the two dying men who had fought in the Great War, almost uncannily symbolic.

At Ypres in France, during one of the major battles of World War I, Roland had been chlorine gassed; the chemical burns made him lie unconscious for six months in a hospital in England. He survived, but during the fighting in the trenches, his brother had died in his arms after being hit by enemy fire. For the rest of his life, Roland had burn scars on his head, but he never wanted to talk about the war. Nevertheless, the scars served as a reminder to all around him of what had happened.

After the war, Roland returned to Canada, where he met and married Jane. He chose to stay in the military, learned to fly, and became a wing commander, though he was not primarily a pilot but an administrator: he never saw combat in the air.

Jane, who came from a simple but warm Irish family, never managed to assimilate into the lifestyle associated with her husband's rising social status. Roland, who had been psychologically traumatized by the war, and who, it seemed, had not come to terms with his experiences, was, like Stephen, wounded for life. In contrast to Roland, Stephen, coming like Jane from an Irish working-class background, did not have the social capital to manage life. Roland developed a respectability that Stephen and Jane never could achieve; they were instead crushed and sank to the bottom of the social pyramid.

During her marriage, Jane became increasingly depressed and developed an alcoholism that did not remain within the realm of the socially acceptable. An incident told in the family illustrates how she combined self-medication with a criticism of military uptight social life.

It was a grand day for the regiment, celebrated with a parade, and all the high brass of the Canadian armed forces were there, with Roland playing an important role. As a column of soldiers paraded by, inspected by the officers, a strange figure tottered after them, a woman with a lampshade on her head, marching with mock formality, obviously drunk. Jane had joined the celebration in her own way.

After Jane had been taken to the mental hospital, Roland employed a housekeeper to take care of their children. She was deeply influenced by English nineteenth-century occultism, inducing Roland to become part of this enchanted world.[3] After a while, she became his partner, but not his wife as he did not divorce but only separated from Jane. During his remaining life, Roland retained a strong interest in alternative spiritualities and was a member of a Rosicrucian society.[4] He read many books on esoteric subjects, which he recommended to Elaine and her family. But, shortly before his death, he renounced his occult involvement and returned to the Church, asking to see a priest on his deathbed, in order to receive the last sacraments. This was something for which his five daughters, all fervent Catholics, had for a long time been praying for.

It was only after the visit to the dying Roland that David and Elaine learned that Stephen had been at the same hospital, and that they could have visited him as well. But, by then, Stephen had already been transferred to a hospital in Toronto, where he shortly afterwards died. At the wake in an Irish funeral parlour in Ottawa, Michael saw a man with a face that he did not recognize, lying in a coffin. Just a few people came, mostly family. At Roland's funeral, on the other hand, there was a large crowd, as he was a highly respected man and a figure of some importance in the Canadian air force.

David's relationship with his father had not been easy after the break between his parents, but Elaine visited Stephen with the children without David knowing it, because she wanted him to see his grandchildren. The first time she came for a visit was when Michael was only a baby and the second time was when he was two years old. At the second visit, Stephen gave her a golden locket ring, with a miniature photo of Hilda welded into it, and asked Elaine to give it to Michael when he reached twenty-one years of age.

In his final year, Stephen lived in the basement of his sister's house, where he returned to the religious faith of his childhood, though he still struggled with alcoholism. His life had been one of continuous suffering and failures, but after his death, David and Elaine inherited his wallet and found that it was full of religious medals and prayer novena cards.

Though both Elaine and David came from broken families with an alcoholic parent, Michael remembers their marriage as serene and companionable. Perhaps their experiences made them work hard to make their own marriage peaceful, though they did not become tee-totallers. Michael cannot recall that they ever argued or fought about anything, but that they instead always discussed things. In hindsight, he knows that they had many worries and had to make difficult decisions, but they kept such tensions to themselves.

Every Sunday, Elaine and the children went to Mass, which was normal in her family, and besides her own prayers in the morning and when going to bed, she said the Rosary with the children every evening, at least before they went to the Arctic. With the onset of the changes in the 1960s, the support for such a standard devout Catholic life changed, as described by Robert Orsi, professor of Catholic studies:

> People looking back on these years from the perspective of the present invariably remember how surprised they were when all of sudden the altar was turned around, new movements were required in church, they could eat meat on Fridays!!! One day the saints disappeared, the rosaries stopped, the novenas ended, just like that.[5]

The combination of dramatic liturgical and devotional change with a new public dissent within the Church gave rise to the feeling that everything was being turned upside down, and Elaine's faith began to falter. After the period in the Arctic, although she never ceased her religious practice completely, it became thinner and more haunted by doubt. In the early 1970s, however, she regained her religious strength through the Charismatic Renewal.

When asked by me to comment on his double British-Irish heritage, Michael remarked that he tends to see himself as Irish due to the creative and poetic gifts of that nation, its Catholic sensibilities, and the moral underdog perspective in relation to the British, as manifested, for example, in the great famine of 1846–1851.[6] In Michael's novels, the marginalized, suffering person is in focus, and in his novel *Strangers and Sojourners* (1997) this English-Irish duality is central to the novel's narrative. The main character, Anne Ashton, coming from a wealthy English family, marries the troubled Irish man Stephen (Stiofain) Delaney, who is fleeing from a crime he had perpetrated while in Ireland. The marriage of Stephen and Anne is certainly depicted as having its tensions, but, in the end, she comes to understand his mythopoetic Irish nature; and he becomes reconciled with his violent history and traumatic memories from Ireland. In his fiction, then, Michael gives form to a reunion never realized between Hilda and Stephen nor between Jane and Roland. In this way, their reconciliation was finally achieved in the literary imagination of their grandson.

After the two grandfathers died, only Michael's grandmother, Hilda, was left, besides Elaine's four sisters and their families. Michael had twenty-five cousins, and he remembers them as a loving family environment in Ottawa, with David as the centre of family parties playing the accordion and singing. However, as the social and religious crisis of the sixties and early seventies gained momentum, it affected the extended family, as it did so many Catholic families at that time. Only a small minority of Michael's cousins are still practising Catholics. Although the family environment was merry, it did not offer much support for the faith of Michael and his siblings to withstand the onslaught of mid-twentieth-century modernity.

Terry Takes the Train

After a year in Ottawa, David and Elaine began to think that the inner city was unsuitable for their family, worrying about, among other things, the increasing crime rate. In 1966, they decided to leave the Victorian house on Gilmour Street and move to the newly built suburb of Bayshore in the west end of Ottawa.[7]

David and Elaine were settling down in Ottawa, but for Terry the transition to city life proved to be too much. He was filled with an urge for travel and adventure—for him school was like a birdcage. In March 1966, only sixteen years old, he therefore decided to quit high school and leave home to search for a job in Montreal. When he told Michael about his secret plan, the latter became very worried and made him tell their parents. At first, they tried to talk him out of it, but they rather quickly gave in. Nevertheless, they made Terry go west to Calgary, Alberta, instead of eastward, as they thought that Montreal, as a bigger city, would have a bad influence on him. They paid his ticket and gave him thirty dollars in pocket money; Elaine

also made a pile of sandwiches for him to survive the three-day journey, and she followed him to the train station. Having said goodbye,
she cried when the train left the station.

Years later, she told Terry that standing at the platform worrying about his future, she had a vision of a huge angel sitting in the
seat beside him, and with one of its wings, the heavenly guardian
was sheltering Terry—she thus felt reassured that her son would
be protected.

An hour after departure, the train passed the western outskirts of
Ottawa, including the neighbourhood of Bayshore, where they lived.
Terry thought he saw his younger brother Dan by the tracks wav-
ing; Terry waved back and continued on his adventure.

Losing His Religion

To return to the modern world after having lived a premodern life
is disorienting in itself, but the timing of the return of the O'Brien
family was also important. The revolt of the 1960s was brewing and
Michael, as a sixteen-year-old, entered it at the most receptive age,
while being at the same time inoculated with something radically different. Both of these powerful ways of living (Inuit and Ottawa city
life) became part of him, but they also built up an unresolved tension.

The new youth culture with the Beatles, who came to Canada in
1964 and 1965, was sweeping through society. The openness to sen-
suality and drugs alienated Michael, as he tried to convey his experiences in the North to his peers:

> They were entirely urban people, with little taste for nature, and
> absolutely no interest in the stories of my northern experience that
> I wanted to share with them. It was a reverse culture shock for me.
> Their minds and what they valued were entirely different from mine.
> I had become a stranger in a strange land—and worst of all, it had
> once been, long ago, my homeland—this city that I had thought of,
> and felt, was my home when I was a child, had become alien.[8]

Instead, Michael turned toward literature. Age sixteen is the period
when intellectual life usually awakens and the move to manhood

starts in earnest. He began to read extensively in modern philosophy
and became excited when discovering the existentialists, especially
Albert Camus, who led him to the writings of Jean Paul Sartre. As
a result, the Inuit and the existentialist met and had to sort out their
differences. Existentialism, in Michael's understanding, expressed a
vision of the world as a place of alienation and darkness, of man alone
within himself. This harmonized with his own experience of life and,
in the process, his childhood faith slowly eroded. At the same time,
he felt a certain pride when in a SAT test (Scholastic Aptitude Test) he
scored among the top 1 percent in the province of Ontario. Yet this
was not reflected in his achievements in high school, as he was generally failing except in history and literature.[9]

In 1967, Michael finished school and went to work at the Ottawa
Public Library, main branch, and then for two years in the west end
of Ottawa, at the Carlingwood branch. His mind was set on books,
on reading and writing. He had begun to smoke a pipe during high
school, and there is a photo of him puffing on it while reading a
thick, hardcover book—he was clearly adopting the intellectual pose
of his time.

In the summer of 1967, he took a job in Yellowknife doing construction work, and, at the same time, he stopped going to Mass.
He was now losing even the outward aspects of his religion. His
father was not home much, as he had recently left his government
job and started a little company in Toronto. It was, however, failing,
and David stayed in a tiny room in Toronto, living on crackers and
sardines during the death throes of the company. Meanwhile, Elaine
worked hard so they could pay the bills. Terry had left, and in the
next year, Patti also moved away from home to work in Vancouver.
Eventually, David returned to work for the government but now
focused on marketing Inuit art.

Conversion

Besides the existentialists, Michael began to read about different
forms of esoteric religion and the evolutionary theology of Teilhard de Chardin, promoted by his grandfather Roland as the bridge
between esotericism and Catholicism.[10] Elaine had also begun to read

the books promoted by Roland as her own faith weakened, but she still tried to keep them away from the children.

When he was fifteen years old, Terry asked Roland about his faith; in answer, his grandfather gave him some of his favourite spiritual books. Elaine, however, quickly confiscated them and said that they went against the Catholic faith, with no explanations added. Terry was disappointed because his main concern was to see grandfather Roland levitate; but he told Terry that he could only do that if it was necessary in the cosmic scheme of things, and Terry's curiosity clearly did not qualify.

Michael had begun occasionally to visit some high school friends north of Ottawa, who were spiritual seekers in the style of the 1960s, opening up to Eastern religions such as Hinduism and Buddhism. This was the beginning of the very diverse phenomenon called New Age that had been spearheaded by the spiritualist movement in the nineteenth century, and the Theosophical Society founded by Madame Blavatsky and Colonel Henry Steel Olcott in New York in 1875. The latter was characterized by its fusion of Western esotericism and elements of Eastern religions.[11]

One night at his friends' place, Michael took part in a séance in which they experimented with a Ouija board. They all put their fingers on the wooden heart-shaped planchette and waited to see which letters it would mark and which words would be formed. They were not completely serious in this: to them it was simply a parlour game.

However, Michael had participated in an Ouija board session previously with his brother and mother. It had been brought to the house by a friend exploring spiritualism. Elaine had begun by asking if her mother were present. The marker with the fingers traced out an affirmative yes. Then she asked, "What is your name?" and the answer came as, "J-e-n," which was her mother's nickname, not known to her sons. Amazed, and also disturbed, they did not pursue it any longer, but Michael had gained a sense that something more than a bit of fun was involved.

At the home of his friends, he anticipated that something unexpected could happen. The room was lit only by a single candle, and they were all set to begin. Then without any movement or any draft in the room, the light suddenly went out, and it became pitch black. The candle had not been blown out; it had merely been extinguished.

The girls began to scream; somebody turned on the light, and the séance was terminated. Michael was frightened but at the same time fascinated.

One of the girls present had brought a friend who lived in a community in Toronto that was dedicated to exploring the spiritual world. He invited Michael, who then was an atheist but not a materialist, to come for a visit. Perhaps the proper label for his worldview was an agnostic seeker, as he believed in cosmic forces and that there was some kind of spiritual world. He was weighing many ideas in his mind on the ultimate makeup of the universe, and his curiosity impelled him to explore this option.

Before leaving, he spoke with his mother and his godmother, and they asked where he was going, whether this spiritual centre was Catholic. He answered that "no, it isn't; it's more a kind of Buddhist, Eastern-style place." His godmother clearly became worried and tore a piece of paper from her prayer book. She gave it to Michael, saying, "Please, take this with you." He did not think much about it, but put the page from the prayer book in his pocket anyway.

In July 1969, Michael took a bus to Toronto to visit the community of seekers for a weekend. A number of young people lived there, guided by a leader, a spiritualist guru. Michael was welcomed, and he was impressed by their efforts at achieving contact with the other world. He stayed up long into the night speaking with them about spiritual matters, especially reincarnation. They did not look like hippies at all and there were no drugs; they were "clean-cut guys", as Michael later recalled.

In the middle of the night, while sleeping on a mattress, alone in a tiny room, Michael suddenly awoke with the terrible feeling that there was an evil presence in the room. Approaching him, he felt, was an extremely malevolent spirit who wanted to devour his soul. He, who had rejected the personal Christian God, replacing him with vague cosmic forces, was suddenly confronted with an experience of an intensely powerful and hostile spiritual presence, which seemed impossible to resist. Feeling like a defenseless prey in front of a large predator, Michael went through a complete religious transformation. Utterly terrified, he cried out from the depths of his soul, "God save me!" Instantaneously, the evil presence withdrew. It was still there, but backed off, and a supernatural peace filled Michael—something he had not felt for many years.

In that moment, Michael recalls that he saw, as if lit up by a flash of lightning, the inner landscape of his soul and the great darkness that enveloped it, but he also perceived divine grace at work. He now believed that God was real, that everything the Church had given him and taught was reality—ultimate reality.

After a while, he stopped praying, thinking that now he could go back to sleep. Immediately, he felt the evil presence resume the attack with full force, hammering on his mind; so he had to continue to pray throughout the night. Spontaneously, he began to pray the Twenty-Third Psalm, "The Lord is my shepherd . . ."[12]

Michael's inner life is rich with spiritual insights, dreams, and visions, which sometimes seem closer to the powers of his imagination, and, at other times, more clearly appear to be of a purely spiritual nature. As a biographer trained primarily within the field of religious studies and not theology, I cannot judge where the exact line is to be drawn; this is something that is not clear even to Michael himself at times. As I see it, my task is to present to you such experiences when they are important for Michael's life and work. You then must decide for yourself the extent to which they are the outcome of the subconscious, his powerful imagination, or real spiritual interventions, or the result of a combination of all three.

What we, nevertheless, can determine is that the turnaround in 1969 was decisive, and that it has withstood trials and temptations for nearly five decades. The simple truth is that inner experiences are not accessible to us, except when they manifest themselves in exterior actions. Thus, according to the Gospel of Matthew, Jesus said: "You will know them by their fruits" (7:16). In a sense, the rest of this book is an account of the fruits of this particular conversion.

Michael did not merely experience an all-embracing, loving-kindness that melted away his darkness and sins. He realized, first, that he, and mankind as a whole, was under attack from an absolute evil, mostly disguised as good. Then he felt the undeserved grace of God, which rescued him from falling into the abyss. This experience provided Michael with a sense of urgency, I would say with a sense of prophetic mission, which became clearer to him as the years progressed.

The word emerging later in his self-understanding is that of a watchman. Humanity, but especially the Catholic Church, needs, according to Michael, to wake up and understand the danger it is facing, and turn back to God. The characteristic exhortation of the prophet, and vital for Michael's work, is, hence, "Repent!"

In the middle of that night, Michael became aware of what he calls the Great War in the Heavens, which is an allusion to Revelation 12:7–13, in which his namesake, the archangel Michael, plays a leading role.

> I realized in that instant that there was a great war in the heavens and that part of it occurred, was occurring in the realm of human individual lives and in the realm of human society. We were at war and we would be at war until the end of time.[13]

Early the next morning, Michael said goodbye to his hosts and took the bus home. He remembers that when he passed the central plaza of Toronto's city hall, he saw thousands of people staring at large screens displaying the moving black-and-white videos of a man walking on the moon. It was July 21, and a small step on the dusty surface four hundred thousand kilometres away was matched by a giant leap in Michael's soul.

On the bus trip back to Ottawa, he found in his pocket the page torn from his godmother's prayer book, and when unfolding it, he saw that printed on it was the Twenty-Third Psalm. Throughout the journey, he read it over and over again, and each time he was filled with peace: "The Lord is my Shepherd; I shall not want. He maketh me to lie down in green pastures: he leadeth me beside the still waters ..."

Arriving home, he told his mother what he had experienced. She became very happy, although she was still struggling with her own faith. Michael said to her that the books and materials provided by Roland, which they had read, were poison. From then on, she stopped reading them, and the following year she joined the Charismatic Renewal.

There was a little parish on McLeod Street where Michael went to Confession, and he began a routine of religious practice, which included daily Mass and Communion. Despite his new faith, the psychological turmoil that preceded it was still very much alive. His inner life continued to rage, plunging him repeatedly into near despair— but there was always a recourse to the Eucharist, providing powerful consolations in the midst of turmoil. As in his conversion experience, there were sharp contrasts; a drama, a real struggle, was going on.[14]

He was twenty-one years old, drifting, taking odd jobs, reading voraciously, but not on the way to a university education or a steady job. He had found his faith again, but had not discovered a concrete way forward. The times were also a-changin', with the young generation in the mood of revolt, leaving the world of their parents behind. Michael had marched with them for a couple of years, but now he suddenly turned in the opposite direction: that of tradition, obedience, and faith.

The Drawing of a Tree

Michael remembers his atheist period as having been creatively barren, but with his rekindled faith something was stirring. As with his conversion, the awakening of creativity came as something of a revelation, but now through the medium of nature.

One day in the spring of 1970, eight months after his conversion, while he was wandering in the woods of the Gatineau Hills north of Ottawa, he saw a little tree with a few new leaves on it. It was a beautiful little sapling, growing from a pile of rocks, out of apparently barren, sterile soil. To him it seemed to carry a message that God was speaking through nature. He was then struck by the thought that it was a metaphor of his life, which had been sterile and barren as the rocks. Yet, here was a new life of love and hope springing from his faith. Even so, he did not know who he was, or what he was to do in life. Standing there wondering, he took out a pen and a paper and just drew the little tree, so he would not forget it.

Michael continued to draw other things he saw in the forest. Nature became for him a medium of experiencing God. The more he drew and painted, the more the inspirations flowed; it was like an old well that had been clogged by debris: stick, stones, and dry leaves. The more he cleaned it, the more the spring of water poured out.

To Become an Artist

Michael's diary begins on New Year's Eve 1970, when he was twenty-two years old. At that time, he looked back to his conversion in 1969, and the beginning of his new creativity in the spring of 1970.

As we follow him into 1971, his main activities are painting, visiting art exhibitions, and cultivating relations with friends. It was a situation with no security or firm foundation; he was still living at the home of his parents, considering the idea of becoming an artist.

Riding his motorcycle, he often returned to the Gatineau Hills, where he had access to a cabin belonging to one of his friends. He wandered and did drawings in the hilly, wooded, and sparsely populated landscape. Sometimes Gregory Bourassa, a friend sharing his interest in drawing and spirituality, joined him. They hiked in the woods and engaged in wide-ranging discussions and occasionally tried to play music together, Michael on a rusty harmonica and Gregory, who later became a professional musician, on a silver flute.[15]

In late winter, Michael visited some friends who had just moved to a house in the high hills of Quebec about sixty kilometres north of Ottawa. They knew no one else in the area, nor did Michael, and their new home was beside a river in a relatively wild region of forest where few people lived; there were just a few lonely farmhouses and cabins.

Michael had brought with him his drawing pad and some sticks of charcoal because he wanted to spend the whole day alone, walking for hours and stopping from time to time to sketch the winter scenes in the cold but sunny weather. The best landscapes were on the other side of the frozen river, so he decided to cross over on the ice, because the closest bridge was several kilometres away. The ice usually began to thaw at that time of year, but he thought it was probably still thick enough to walk upon. However, as he walked across, he could hear the ice cracking like broken glass beneath his feet, but it supported his weight and he made it safely to the other side.

All day long, he walked and sketched without seeing a single soul. When the afternoon sun began to sink toward the horizon, he turned around and headed back to the river, where he hoped to again cross over on the ice. He hesitated a little because the sun had been beating on the ice all day, but he was tired and hungry, and to walk more kilometres to the bridge would mean he would have to go a part of the way in the dark.

He had just reached the edge of the river and stepped off the road, when a car came along the road and stopped beside him. Inside the car were three young men, about twenty-one to twenty-five years of age.

"Where are you going?" asked one of them.

"I'm going to cross the river on the ice, and get home before sunset," Michael answered.

"Come with us," he said; "we'll drive you to the bridge."

Michael got into the car beside the driver, and for the next fifteen minutes as they drove along, he observed the three men closely. They seemed to have come out of nowhere, and they looked rather unusual. They were all exceptionally handsome, Michael thought, with manly, wholesome faces. They did not seem to have embraced the revolutionary ethos of the 1960s and 1970s; it was as if they had stepped out of another era of history. Their clothing was neat and clean, their faces flawless, and their hair clean-cut and short; their mannerisms and facial expressions were full of politeness, kindness, and open-hearted goodness, Michael recalls. They struck him as highly unusual.

Finally, the driver stopped the car at the entrance to the bridge. Michael opened the door and stepped out onto the road.

"Thank you very much," he said. "God bless you."

All three of them looked at him with shining faces, and one said: "God bless you, Michael."

He was startled, because he had not told them his name.

"How do you know my name?" he exclaimed, astonished.

Without answering, all three smiled at him, and then they drove away.

Michael crossed over on the bridge and made it home to his friends' house before dark. The next morning, he went down to the river and saw that during the night all the ice had collapsed and been swept away by the roaring waters. He realized then that if he had tried to walk back across the second time, yesterday afternoon, he might very well have died.[16]

Michael sometimes wonders if the men in the car were angels, like the "three young men" who visited Abraham and Sarah (Gen 18:1–10). Or if they were human beings whom Divine Providence had arranged to come to his rescue at exactly the right moment.

In February 1971, Michael wrote down his alternatives: either the New School of Art in Toronto, but it was expensive and required a job on the side—besides, not much help would be forthcoming as this was a "free" school focused on modern art—or he could remain in Ottawa, live at home, and develop his art on his own. Perhaps he

could study under another artist—but he would miss the art environment of Toronto. The two other alternatives were either to travel in
Canada and develop landscape painting or to travel in Europe and
perhaps enroll in an art school in England or France. He clearly leaned
toward the last option, which he thought was a "very exciting idea".

At the same time, he rebelled at his own tendency to plan a career
as "a great artist".

> Be ruthless now—not success, not approval, nor self-approval through
> the world's standards or the consensus of the artistic community—
> (look what's happening *there* for heaven's sake) nor security. Rather
> honesty, beauty, freedom: or, in other words, Goodness, Beauty,
> Truth. O yes, yes, yes, Michael, these above all else are the roots
> which go deep deeper deepest, making the branches go high, high.[17]

In April, he was thinking about poverty as an ideal, but shied away
from solitude.

> I've been strongly drawn to poverty lately; (to have the *choice* is for-
> tunate) as more and more I find the wealth of simple beauty in little
> things, silences, listening, creating—yet, I know too how very much
> I need to be loved and to love and am in no way ready for solitude.[18]

He was also alienated by the condition of modern art. In the back
of his mind, the experiences in the Arctic served as a powerful anti-
dote to the often-overintellectualized avant-garde.

One day, after attending an art history lecture on post-painterly
abstraction together with one of his friends, he was in a low mood;
most of the paintings had looked to him like rug design. On the way
back home, he came across a little photographic exhibition, and to
his excitement, it was a National Film Board display of the Arctic. He
was overjoyed by the beautiful pictures and the feeling of a land and
people so full of life. Then he came to a photo of an old Inuit couple,
and was astonished when he realized that it was of James and Annie
Koihok, who often had visited the O'Brien house in Coppermine,
drinking tea and eating Elaine's homemade bread and jam, communicating with smiles and gestures, teaching the children a few words
of the Inuit vocabulary.

Memories resurfaced in Michael's mind with great intensity, as when he visited the warm-hearted and humorous couple in their igloo one winter and ate raw fish and seal liver for the first time, or when in the summer he had paddled the family kayak across the Coppermine River to visit them in their caribou-skin tent and saw Annie carving a soapstone sculpture. Standing in front of the photo, Michael said to himself, "This seems to be an answer. What a strange day!"[19]

Robertson Galleries

Throughout 1971, Michael continued drawing, but he also developed his painting skills. David then worked for the government promoting Inuit art and had therefore some contacts in the art world. Impressed by Michael's drawings, he spoke to John Robertson, the owner of Robertson Galleries in Ottawa, who agreed to look at his son's work. After going through his portfolio, Robertson offered Michael an exhibition in the spring of 1972.[20] And the next time Michael saw him, he moved the date forward to November 1971. Michael, quite naturally, felt happy and grateful for this opportunity: he had bypassed art school and entered on the professional scene after only a year of dedicated drawing and painting.

The opening of the exhibition on November 18 was an overwhelming experience for him. In his diary, he tried to make sense of it.

> Last night was my first exhibition at Robertson's Galleries. What incredible memories I have of it. I could weep when I think of it—but I don't think I'll go through with it again—too much to overwhelm and seduce. But wonderful. There are a thousand comments encouraging and otherwise which are swirling around in the ole noggin. Mr. Robertson was elated by the sales—10 in 36 on the first night. "almost unheard of . . ." response for a first showing. Will success spoil Michael O'Brien? I pray to God it won't. I do most earnestly, for if it does, it is one more soul-killing victory for nihilism and the dehumanizing forces of our society. Privacy, constant reassessment and reflection—deeper roots in service to God and fellowmen, humility, absolute honesty.[21]

There was a favourable review of the exhibition in the *Ottawa Citizen* five days later under the title "Delicate Pen Drawings Depict Natural Things". The reviewer was particularly impressed with the detailed studies of nature and Michael's sympathetic rendering of "the smooth solidity of time-worn pebbles, the brittle, transient beauty of dead, dried twigs and the pleasing repetitive patterns of old stone walls".[22] However, she considered the portraits less successful. Here the original inspiration that had released Michael's creativity became apparent; it was in the small details of nature that God had spoken to his soul, not in the depths of human personality and presence.

At the same time as he appreciated the positive response to his art, he wanted to take a decisive step away from the art world.

> I'm resolved to avoid involvement in "society circles", and they were there last night and mostly friendly. I don't deny that for the most part, these "important" people are fine and good, but I am afraid of what being absorbed into their perspective in the culture would do to me. Poverty must be my mistress, as St. Francis said. Constant work and interior search for light.—To grow in it and give what I can. Reputation, relevancy (social), entertainment, are things which mustn't influence my work. The thing is to work on steadfastly as I have been.[23]

In other words, he decided not to ride on the wave of success but instead to follow the way of material simplicity and service to God. Already here, the main theme of Michael's life project is present. Yet, one can sense a tension between a radical ideal of sincerity and of spiritual purity, which he decisively embraces, and his will to live the life of an artist, which, of course, includes making a living from it. This tension was very strong for him: on the one hand, he felt happiness at the reception of his art, and, on the other hand, he feared being contaminated by the art world and its inherent values. He was clearly torn in two directions.

Because of this apparent contradiction between art and God, he entered into an inner darkness and spiritual dryness, wondering if this was a natural down after the exciting high of the exhibition's opening night—or, worse, if he had chosen the wrong path, or, better, if he was being tested by God. He looked back to the summer of 1970, a year after his conversion, when his prayer experiences had been so powerful and beautiful, but, he wondered, "Why are there no inner confirmations now?" When he began to think about it, also during the months preparing for the exhibition, he had felt far from God.[24] The inner light will return, he wrote in his diary to reassure himself, but a few days later, the existential uneasiness had developed into a solid creative block. There was no way he could feel the inner quietness so necessary for his flow of creativity; the sight of the way forward had been lost in the inner turmoil.

4. Blue River

Going West

At the very beginning of what could have been a successful art career, living strategically in the capital of Canada, Michael desired to withdraw. Unwilling to stay in Ottawa, he decided to go west on a great train journey across Canada, using the money he had earned from his first exhibition. As Terry had, he went in search of adventure, instead of staying in the city, going to art school, and carving out a career.

His strong, emotionally arduous spiritual struggle was driving him toward an undivided religious dedication, toward the periphery, far away from modern civilization. Perhaps his religious quest was influenced by his childhood experiences, acting from the depths of his personality, but we also have to factor in the spirit of the early 1970s, with its focus on alternative living, closeness to nature, and an aversion to mechanical modernity. It was the time of the "Jesus people", Christian hippies, who, as many others during this time, tended toward an ideal of communal living.

Next Stop: Valemount

During his travels from Ontario over the immense flat expanse of the prairies to the mountains and the Pacific Ocean, Michael stopped in Valemount, a small village in the Rocky Mountains of British Columbia. By a coincidence, which he considered extraordinary, he had just received letters from two of his friends whom he had known from different parts of the country. Neither of them knew each other, and both had moved to Valemount to do different kinds of manual labour. Both had written to invite him to visit them. Michael thought that this was something more than a reunion of friends, that perhaps it was divinely inspired.

In Valemount, he learned that the resident Catholic priest, Father Emil Sasges, had begun to invite young people to come and stay as part of a local, evangelizing mission that he had initiated. Father Sasges asked Michael to join the mission, which at the time consisted of eight young persons: "to work and pray—to be one with the poor and act as a leaven in the little community". There was no formal rule; it was more like a loose gathering of people with a vague common calling. The idea attracted Michael, whose artistic and spiritual instincts had been kindled by the dramatic mountain landscape, and the call to a life of simplicity and religious dedication. He did not hesitate to answer yes, but Father Sasges told him to first go back to his parents and consult with them.

When Michael arrived home in January 1972, he told his parents that he wanted to go back to British Columbia and join the apostolate of Father Sasges and work in a lumber mill in Valemount. Naturally, Michael's father was concerned and asked what would happen to his art. Naïvely, or as an excuse, Michael replied that the stay in the mountains would be an excellent opportunity to develop his artistic skills by doing nature studies in his free time.

Sheila

During the spring of 1972, while Michael was piling logs in the lumber mill, a friend told him that a friend of hers, Sheila Mercer, was the girl Michael was going to marry. He scoffed at the idea as a silly, manipulative attempt at matchmaking. To make things worse, without Michael knowing it, she had said the same thing to Sheila about him: "I have met the man you are going to marry." When Michael and Sheila first met in Valemount at the farm of their common friend, Sheila recalls that Michael was bent over untying his shoes, so she could not see his face; but she heard his deep, resonant voice and immediately felt drawn to him.[1] Michael, on the other hand, had his guard up, as he was determined not to be manipulated. But after looking up and seeing a beautiful girl in hiking boots standing there in the hall, that resolution weakened substantially.

Sheila, twenty-two years old at the time, had spent her childhood in McBride, a village eighty kilometres north of Valemount in the

Robson Valley region. The village was founded at the beginning of the twentieth century as a stop on the Grand Trunk Pacific Railway and had until 1968 merely a summer highway out; during the winters, it was very isolated and dependent on the railway.[2] She lived there until she was thirteen years old, when her father, who was the local RCMP (Royal Canadian Mounted Police) official, was transferred to North Surrey in the lower Fraser Valley, closer to Vancouver.

For Sheila, to move from a remote village to suburbia entailed culture shock. Ever since, she has treasured her childhood experience of village life with its material simplicity and beauty of nature, especially the majesty of the mountains. In a similar way, Michael's time in the Arctic had been deeply imprinted in his personality. They thus shared a lived ideal of small-scale life in the countryside, if not the wilderness.

After high school in the town of Chilliwack, Sheila began to study liberal arts at the University of British Columbia (UBC) in Vancouver. Yet she returned to the Robson Valley in the summers during her late adolescence to work at Mount Robson Ranch, which is a mere half-hour drive away from Valemount. At that time, it was a fully functioning ranch supplying packhorses for climbers and tours.[3] The attraction was, and still is, Mount Robson, the highest mountain in the Canadian part of the Rocky Mountains.

The move from a rural village to suburban life of the 1960s, and then finally to studies at a university in Vancouver, which at that time had four hundred thousand inhabitants, was challenging for Sheila. This was also during the end of the 1960s, when revolutionary zeal gripped the souls of the baby boomers. In October 1968, one thousand students at UBC, encouraged by an American activist, stormed the faculty club and "liberated" it, as they claimed. They drank the faculty liquor, burned dollar bills and an American flag, and swam nude in the patio pool.[4]

Though Sheila did not participate in such outbursts of protest against hierarchies, the ideological milieu around her was aggressively atheist, weakening her childhood faith. She embarked on an existential quest and began exploring what life would be without God. Eventually, it brought her to a state where she had to face the question of the ultimate meaning of life head-on. A world without God seemed inevitably to lead to nihilism. "Is this it?" she thought. "Is life a mere nothingness? Is it worth it, or not?"

These were not mere abstract questions for her, to be entertained as interesting philosophical puzzles at a seminar; they cut to the core of her being. To live life knowing that death would be an absolute end—that despite all her gifts and efforts, she would just cease to exist at maximum a few decades into the future—filled her with existential despair. She came to the point where sleeping was difficult, and one night she could not sleep at all or rest during the next day. In the evening, alone in her room in the student residence, interiorly tormented by life's ultimate question and dazed by sleep deprivation, she finally called out to God, "If You are there, help me!"

There was no immediate response, but she managed at least to sleep that night. When she woke up the next morning, feeling somewhat better, the sky was completely overcast and dark. Then, to her amazement, a ray of sunlight beamed through a gap in the clouds and shone through her window, making a sun puddle on the floor in front of her. The drama of the scene was heightened by a white pigeon, sitting on her windowsill, silhouetted against the strong light. She felt that there was something strangely symbolic in all this and wondered, "Perhaps the white pigeon is a symbol of the Holy Spirit?"

In the middle of the sunlit area on the floor, she then saw that there lay a small paper note. She took it up and read the message, which had been left by a friend who had noticed that she had not been completely herself lately and was worried about her. It contained a quote from Psalm 30:5: "Tears come in the night, but joy comes in the morning. God bless you, dear Sheila."

The experience of such a dramatic and symbolic answer to her heartfelt prayer restored the basis of her childhood faith at a stroke. Once again, as before her faith crisis, she believed that there was something beyond death, that atheist materialism was not the solution. However, she did not immediately become a devout, daily Mass Catholic; but the atheist professors had no power over her anymore. To her, they now seemed shrunken and pathetic in their outlook.

Sheila's conversion experience in 1969 took place the same year as Michael's. They both regained their Christian faith after facing the nihilism of secular modernity in the middle of the confusion that followed in the wake of the Second Vatican Council. They were in this sense "born again" Catholics. Their reconversions also had a decisive dramatic nature. For Michael, it was the experience of a diabolic attack, while, for Sheila, it was an answer in the middle of an

existential crisis. For both of them, a biblical psalm written on a piece
of paper had been central. For Michael, it was Psalm 23, "The Lord is
my shepherd ...", with its main theme of protection, while for Sheila
it was Psalm 30, which is a song filled with gratitude for divine help
rendered in the hour of need.

After this spiritual turn of events, Sheila took some time off from
her studies and went for half a year to Europe, travelling in France,
Belgium, England, and Wales. Especially important for her was to
connect to her family roots of recusant Catholics in England, one of
whom was St. Anthony Turner, a Jesuit priest who, like St. Edmund
Campion, had been martyred on the infamous gallows at Tyburn.

During her time in Europe, Sheila thought about what to do
on returning to Canada. Her dream was to work with young children in native schools in northern British Columbia, giving them
a firm foundation of reading skills, as she had been deeply moved
by her friendships with native people over the years and was concerned about their marginalization. When returning to Canada, she
transferred from the liberal arts program at Simon Fraser University,
where she had been majoring in anthropology, to a teacher's college.
During her practicum (teaching year) in Victoria, on the spring break
of 1972, Sheila visited a friend in Valemount with whom she had
worked at Mount Robson Ranch; and there in the hallway, she met
Michael for the first time.

Although Michael and Sheila did not talk a lot in the beginning,
a friendship began to take form during subsequent visits, and they
began to exchange letters. They did not see a lot of each other in
the summer of 1972, because Michael was working on a Chilcotin
(Tsilhqot'in) ranch at the request of Father Sasges. The owners of
the ranch, an elderly couple, had rescued the priest three years earlier when he had crashed his home-built airplane in the mountains
and was lost for three weeks. Returning a favour, Father Sasges sent
Michael to help them manage during the ranch's busy summer season; Michael loved the hard work, good food, and natural surroundings of ranch life.

In the autumn, after visiting his sister, Patti, in Vancouver, Michael
decided to stay in the city. He was beginning to feel physically unwell
and saw a doctor who diagnosed him as suffering from a severe case
of glandular fever (mononucleosis). Throughout that year, he was

continually ill with colds and fevers, and unexplainable extreme fatigue—a recurring symptom that has plagued him for much of his later life.

Patti and her husband gave him a room in their basement. He found work in a bookstore and also did some painting and kept in contact with Sheila through letters. She had just accepted a teaching position among the Nisga'a people at the First Nations village of Aiyansh (Gitlaxt'aamiks) in northern British Columbia, to begin in September. At one point, she travelled the fourteen hundred kilometres south to Vancouver to see Michael, and they walked together holding hands. Clearly, a relationship was forming, though they were still at the stage of getting to know each other.

Feeling some restoration of health, Michael returned to Valemount in late summer of 1973, but Father Sasges asked him to move to Blue River instead, a village ninety-one kilometres to the south, to become the manager of an old, unused pool hall. The idea was that it would be reactivated and function as an alternative to the bar, with no alcohol served.

Under Father Sasges' influence and at his invitation, Sheila finished her job in Aiyansh and moved to Blue River in June the following year. She left the village with good memories, especially of the children, whom she had really loved. As the ordinary white middle-class education was not connecting well with their lives, she had written a series of little books for her students, based on their own culture and on daily events of their lives in the wilderness. The people of Aiyansh showed their appreciation of her work by formally adopting her into the community and giving her a new name, which in the Nisga'a language meant "Big Nest".

It was thus with some reluctance that Sheila left the North, but throughout her time there she had been troubled by the unavailability of the Mass and, of course, she wanted to get to know Michael better. Both of these longings came together in the search for a Catholic community in which her faith could grow and find support.

In Blue River, she lived with some other girls who took part in Father Sasges' vision of community. They did odd jobs and ran a little café in an old garage, as a place where local young people could come together for coffee and snacks, music and discussion. One can say that they were Catholic "hippies", embracing the ideal of alternative living. Still, they were "conservative" in their values; their context was the Charismatic Renewal with a focus on listening to the Holy Spirit within a Catholic sacramental framework.

Sheila mainly lived on the savings from her teaching in Aiyansh, and she managed to support the other girls too. However, the work within the apostolate of Father Sasges was fuzzy in its institutional form, and not economically stable in the long term. As her savings began to dry up, Sheila decided to take training at the Department of the Environment to work as a weather observer in the local meteorological station. During the previous winter, the pool hall had collapsed into ruins under a heavy snowfall, and though no one was hurt, Michael realized he had to find alternative work. He had applied for a position at the weather station in Blue River and took a training course at Vancouver Airport. Now, Sheila would join him on the job. It was a way to support themselves, while at the same time continuing to be active in the apostolate.

At the little weather station, Michael read various instruments that measured clouds, precipitation, temperature, and wind, and then translated the readings into code, punched holes in a ticker tape, and ran it through a teletype machine that transmitted the data to Vancouver Airport. There the signal was decoded with many other such daily readings from all over British Columbia, forming the basis for the province-wide weather report.

At the weather station, three people worked in shifts, so despite being co-workers, Michael and Sheila did not really work beside each other, but met outside of the shifts. Their relationship continued to deepen, but Michael was still not sure about his vocation.

In the Catholic tradition, a deeply felt religious vocation often leads to a consideration of celibate life: for a man, either as a priest or a monk, or other alternatives, such as a celibate layperson or hermit. Therefore, during 1974, Michael attended weekend retreats at the Benedictine monastery in Mission, British Columbia, hoping to discern whether it was God's will that he become a monk or a priest, though he felt increasingly drawn to Sheila.

To add to the complexity of his life choice, he did not know whether he was to be an artist or continue with weather observing. Art as a vocation was a theme of his thoughts, as can be seen in his diary. For example, in December 1974, he wrote, "I have a growing

conviction that creative work is valid as a life's work, my life's work."
Despite these thoughts, he did not decide to resume painting again in
earnest. The question of art had to take the back seat for a while, as he
tried to find out whether his vocation would be a life solely dedicated
to God in a monastery, or whether he should remain a layperson and
start a family.

To sit passively waiting for God's decisions was not Michael's cup
of tea, or coffee; instead, he bought a shack in Blue River, measur-
ing twelve by fifteen feet, with money earned from his new job.
He developed it into a little Catholic centre and named it the Ark,
where, besides offering free coffee, he sold used clothing, Catholic
books, rosaries, and other religious items. The aim was not to make
any profit, but to evangelize. The bar had competition once again.

Michael lived in another one-room shack that he rented for fifty
dollars a month; it had a single overhead light bulb, but no running
water, and hence only an outdoor toilet. It was radical simplicity and
according to his taste.

While both Michael and Sheila were praying for discernment,
Sheila had already decided that if Michael asked her to marry him,
she would say yes. Nevertheless, she did not want to take him from
his vocation—that is, if he had a priestly calling—so she waited for
God's will to be revealed.

The Retreat

In March 1975, Michael took a four-day retreat, based on the Spiritual Exercises of St. Ignatius of Loyola. It took place in the cabin of
the hermit Brother Leonard Gibbs, a layman from Tennessee who
had received permission to build a cabin in Valemount with small
living quarters on one side and a humble little chapel on the other.
During the retreat, the hermit slept in the chapel and Michael on
the other side. They met in the chapel for prayers and some brief
discussion. The structure of the retreat was that of a *pro et con* interior
dialogue: a simplified version of a thirty-day Ignatian retreat.

The first day was dedicated to considering the reasons against marrying, the next day the arguments in favour of marriage, and then followed a day for conclusions, and a final day for confirmations. I think

few people take the decision to marry so seriously, but it is also typical of Michael's decision process, which includes a back-and-forth between yes and no, accompanied by requests for divine assistance.

Friday, March 21, 1975, was the day for arguments *against* marrying. The sun was shining from a clear sky on the snowy landscape; a gentle breeze blew the smoke from the chimney of the cabin into graceful curves. Michael ate a simple meal of tea and bread, and felt a great peace in the beautiful natural surroundings. He took up a pen and began noting down reasons against marrying. In the forefront of his mind was his own weakness, his emotional ups and downs caused in part by his years of unbelief, and also by his uncertainty about his ability to support a family in these unstable times. He then wrote about the possibility of celibate life in the lay state in combination with a vocation as an artist.

This idea of lay celibacy was an option that the hermit on the other side of the wall had proposed to Michael in a talk the same day. In this notion, we can see a tension between, on the one hand, an ideal of sincere Catholic practice founded on the total dedication of celibate life, and, on the other hand, a life in the middle of the hustle and bustle of secular modern life. The solution of celibate lay life was a compromise, or, phrased in another way, a radical innovation, in which the monk dons civilian clothes and lives among the people. This has its place, but was not sufficient as the primary solution for the crisis affecting Catholicism, and especially the Catholic family, beginning in the late 1960s in the industrialized world. What was urgently needed was a new way forward for the traditional Catholic family, when what had appeared rock solid dissipated with amazing speed. What was happening, and what Michael had experienced as a teenager, was the onset of the collapse of the traditional Catholic world in the West.[5]

The next objection against marriage was whether it was wise to bring children into the world considering its present state; and, finally, he posed the question of how deep his love really was. Nevertheless, toward the end of the day, he remarked that even if the task was to search for reasons *contra*, it had almost seemed like a day of *pros*.

After supper, he stayed up quite late and gazed at the starry night, which included an almost full moon. Lit up by the silvery light, the chapel stood as a haven of peace in the middle of the majestic natural surroundings.

On the next day, which was dedicated to arguments in support of marrying, he looked out from the cabin at the surrounding mountain peaks of the Cariboo range rising above a dark pine forest; their white tops glistened against the clear, intensively blue sky, while below in the valley, the creek was melting. He took a cup of tea and noted down the liturgical readings of the day, and then a long list of arguments. The contrast was stark when compared to the few lines against marriage that he had managed to produce the day before. The first reason was the simple but powerful "I love her. 'This love awakens my heart' and though I feel keenly my heart's wounds and walls, I know there is healing too."

He remarked on how the Holy Spirit had been so strongly present when they prayed together and how her wisdom and insights compensated for his own foolishness. Then, he countered the argument against bringing children into the ever more decadent modern world.

> Children of our love would be raised, by the Grace of God, to Love the Lord, would be gifts to this world.
> We know from our own wounds, that what was lacking in us, through the healing of Jesus can be given to our children.

Finally, he painted a picture of the family as a vocation to holiness based on total trust in God's Providence: "I believe that if we can, through all things, trust in the Lord, trust absolutely that he is leading and healing, even through possible times of distress and emptiness, then our marriage can be a holy path."[6]

"Perfect Love Casts Out Fear" (1 Jn 4:18)

When on the last day of his retreat Michael sat down to reach a decision, Sheila felt restless at home. "I can't just sit in church and pray all day," she thought. Said and done, she put on her hiking boots, filled a backpack, and set out on a pilgrimage on foot from Blue River to Avola, a distance of forty kilometres to the south. It was a full day of praying and walking.

She followed the valley with the mountains on her left and right, enjoying the scenery. However, when she was striving up a particularly steep hill, there came a surprise snowstorm. She had no gloves with her, and her hands were freezing in the wind and the heavy snowfall. Suddenly, she saw two sparrows on the path in front of her. They had just died but were still warm. She took them up and carried them in her hands to keep herself warm. Somewhat overwhelmed by the symbolic nature of the two birds, she could not quite grasp what the meaning was. But firmly believing that God would help Michael, as He had helped her, she braved the snowstorm and reached Avola in safety.

The same day, Michael realized that the arguments against marriage were primarily based on his own fears. The minor conclusions and confirmations of the final days of the retreat taken together made a very strong case for marriage. At last, he made up his mind.

Proposal

In late March 1975, after the clear discernment of a decision for marriage, Michael went back to Blue River with the intention of proposing to Sheila. When he opened the door and walked into the weather station, Sheila became so nervous that she had to lean on the barometer to keep from falling over, but noticed that he appeared joyful and peaceful, so her hope was awakened. "But what is God's will?" she wondered. As he told her what had become clear during the retreat, she became very happy, and even more so when he proposed. Without hesitation, she answered yes, and they hugged. They were now engaged. Michael then used the ticker-tape machine to make a code version of the proposal. It was never sent to Vancouver Airport, otherwise the weather report that day would have warned of strange atmospheric phenomena over the small village by the name Blue River, at the same time as a young couple deep in love went for a long walk.

Later in spring 1975, Michael moved into a three-room cabin owned by Father Sasges. He shared it with Tom de Paul, another young person in the Sasges apostolate. Tom was crippled, but was able to walk with crutches, though the process was very laborious. Michael frequently had to help him move around, to go over snowbanks, and to climb stairs. Returning the favour, Tom would sit in the Ark to keep it open while Michael worked at the weather station. Michael remembers him as a person equipped with both a keen mind and a good-humoured heart, bringing a lot of cheer into people's lives, through a kind of personal apostolate of counselling and friendship.

In April, Michael and Sheila began to talk of marriage, and Michael felt peace, joy, and a growing excitement. But, in May, his old fears began to grow again, and he sometimes felt tired, depressed, or sad over his imperfections. In prayer together with Sheila, he slowly opened up and began a process of reconciliation with his inner pain, as recorded in his diary.

May 13, 1975

I told Sheila tonight about my past, and as she gently lovingly helped me open my tightly clenched fists, she blew away the bones they held. Later, the rosary and prayer was so rich and peaceful for both of us.

May 25, 1975

A week of anger, frustration, temper, emptiness, exhaustion, feeling far, far from God. Sheila shows me how I clutch my hurt to myself, erect walls to hide anything I hate about myself—and find myself behind those walls—alone.

Sheila thought that perhaps the long forty-eight-hour shifts they had at the weather station were affecting him: Michael was not very good at managing sleep deprivation. But the diary suggests that this fight with emotional confusion and darkness was a recurring phenomenon, depending on deeper spiritual and psychological forces, aggravated by his poor physical health and the lack of sleep.

During the same time, they came to the decision to stay in Blue River and be professionally inactive: he as an artist and she as a teacher. Their dream was to own a piece of land, to live at a quiet pace with animals, and to do manual work: the vision of a simple rural life.

Despite their common decision not to pursue their professions, in the diary one can see that Michael had not completely abandoned the thought of being an artist. His had very much a wait-and-see attitude, based on a careful discernment of the will of God, as he had done in the choice of marrying—and of course, the wedding was only two months away. In July, during their marriage preparation course, the priest said that they were the only couple he had met who had asked the Lord in prayer whether they should marry.

Something more was needed to give Michael the necessary push to dedicate himself to art, and escape the vicious cycle of *pro et cons*. As he had ruled out the possibility of being a secular artist, to pursue art as a vocation for him meant also to take it seriously from a spiritual point of view. And, at that moment, it was not clear to him how that could be done—especially as their common ideal was the life of small-scale farming. Weather observation seemed to be the pragmatic option.

Marriage

The preparation for the wedding began with an open invitation to the whole Blue River Village: everyone was welcome. Invited, of course, were also Michael's and Sheila's extended families, as well as friends from various stages of their lives. They wisely decided for a potluck wedding feast, but they were somewhat worried whether the local kitchens would suffice if everyone showed up.

August 2, 1975, was the big day. Sheila had sewn Michael a folksy, grey-blue long shirt, with wide arms and wooden buttons. He had completed the outfit with a pair of shoes and trousers from the Ark, his secondhand store, as he thought they looked "good". His half-long, curly brown hair and short beard completed the hippie style and made him appear very different from Sheila's father, who looked solemn, if somewhat confined, in his dark suit, white shirt, and checkered tie. Sheila was beaming with happiness in her more traditional but simple white wedding dress, and wildflowers in her hair.

So many people came that the marriage ceremony was moved to the town hall, which was temporarily transformed into a sacred space. They installed the altar from the tiny parish church and made flower decorations with slender, light purple fireweed, green fern, and daisies, all growing wild in Blue River.

When Michael stood in front of the altar and looked down, he saw to his dismay that the trousers had a hole on one of the knees and that the shoes curled upward like oriental slippers. He understood that this was going to be rough on his relatives, especially Granny Hilda.

The music was a mix of communal folk music and a choir put together by a professional conductor from Boston who had given a year of his life to the Canadian missions. From the local raw talent, he had managed to create something similar to a sophisticated urban choir, Sheila thought, impressed and joyful.

The wedding Mass was concelebrated by Father Sasges; Father Damasus Payne, a Benedictine monk and friend of Michael's; and Father Joseph Murray, O.M.I, an old friend of Sheila's family. For both Michael and Sheila, the high point of the liturgy was when, during the vows, they looked into each other's eyes—and then, during the Consecration and elevation, when both of them experienced a sense of suspension of time as they gazed on the uplifted Sacred Host.

When they greeted their parents during the sign of peace, they saw that they were visibly touched. When Michael embraced his father, who was speechless with emotion, Michael noticed that he had tears in his eyes.

During the whole ceremony, a pig (which Michael's best man, Harry Heemskirk, had brought) was being roasted outside; unfortunately, someone put too much wood on the fire, so the pig went up in flames and turned to carbon. As the mood at the wedding was relaxed and much was improvised, this was no catastrophe, and despite the incinerated pig, everyone ate to his heart's content.

The wedding dance was a spontaneous affair held in the village hall, backed up by folk music: Michael's father played the accordion, friends played fiddles and flutes, and there was a band staffed by Sheila's cousins. In the large ring dance, everyone participated, even the local police constable, hand in hand with a petty criminal whom he sometimes locked up for various offences.

After the wedding, Michael and Sheila left for a two-week honeymoon in Western Canada. The first stop was in Calgary, Alberta, where they stayed in a large house borrowed from some friends; the remainder of the time they spent in Blue River, climbing and camping in the mountains. Then they moved into Michael's little house, which Father Sasges had given to them as a wedding present, while Tom moved in with a local family.

The Weather Observers

Michael and Sheila were now two happily married weather observers. Sheila bought goats and Michael built a log goat shed, rabbit hutches, and a chicken coop, in this way hoping to lay the foundation for their common agrarian life. They were praying for a child, but, in November 1975, Sheila began to worry why she had not yet become pregnant. Feeling panic at the thought of not having a child, and realizing that it was presumptuous to take children for granted, she ran to the Blessed Sacrament and asked for forgiveness, praying again that they might conceive.

A month later, the doctor confirmed that Sheila was pregnant. She and Michael were overjoyed. Michael had thought about children a lot and even had dreams in which he saw his future children. In his diary, he wrote that he knew deep within himself that the first child would be named John. However, in late winter, Michael was not completely at peace with the situation, and his urge to create, to dedicate himself to art, was resurfacing. In February 1976, he wrote: "Increasingly frustrated, confused, unhappy, depressed— my thoughts revolving around the job, the art, the community problems—so topsy-turvy inside."[7]

Again, exhaustion and uncertainty about providing for his family were taking their toll. He went for a long walk through the forest on snowshoes to clear his mind, praying for wisdom. The answer that he experienced interiorly was to wait patiently for the Lord's wishes—to trust Him; to be silent and praise; then he would have peace.

In Blue River, Michael was involved in the Charismatic Renewal, being the leader of a little prayer group among the volunteers working in the Sasges apostolate. Besides speaking in tongues, they experienced other charismatic gifts such as prophecy and interior words. Sheila was reticent, as she was not comfortable with the exterior manifestations of Charismatic Christianity. At first, she did not take part in meetings, but with Michael's encouragement, and that of a trusted friend who invited her to come and to just relax and not be afraid, she went to one meeting and prayed quietly throughout the whole event. To her surprise, later, in the middle of the night, she woke up praying aloud in tongues, and the next day, she felt a desire to read Sacred Scripture.

5. Sacred Art

The Brushes under the Altar

Before the wedding, the thought of working with art once again had been percolating in Michael's mind. During the beginning of 1976, these thoughts returned with a subsequent interior turbulence characteristic of his process of discernment. In one sense, Michael's and Sheila's situation was idyllic. They had a steady income, a little house, and they were expecting their first child in August. To choose art in such a situation was to venture into the unknown: to embrace uncertainty and most probably financial instability, instead of trying to make the most of what they already had.

For Michael, this tension could not be resolved by introspection; a force from the outside was needed, as he clearly felt his responsibility as a married man and soon-to-be father.

For Sheila, the idea of trying to make a living by art was frightening— she clearly saw the uncertainty that such a path entailed, but did not let herself be dominated by her fears, choosing instead to trust in the Providence of God. She had browsed Michael's portfolio of older works from 1969 to 1971 and had seen that he had a special gift. In late spring, she said to him, "Michael, you are an artist. God has given you this gift; this is what you must be."

He answered:

You know, I am now a married man, and we're expecting our first child, I have to be responsible. It's very difficult to be any kind of artist and support a family. To be a Christian artist is impossible, *absolutely* impossible, and with a family it is impossibility squared.

Sheila replied:

Nevertheless, God is God. He can do anything He wants. I think we should at least offer Him a year of our lives for you just to paint; paint

67

for the Lord; paint for Him, and let Him deal with success or failure. We can't make a success of it, but you can paint. You are able to paint: so, let's paint.[1]

This was the push Michael needed, and they took the plunge together. He resigned from his job as weather observer, and on the feast of St. Joseph the Worker, May 1, 1976, they went to the small Catholic church in Blue River, Our Lady of the Snow. Sheila was then six months pregnant, and they were choosing a life with no certain income. Michael was an unknown artist in a remote village in British Columbia—the odds were clearly not stacked in their favour.

Michael brought his brushes with him to the church and on entering put them under the altar. After Mass, they consecrated their whole life and marriage to the service of God. The intention was to do Christian art: to be a Christian artist. But what did that mean in the middle of the 1970s? The Western art scene of the twentieth century was, if anything, not Christian; very little inspiration was hence to be found there. Not since the baroque era in the seventeenth century had Western art been clearly Christian. On what tradition could Michael possibly build? Where would he start? In Ottawa, his art had been secular in themes and realistic in technique. He was not prepared for Christian art.

Anyway, Michael went home and thought to himself, "Okay, now. Let's do something wonderful for God. It may go nowhere, but at least we will have done it."[2] On the day of consecration, he notes in his diary:

St Joseph's day is our first day of freedom from the job, freedom to work on art for the next 6–8 months.... I could only cry in gratitude to God for supplying this time in my life, for a place to work and a host of other gifts.

At a prayer meeting a few days later, a man known to have prophetic gifts prayed over Michael and said, "I am calling you into the desert. You will be tested by fire." This proved very much to be the case, as contrary to expectations, the newfound freedom did not allow the pent-up creativity to flow; instead, it only laid bare an inner desert. Michael found himself incapable of painting anything at all; he merely sat in front of the easel in the Ark, which had been transformed into a studio, and could not draw even a single line. The situation was frightening: he had just quit his job and had a family to support—the baby was due in a couple of months. He thought, not unreasonably, "Am I crazy? Is all this in my imagination? Have we made a huge mistake?"

Michael is a man of strong emotions, born with the gift of high sensitivity. This is a vitally important capacity when portraying the human condition, but he also has a remarkable stubbornness and strength of willpower grounded in prayer and in reasoning. In those early years, he often felt suspended between darkness, bordering on despair, and a naked trust manifested in a steady march toward a goal irrespective of the opposition he faced. But it is doubtful if he could have pulled through the more severe trials in the way he did if he had not been blessed with a wife who supported him so wholeheartedly in taking the difficult path. For Sheila, a comfortable middle-class life was never really an option, drawn as she was toward alternative ways of living, but the squared impossibility was still there.

Despite the creative blockage, Michael went to his studio every day for three weeks. He mostly just sat there in emptiness, unable to create. He waited, prayed, and read Scripture. Sometimes he cried when seeing nothing except the dense darkness of the future lying before him and his family. He feared that his gifts had been taken away or that they had simply dried up.

Icons

At last, after three weeks, Michael recalls, within the space of twenty-four hours he received two letters and one telephone call, all pointing him in the direction of icon painting. Two of these persons did not even know that he had taken up art again. A letter from Eastern Canada told him, "Michael, you are an artist. You should paint Byzantine icons." Another person calling said, "Michael, what are you doing these days? Have you ever thought of painting icons?" A friend from farther west in Canada sent him a book of icons and wrote in her letter, "Have you ever thought of painting icons?" Michael took these "coincidences" as a confirmation from God that he should begin to paint icons in the Eastern tradition. To do so became a question of obedience for him. He wrote in his diary, June 1, 1976, "Feeling drawn to icons—expressing in a more definitive way the sacred image—the signpost pointing to God."

In this way, the loss of the sacred in Western art, and the lack of a living tradition of Christian art in the West, was to be remedied by a blood transfusion from the East. With icon painting, Michael could connect to an unbroken tradition of Christian art with strict rules separating it from secular pictures. The icon satisfied Michael's thirst for the radical and the explicit choice he had made for God and the spiritual world. At the same time, the basic problem of the lay monk came to the fore again. For the time-consuming and contemplative work of creating icons is traditionally an integrated part of the celibate life in a monastery. Icons are not signed—in a sense, the icon creates itself with the help of the painter, whose personality is subordinated and hidden. To be a layperson painting icons—in a sense, trying to make a career and supporting a family on the income of the sale of icons—was an attempt to combine two very different worlds.

To make matters worse, icon painting is a tradition, which means an inheritance handed down from the preceding generation to the next as a gift, a patrimony. It is not something one is supposed to learn from a book, like *Icons for Dummies* or *Icon Painting: Step by Step*. A tradition needs to be taught by a master who stands in an unbroken chain reaching back to the legitimizing source. The critical point of a tradition is when that chain is broken; then there is no possibility to continue—that is, if the source, for example, God, does not make a new foundation. Without standing in a living, concrete tradition, one can always fall prey to the argument that this is not *real* icon painting; because as you are not born or initiated into the tradition, you cannot possibly pass it on or practise it in a genuine manner. It will look like an icon—but it will not be an icon.

What Michael embarked upon was, however, not the path of becoming a true, in the sense of a traditional, icon painter; he was instead attempting a transfusion of life into the Western tradition and, at the same time, probing Christian art as a lay apostolate. Once again, it was impossibilities squared twice, and Sheila sensed that this was going to be a rocky road. From the difficult to the impossible, one might say. Nevertheless, she continued to trust in God's Providence.

Michael felt this challenge too, despite the confirmations he had sensed in the advice of his friends. In the beginning of June 1976, the postmaster's job in Blue River was open.

> I am greatly attracted to it—it's a "sure thing"—well paying and permanent—a real temptation, but one I must resist despite all its attractiveness—I have promised the Lord to do this act—to really submit it to his Lordship.[3]

Life and Death

In the beginning of June, just as Michael had emerged from his initial creative desert and begun to explore the world of icons, David, his father, suffered a heart attack and was hospitalized for a couple of weeks. When Terry visited him in the hospital, David said that he had recorded a message for Michael that he wanted Terry to hear. This was not strange, as Michael and Sheila used to exchange tapes with Elaine and David. The long distance between Ottawa and Blue River made it difficult to meet, and telephone conversations were expensive, so it was a nice complement to letters. David also said to Terry that he had received a visit from a priest due to Michael's intervention.

I have not found that particular tape, but have listened to another, recorded on July 18, when David had been at home for two weeks. One hears first Elaine saying that David is improvingly wonderfully, and that the doctor has said he can return to work again on August 3. She says that his spirits are good and that he attributes his recovery to the prayers of the family. She ends by wishing Michael all the best in his present painting project of five small portraits of saints, on which he was working.

Then David begins to speak and he mentions a letter that Michael sent July 10, which he has been reading and rereading, enjoying it very much. After a comment on a book on cheese making, in which one glimpses his sense of humour, he thanks Michael for his advice on two paintings that he is working on. And he asks for photographs of the five saint portraits when Michael has finished them. He ends with the wish that he will be able to come for a visit to Blue River next year.

A conversation on art was emerging between father and son. David, an amateur painter, had shown Michael when he was a young boy how to paint, and now he was taking advice from his own son.

Michael's life is full of strong existential and religious contrasts. The same summer as David fell ill, Sheila was preparing for the 176-kilometre drive to the hospital where she was to give birth. On July 25, she was beginning to have contractions and, among other things, packed in her travel bag the book *The Womanly Art of Breast-feeding* beside Chesterton's *The Everlasting Man*.

While new life was on its way, another was leaving. In the evening, two days later, Michael's father suffered a second heart attack and died.

After Michael received the telephone call about David's death, he knelt down by their home altar in Blue River, and interiorly he sensed his father's presence and heard his voice strongly in his mind: "Don't be afraid, Mike; I am very happy now; God loves you very much." Michael later wrote in his diary, "Joy and sadness mixed—it is so hard to believe—we are so far away." The grief of the loss of his father was mingled with the joy of knowing that he, like his own father, Stephen, had returned to the Church at the very end.

David was only fifty years old when he died. At a time when Michael and his newly founded family needed it the most, he was left without the support of a father; when he chose art as a vocation, the support of his artist father disappeared. Such an event can easily derail a new and insecure venture, such as a dedication to icon painting in the wilderness, but instead it led to new opportunities. Perhaps not the least because death at the end of July was followed by the birth of a son in the morning of August 14, at the hospital in McBride. The baby was, as Michael had been so sure, a John.

It was a long labour, nineteen hours. The baby was healthy, though there had been complications, as he was born with the cord wrapped around his neck, and a section of it was knotted. Michael cried at the sight of his newborn son, and Sheila was excited and joyful. Despite their exhaustion, they felt welded into one, rejoicing together over their newborn son. For safety's sake, Michael baptized him there on the spot when he saw that the face of the baby was dark blue. Two weeks later, John was conditionally baptized by a priest, and his first smile came a week later, to the delight of his parents.

6. Iconography

In the beginning of the fall of 1976, Michael and Sheila could look back on a momentous half year. They had made the courageous act of staking their future on Michael's career as a Christian artist, and David had died merely two weeks before the birth of their first child. The question was, how to go from here? They were, after all, living in a remote village in the Rocky Mountains, British Columbia.

Their decision was to go east, to Ottawa. In this way, they could give some support to Elaine, who now was alone, while Michael would try to find a way to learn icon painting. Once again, it was the better-education possibilities that drew him from the periphery to the centre.

In 1972, Michael had moved west to British Columbia, to the wilderness away from the art and city life of Ottawa and Toronto. Five years later, he was coming back with a young family and the idea of connecting to the tradition of icon painting. This fusion of East and West was not wholly new for him. Although he lived within the realm of the Charismatic Renewal in Blue River—with prayer meetings in which prophetic words were spoken and persons were prayed over—the Eastern tradition had been present in his life through the Madonna House Apostolate in Combermere, Ontario, located two hundred kilometres west of Ottawa. It was founded in 1947 by Catherine Doherty, a Russian Catholic émigré who came to the United States during the First World War. She had begun her apostolate in the early 1930s by founding a "Friendship House" in Toronto to work among the poor. Ironically, she was made to leave due to accusations of Communism—she, who had barely survived the revolution of the Bolsheviks. After a year in Europe as a reporter, she went to Harlem, New York, and opened a Friendship House there; but, in 1946, she was once again forced to leave, now due to opposition among her own staff.[1]

The following year, she moved to Canada with her husband, Eddie, seemingly completely burned-out after all her work and disappointments. Nevertheless, a new foundation was slowly laid for Madonna House, which developed into a worldwide movement.[2] Michael had contacts with the Madonna House Centre in Combermere before going west; and, when he was on a retreat trying to discern whether to marry or not, he referred to the cabin as a *poustinia*, a Russian word for hermitage (literally "the little desert")—a notion introduced into the West by Catherine in a book published the same year.[3]

We can see how different Christian traditions came together in Michael's life. Since his conversion, the Catholic Church with its sacramental life had been foundational for his Christian faith, as seen in his eucharistic devotion, which functioned as the beating heart of his religious and mystical life. Moreover, the Charismatic Movement with its focus on openness to the Spirit, religious experiences, miracles, and contemporary prophecy was important for his intense, interior, spiritual life. To these two, Eastern Christianity was united with its aesthetic tradition of religious images, the icons, and the experience of the desert: *poustinia*. This welding together of different traditions (Charismatic, Western, and Eastern Christianity) took place in the context of the 1970s, when there was a movement both in the Catholic Church and in the Western world, more generally, toward alternative lifestyles. A cultural current was making people long for the life of nature and farming, but, in 1976, Michael and Sheila were going in the opposite direction: to the capital of Canada.

Going East

The decision to move back to the city was taken in October 1976, and, in November, Michael and Sheila set about arranging the practical details. Michael managed to sell their little house for a few thousand dollars, and with the money from the sale, he bought a rather battered pickup truck. He also sold a painting, which provided them with some extra money for the trip. After saying goodbye to Sheila's parents, they began their drive with a prayer for protection. Divine assistance was of the essence: winter had set in, and their baby was only three months old. The truck, named by its new owners, "the donkey", was loyal and steadfast, but not new and shiny, lacking among other things a heating system. Snow was beginning to fall, and the drive to Ottawa was forty-two hundred kilometres long. Baby John, swaddled like an Inuit Christ Child, was nonetheless warm in his cardboard box in the front seat between his two adventurous parents.[4]

As you have perhaps guessed, after the donkey had climbed the first mountains and was rolling down a long hill, they heard a loud thump, and it began to squeak in a most ominous and agonizing way. The donkey was clearly hurt and in need of instant care. They managed to hobble to a garage farther along the highway, and, after having investigated the truck, the mechanic said, "Boy, were you lucky, the right front tire was just about to fall off and the left one any minute!" Michael praised God, and after a long wait, they resumed the days of driving across the prairies to Ottawa.

During the winter and spring of 1977, they lived in the house of Michael's mother, Elaine. She had been widowed at only fifty years of age and was grateful for Sheila's support, and baby John was a real solace in her grief. The house was not big: a mere one-bedroom cottage in Manotick, a village a half-hour drive south of Ottawa, with a view of the Rideau River. While Elaine slept on the couch, Michael and Sheila had the only bedroom. They did not have to pay any rent, and Michael used the garage as his studio. It was unheated, so during the winter the varnish on the paintings never really dried. This brought with it a surprising antique effect; the surface became warped, which made the icons look old.

For Sheila to come to Ottawa was an adventure; she had never lived east of the Rocky Mountains. Still, she had to leave all her family and most of her friends in British Columbia. To live in Elaine's little house was also no long-term solution, so the feeling was that of being on a journey, of not having settled down yet.

William Kurelek

The main motivation to move east was so that Michael could begin to learn icon painting in earnest. He therefore had to find a teacher who would agree to take him in as an apprentice, or at least show him the fundamentals. The search took him to Madonna House in

Combermere, where there was an icon painter, Joan Bryant. She had studied fine arts and worked as an art teacher, but, in 1969, she became a permanent celibate staff member of Madonna House. When Michael came for a one-day visit, she was forty-three years old and had painted icons for approximately five years.[5] She introduced Michael to tempera painting and showed him some icons; he was overwhelmed by their beauty, comparing them in their brilliant colours to gems. Then she instructed Michael in the basic process of making an icon: the use of a maple board aged one year; the first covering of linen and gesso—that is, a traditional white underpainting; the drawing; and the painting itself with tempera paint—the final touch was the varnishing. Bryant emphasized the importance of careful work and being true to the essentials of icon painting, which included the absolute necessity of prayer—she also fasted before beginning each new project. The ideal presented to Michael was that of meditative craftsmanship relying on a prayerful relation to God and a denial of one's desires. This was sacred art as a vocation.

According to Michael's diary, Bryant was enthusiastic about his work and said that he had great talent, and that he should work on. This was the encouragement he had hoped for, and he was happy about it. The next visit to Joan was on his birthday, April 2, and he brought Sheila and baby John with him. Bryant continued to encourage Michael to paint, and emphasized that he should write to the famous painter William Kurelek, who was a friend of the Madonna House community, and tell him of his desire to be an artist totally dedicated to work for the Lord. Michael's thoughts were, "What on earth could I say to him. Okay, I will write."

William, "Bill", Kurelek was a second-generation Ukrainian immigrant born in 1927 in Whitford, Alberta, Canada. His childhood during the Great Depression with parents disapproving of his interest in art, in combination with bullying in school and an innate high sensitivity, led to psychological problems, and he was eventually diagnosed with schizophrenia. In 1952, he moved to England for treatment, which included both art therapy and electroshock therapy. This did not seem to work, and Kurelek repeatedly tried to take his own life. The turning point instead came when, after having reached the darkest moment of his descent into madness, he began to pray. With his return to the Christian faith, he improved to the degree that he could leave the hospital and begin making a living by painting small trompe l'oeil paintings. Kurelek was brought up in the Orthodox tradition, but during his youth and the revolt against his parents, he had become an atheist. After a pilgrimage to Lourdes, he became interested in Catholicism and entered the Catholic Church in 1957.

Two years later, Kurelek returned to Canada and began a massive project of illustrating the whole Gospel of St. Matthew as an act of thanksgiving for his recovery. Besides explicit, sometimes jarring, religious themes, he also painted rural Canadian scenes with a warm, slightly naïve realism. His breakthrough came with an exhibit in 1960, after which he achieved fame as a realist painter.

Beginning in 1962, Kurelek became connected to the Madonna House community, and, in 1974, he bought a small farm in Combermere, where he stayed with his family during summers and holidays.[6] When he received Michael's letter, he had been a well-known and appreciated artist for seventeen years, though he was also criticized for his explicit religious convictions and attempts at evangelizing. In this sense, he was a perfect mentor for Michael, combining a serious and explicit Catholicism with successful painting.

A week later, Michael received a reply from Kurelek. Michael had written to him asking whether he could show him his work, and Kurelek answered with a short note that included the following sentences:

> I feel you are a bit idealistic considering you are a married man (about making a living painting icons). However, this world belongs to God and He can work any miracles He pleases, including providing for you as an icon painter—So I'll not say more beyond offering to share my experiences.[7]

He also wrote that Michael should phone him, a collect call at Kurelek's expense. Before leaving for England in the 1950s, Kurelek had himself sought the advice of famous painters, but never received replies. He was, therefore, very generous with young aspiring painters seeking his advice.

Kurelek's scepticism toward making a living as an icon painter and at the same time being a provider for a family was an expression of common sense. It confirmed Michael's doubts—according to all sensible persons, his project was somewhat crazy. We can compare Michael's situation with that of Joan Bryant, who had made a vow of poverty and was living a celibate life in a community, which to a high degree depended on the generosity of benefactors. Still, as Kurelek also mentions, a blind trust in God requires such madness. It does not mean that it will be a smooth ride—it is more like an adventure than a comfortable, secure middle-class life with some extra sprinkling of religion on it. A married icon painter was, and still is, similar to a squared circle.

Two weeks later, Michael visited Kurelek on Balsam Avenue in the eastern part of Toronto. They spent several hours together looking at Michael's work, and Kurelek said encouraging things— for example, that Michael should follow his vocation, because to do otherwise would be a sin. He also wanted to stay in contact and told Michael that when he was going to Combermere, he should let him know, so that they could meet at the farm.

Kurelek came across to Michael as a silent, interior man who when he spoke did so in a gentle and quiet way, but full of meaning. Kurelek also took back what he had written earlier in his letter about the idealism of making a living as an icon painter. He said that Michael's work was much better than he expected. Still Michael expressed some doubts.

> I said perhaps I am being foolish and he replied that I should be a fool for Christ's sake and God will bless you.... He [Kurelek] said that there may come a point where it will not be practical to continue painting without causing pain to my family (that is, shelter, food, a decent living) and that I cannot put painting above the livelihood of the family.[8]

In Michael's reaction to this, we can see his determination manifested. He does not simply acquiesce, but his thoughts went to Abraham's sacrifice (Gen 22); a sacrifice of heart was demanded by God—that is, one has to intend to go all the way in obedience. I do not think that Michael here thought that it was appropriate to prepare the sacrifice of one's family for the sake of art; instead, he writes that he and Sheila needed to be prepared to use all the money they had received from the sale of the cabin to support them in this project. Only when the last penny was spent, and no further support was forthcoming, would he get a "normal" job. It was a kind of religious brinkmanship: living without a safety net, and not giving up until it was totally impossible. Trust is here persistence in the face of overwhelming odds.

After their encouraging talk, Kurelek took Michael out for lunch to a Chinese restaurant, and then to underscore the feasibility of overcoming the seemingly impossible, he brought Michael to the studio of another Ukrainian artist, Mykola Bidniak, living on Gladstone Avenue, a half-hour drive from Kurelek's house. Bidniak received Michael warmly and remarked, "Well, well, well, an Irishman painting icons.... This should be interesting"; and, "If you are crazy enough, you are going to succeed." To which Michael replied, "I am crazy enough to try." Bidniak himself was painting under severe limitations, having lost both his arms and one eye in Europe after World War II, when he was planting trees and hit a landmine.[9] Wielding brushes with his mouth and toes, he painted with an incredible energy and accuracy that astonished Michael. Clearly, one had to go to the very edge and not give up; endurance and perseverance was of the essence. This act of will, however, did not mean that the inner turmoil went away, as Michael was to learn—almost to the contrary, as one pushes oneself to the limit, the conflicting inner voices often increase in intensity.

The move to Ottawa began to produce the results that they had hoped for: Michael now received instruction from an icon painter, and he had established a relation with a serious, well-established Catholic artist. The benefits of being in the centre of things were beginning to show. The next step for Michael was to prepare for an exhibition, but he had no offer yet. He also wished that he had some more space: a real studio.

Two weeks later, he and Sheila received an offer of a little farmhouse near Bancroft, Ontario, rent-free for the summer. It was beautifully situated by a lake, not far from Madonna House and Kurelek's farm, but it had no plumbing or electricity. Such simplicity, however, did not deter Michael; it was almost an added bonus. The "Franciscan" situation attracted him.

On June 1, 1977, they settled in the cabin, and Michael enjoyed the scenery of maple woods, the stillness, and the quiet, as well as the wind blowing fragrant wood smoke from the stone fireplace by the front door, and the haunting calls of loons in the moonlight. He felt his soul was easing, quieting; it was a chance to think and absorb. The setting seemed ideal for contemplative artistic work, to develop slowly his icon painting, but it had the opposite effect on Michael, as when he had made his decision to begin painting he became unable to create anything.

During the night, he thus experienced "fears, anguish, and dark-ness" and could not sleep; he felt like a failure. Sheila tried to con-vince him not to try to force himself to paint many paintings: not to rush things to get material for a whole exhibition, but to paint with love and reverence. However, the anxiety did not disperse, and, on June 19, he wrote, "Unable to work at painting—the springs within have been dried up for weeks and when I think of forcing out some-thing I am filled with distaste and fatigue." He had to be content with relaxing and reading. The blockage continued to the point where he began to wonder whether this was all vain self-delusion or at best a mistake. He was coming close to the edge, but then he got three encouraging letters. One was about an icon he had painted, another was offering encouragement, and a third came with a bundle of icon prints. He thought, "It seems to say, yes, continue—but I feel utterly *shallow* and unworthy."[10]

On June 20, he began to paint a copy of the well-known icon *Our Lady of Vladimir*, and "the streams started to flow and I could paint." Behind this was a total outpouring of his inner troubles to Sheila, which she met with love and prayer. Her support had become nec-essary in his struggle with self-doubt—he also made the conscious decision not to doubt himself, and not to fear; and finally, "I set out and began to work even though it felt empty and pedestrian; then something inside clicked and started to go."[11] I think we can see here how an important foundation for fruitful work was being laid. It was the combination of support from Sheila and a conscious move beyond the volatility of his feelings: to trust and work even when no emotional inspiration was forthcoming. This is what John of the Cross called "the dark night of the soul": to proceed in faith even when the senses, emotions, and intellect are numb and dry, immersed as they are in darkness.[12] It was the coming into maturity of religious life: the Way of the Cross.

During the remainder of June and the beginning of July, his inspiration was flowing, and Michael was joyously working on the icon of *Our Lady of Vladimir*, whose feast day fittingly was June 23 (according to the Julian calendar). His trials and temptations were, nevertheless, not over, and soon he was to experience something that called into question the very foundation of his art project; perhaps an Irishman painting icons was not only crazy, but also inappropriate and doomed to fail.

The Russian Lady

In early July, Michael went to Madonna House to continue his instruction in icon painting with Joan Bryant. While waiting for her in the dining hall, he met Catherine Doherty, the founder of Madonna House, coming downstairs from the chapel. She was at that time eighty-one years old, limping with a cane and rather heavy, moving with some difficulty down the steps. When Doherty was told by a member of the community what Michael's errand at Madonna House was, she was not particularly happy about it. "You, paint icons? Ha!" she snapped angrily at him. "You just want to make money!" Stunned by this groundless accusation, he said not a word. Her mood was perhaps coloured by her fatigue after just arriving home from a six-month working trip abroad, the recent death of her husband, and the physical pain she was suffering at the time, but she was also known to be frank and sometimes brutally blunt. Her charisma, that of a leader, was founded on the self-confidence of her aristocratic background and seasoned with experiences of persecution. Further to that, she had been a refugee, had spent decades working with the poor, and was twice made to leave her lifework behind. In front of her stood a young man beginning a journey in Christian art, but she was not sure about his motives; she, therefore, began to question him with her deep, commanding voice whether it was the "lure of the East", "another temporary fad, or money", that had induced him to make this choice. Michael had difficulty getting anything said at all, under pressure as he was. She said, "You might be able to study under an Orthodox priest in Paris, but he probably wouldn't take you; you're a Roman Catholic." She then said, "Come!" and led him over to an icon on the far wall before which burned a vigil light. She bent low touching the floor with one hand. At her age and physical condition, this was not easy; she thus dropped her cane in the effort and Michael bent to pick it up. She angrily said, "Leave it!" Michael picked up the cane anyway. She said:

> When a Russian or Orthodox does this, it has 2000 years of meaning behind it. But a Westerner, what does it mean ... whsst! You may paint beautiful pictures, they may look like icons, but a Russian could tell you the difference in three seconds.

She then left, and as Michael turned to walk part of the way with her, she said, "We are going two different directions; go see your friend."

Michael went to Joan Bryant's little *poustinia*, her studio cabin, and she said to him that he should not think too deeply about Doherty's words, just pray and paint on, and her words would eventually return to him in a better light. Michael thought, "She would not soften the blow, because she believed Catherine was right—I wasn't an icon painter—that what I am is an artist of fine talent who wants to serve God. He will lead me." Despite his intention to trust, Michael was hurt—a "woman of famous spirituality had found me wanting or, at least, questionable". Later he cried and prayed to God in the chapel.[13]

Despite Doherty's brusqueness with him, she had pointed to something important. To paint icons is to place oneself outside the art world; the essential aspect of icons is adoration, ritual piety, not aesthetic appreciation, while these two can, of course, coincide. Even an ugly icon, blackened and scarred, can be the carrier of great power and majesty, which is acknowledged through devotion. Once again, the finger was put on the weak point in Michael's project: to make a living by something not oriented toward monetary evaluation. The "market" for icons, as for sacred art in general, was primarily constituted by church commissions. An artist of sacred art is very much dependent upon the vitality of the Christian churches in his country of residence: secularization is not good for business. A Christian artist who does not brook any compromise with the spirit of the world can thus unwillingly turn into a sign of the rejection of Christianity by modern society.

Doherty's comments also pointed to the importance of a living tradition—that icon painting is not a skill, but a practice dependent on the culture of a people.

However, at that time, icons were beginning to transcend their original context; they were becoming mass-produced commodities available globally. In addition, with the ecumenical turn of the Catholic Church after the Second Vatican Council, there was a new openness toward Eastern traditions in the Latin Church.[14] To use icons in a Catholic church, or even a Protestant one, had thus begun to be accepted.

Nevertheless, the question was whether an icon was a *real* icon if it was not embedded in the specific ritual and devotional life where it had developed during two millennia. In the postmodern world, fragments of religious traditions travel, dislocated and decontextualized, as Doherty herself had fled Russia and found new roots in America. We find icons in Catholic churches, yoga classes in American suburbs, and rosaries around the necks of pop stars. But what is a genuine transplant? How do you carry a beating heart from one culture to another, so that it can give fresh life to its new cultural organism?

The End of Times

If globalization in the second half of the twentieth century was making traditions come increasingly into closer contact, another theme of the 1970s was the sense of the imminent threat of a global catastrophe of apocalyptic proportions. The most potent of these threats was the risk of a nuclear war. It animated Kurelek, for example, who with his inner eye saw Toronto burning. He tried unsuccessfully to gain a permit to build a large cement shelter connected to his home in Toronto. Eventually, he built one on his farm in Combermere instead. His idea was that after the approaching catastrophe, a new era for mankind and Christianity would begin. This idea was born of a combination of a modern secular fear and the imagery of Christian eschatology.

Since his conversion, Michael had pondered the connection between the technological development of modernity and an end-time scenario leading to a cataclysmic confrontation between good and evil. To look forward to the Second Coming of Christ and wonder if it is imminent is a natural Christian instinct, which began already in the first century as seen in the Revelation to John, the last book of the Bible. All Christian generations since have wondered whether the trials, wars, and persecutions of *their* times were the prelude to the end. At the same time, this focus on being prepared is tempered in the Bible with the warning that a day for the Lord is as a thousand years for man (2 Pet 3:8), and that no one actually knows the day or the time, not even the Son of God (Mt 24:36).

Despite these reservations, the increased power of technological modernity, two terrible world wars, and the secularization of the West in the twentieth century seemed to provide clear signs pointing to the possibility that the end was actually near from a human point of view. The approaching close of the second millennium added even more symbolic weight to these expectations. Among Evangelicals, for example, the publication of *The Late, Great Planet Earth* in 1970 by Hal Lindsey, which was made into a movie in 1979, became an influential interpretation connecting the Cold War and the battle of Armageddon; it was believed the latter would probably take place in the 1980s.[15]

On July 21, 1977, Michael made a note in his diary that there were a lot of prophecies coming from the Charismatic Renewal about a time of darkness approaching, and he wondered if this would involve the increasingly powerful computer technology. The calculating power of computers and the almost complete surveillance society that it made possible became in this way part of a techno-apocalypse, which is a pervasive trope in Evangelical end-time imagination.[16] To Michael it was clear that a basis was being laid for a future totalitarian regime extreme in its reach and capabilities. With the combination of increasing computer power and mass surveillance, the preconditions for the rule of Antichrist, the final and most brutal persecution of Christianity, seemed to fall into place.[17]

Such an eschatological understanding of modern technology is easily connected to another influential critique of modernity, the environmental movement. The current development of global society is then seen both as unsustainable and as increasingly spiritually and socially suffocating. The choice stands between freezing technology at a certain level, like the Amish, or using it—but in a restrained mode and always wanting to dispense with it, in order to return to a more genuine, authentic life based on handicrafts and agriculture. Later we will see how an eschatological framework is crucial for Michael's critique of modernity, and how he repeatedly tries to go off the grid, but at the same time is dependent upon it for his work.

Pro-Life

During the late 1970s, an apocalyptic understanding of modernity, despite differences such as the idea of the Rapture and the role of the pope, cut through denominational boundaries. In this way, it created contacts between Evangelicals and Catholics who were critical of the development of Western societies. Another such unifying set of issues, with a similar agenda of opposing modernity, but which in contrast solidified into ecumenical organizations, was the pro-life movement.

In Canada, abortion was illegal until 1969, when it became allowed if the life of the mother was in danger. The legislation was a compromise satisfying neither the opponents of abortion nor those in favour of a more liberal approach. The pro-life movement began in earnest as a reaction to this change in legislation, but already, in 1968, the first pro-life group, the Alliance for Life, was formed in Ottawa. In 1973, a sister organization, Coalition for Life, was formed with a more explicit political task. However, a conflict was brewing between pragmatists, who wanted to focus on restricting the availability of abortion, and those who wanted to achieve a complete ban of abortions. In 1977, this tension led to the formation of a new organization, Campaign Life Coalition, which worked for the latter goal.[18]

The movement was predominately run and managed by Catholic laypersons, but from 1977 Canadian Evangelicals also joined the struggle in larger numbers. One of the prominent features was the passivity of the Catholic hierarchy in the 1970s in relation to the pro-life organizations.[19] This can be traced back to their stance toward the encyclical *Humanae Vitae*, which was promulgated by Pope Paul VI in 1968. It condemned, besides abortion, all forms of artificial contraceptives, insisting that the sexual act must always be open to new life.

> Therefore We [Paul VI] base Our words on the first principles of a human and Christian doctrine of marriage when We are obliged once more to declare that the direct interruption of the generative process

already begun and, above all, all direct abortion, even for therapeutic reasons, are to be absolutely excluded as lawful means of regulating the number of children.[20]

Toward the end of the 1960s the sexual revolution was in full swing, powered by the birth-control pill, publicly available in the United States in 1960 and in 1969 in Canada.[21] When Pope Paul VI reaffirmed traditional Catholic moral doctrine, he was most decisively going against the cultural and social current of the Western world. Polls consistently show that since the 1960s, a growing majority of Catholics in North America think that the Catholic Church should allow contraceptives.[22]

It was therefore not surprising that the Canadian Conference of Catholic Bishops felt crushed between the hammer and the anvil, between the Magisterium of the pope and the dominant view of Canadian society—and, increasingly, that of Canadian Catholics.

Only two months after *Humanae Vitae*, the Canadian bishops released the so-called Winnipeg Statement, which in effect permitted individual Catholics to follow what their conscience told them was the correct way, even when it was in conflict with Church teaching.[23]

In Canada, the ground was thus prepared for a widespread dissent in the 1970s among laypersons and clergy on questions of sexual morality. However, the resistance to abortion, in comparison with the ban on contraceptives, was able to claim a much greater proportion of Catholics and Canadians in general. For example, it was still possible to collect large numbers of signatures (in 1975, one million signatures were gathered) and organize impressive marches in order to demonstrate the large numbers of people actually supporting the pro-life movement, and to show both politicians and the public that they were a force to be reckoned with. Moreover, it was a way to galvanize the supporters into action, as they understood that they were not alone.

In 1977, Michael and Sheila took part in such a pro-life march in Ottawa, where one of the main speakers was the British journalist and author Malcolm Muggeridge.[24] They carried their own homemade sign with a quote from the Book of Jeremiah: "Before I formed you in the womb I knew you, and before you were born I consecrated you" (1:5). However, when Michael and Sheila later saw the media reports, they were severely disappointed, as they learned that the numbers of those participating were underreported and the coverage negatively skewed.

Exhibit of Sacred Art

Returning to Ottawa from their summer interlude of rural simplicity, Michael and Sheila moved into an old duplex on Selby Avenue. John was now a one-year-old and walked a little unsteadily, holding on to the furniture as he explored the new surroundings, while Michael was painting intensely, "a hundred small details". Toward the end of September, he had finished forty paintings, all framed, and the daily prayer intention was that he would find an exhibition spot, or an interested gallery curator.

Before going back to Ottawa, they were invited for lunch at the Kurelek farm in Combermere. When they arrived there, Kurelek said he hoped that Michael would not only preach to the converted—that is, have an exhibition in a church basement—but that his art would be a light on a hilltop. Kurelek had achieved his own position in the public space through painting in two different keys, to borrow a musical metaphor. He achieved popularity through his illustrations of Canadian rural life such as in his 1975 book *A Prairie Boy's Summer*, which was based on his childhood memories. In this way, he was able to escape the ghetto walls of Christian culture that secularization made increasingly confining. On the other hand, he also painted explicit religious themes such as intense pictures of Christ's Crucifixion. Sometimes these keys were blended successfully, as in the book *A Northern Nativity*, published a year before he met Michael. In it, the birth of Christ is portrayed as taking place in different marginal places in Canada: in an Inuit igloo or in a lumber camp stable.[25]

Michael decided not to hide his religious convictions, by allowing them to be merely the unspoken basis of his work, which would be allowed to surface only in certain genres such as church commissions. He instead took it upon himself to paint Christian themes in a medium designed for that purpose. The icon was uncompromisingly religious, but there was little room for it in the secular art world— that is, without a frame of irony signalling critical distance. One can say that Michael's paintings were destined to be displayed in church basements—well tucked away inside the ghetto. His uncompromising decision to do sacred art made him disinclined to paint both secular and religious themes, and then try to evangelize the world through their relation and combination, as Kurelek had done. His position was that of no compromise, and, if postmodern people did not like being preached at, that was their choice and responsibility. It is uncertain whether Kurelek was trying to point Michael in the direction of including a secular form of address, or if he was merely hoping that there was a hilltop somewhere hospitable enough to allow the light of Michael's art to shine.

During October, Michael and Sheila searched for a place to exhibit Michael's art; it was frustrating when nothing seemed to come forward. But toward the end of the month, they found the parish hall of St. Patrick's Basilica on Gloucester Street, and the exhibition was planned for November 1–7, 1977. The hall was huge, and to Michael it seemed ideal. At the same time, the Dominican monastery, through the prior Father Belanger, rented Michael, for a nominal sum, an empty monastic cell as a studio. It was located deep within the monastery on the fifth floor; it was quiet, peaceful, and full of light, and it had a splendid view of the city. Above Michael's window, the word "Veritas" (truth) was chiselled on the frieze beneath the battlements. For the next three years, five days a week, he would attend daily Mass with the Dominicans and eat lunch with them and the students of their college.

On November 1, the exhibition of Michael's new kind of art opened. Many people came; several paintings were sold, and he received some commissions. It was a promising start, and he calculated that the income would keep them afloat for at least six months. The day after, there was a review of the show in the *Ottawa Citizen*, and a larger article on Michael appeared three days after that. Sadly, in the same paper, there was also a note on the death of William Kurelek. His wife, Jean, had written to Michael the first day of the show, as he had been unable to write the letter himself because of his late-stage cancer. The doctors had, Jean wrote, only given him a few days to live.

Kurelek's funeral in Toronto was on the last day of the show, November 7. Michael wanted to go, but could not make it. Once again, joy was mingled with the sorrow of death. He wrote in his diary that this "loss of another father in the spirit" filled him with grief, and

> created an intense hunger for fatherhood, to be understood and consoled—it raises so many questions—especially the mystery of death rises up and cries for understanding—why, why?!!! Thank God for this peaceful monastery, for the Mass.[26]

The review in the *Ottawa Citizen* was titled "Icon Show Not for the Cynical", but it was generally positive in its comments. It congratulated Michael on his "finely developed painterly skills" and for not sacrificing quality for quantity, though this was a large show with forty-six icons. However, the reviewer, Martha Scott, ends with a reservation:

> The *Images of the Lord* exhibition appeals to a specific audience. The cynical and non-religious segment of the population might not be able to fully appreciate it, but for those who enjoy religious art this is an interesting show.[27]

Compared with his first exhibition, which was an unreserved success, Michael had now been placed in a specific compartment, that of *religious* art.

The article on Michael's art and life, published a few days later, was titled "Painter Risks All to Develop Religious Art" and describes his and Sheila's decision to embark on their adventure with little promise of financial security. In the interview, he says, "A painter expresses what is precious to him, what is a profound experience. That's why I expressed Christ. He is a reality to me, a presence."[28]

One of those who came to the show was Patricia Morley, a forty-eight-year-old professor of English literature at Concordia University. It was Kurelek who had encouraged Michael to invite her. At the time, she was working on a biography of Kurelek, which was published in the 1980s.[29] In what she saw at the exhibition, she perceived something similar to that which had fascinated her in Kurelek's life and art. She introduced herself to Michael, and from that day began to collect his art and follow his career. During the following year, she asked him if she could write his biography; Michael, who then was only twenty-nine years old, was, of course, both somewhat perplexed and flattered. He had not really lived a whole life yet, not even a half; and if he lived until, at least, sixty years of age, then she would be ninety years old! He, therefore, answered somewhat vaguely, well, yes, there is a possibility. Upon which she exhorted him to save all his letters and reviews, and send them to her. Michael never did send them, but they continued to correspond through letters.

The Altar Piece of St. Barnabas

After the show at St. Patrick's hall, Michael continued to paint in his quiet monastic studio, while the family was living on the income that the show had generated. He was thus a married man working among monks, in a sense combining the two roles—but monks do not have children. In February, Sheila was expecting a new child to be born in September—the family was growing. At the same time, little John fell off the couch and broke his collarbone; he had to wear a sling around his arm. As Michael continued to balance contemplative work life in a monastery with family life, the situation, of course, increased in difficulty and according to the number of children. One child is still child's play.

In a conversation with the Dominican theologian Jean-Marie Roger Tillard, who was a peritus (expert) at the Second Vatican Council, Michael was surprised by his reservations toward the Charismatic Renewal and by his view that the icons being painted at Madonna House were not authentic icons.[30] Michael answered Tillard,

> What a difficult, even more dubious, light a Roman Catholic Irishman would be in, compared to the Madonna House Eastern rite hermits (Joan), who have studied extensively and fast and pray as the foundation of their work.[31]

Despite Michael's reservations about the opinions of Father Tillard, he and Sheila began at this time to drift away from the Charismatic Renewal, while retaining some elements of it in their prayer life. Michael also began to think about finding a synthesis of the discipline of the Christian East and the mystical emotional expression of the West. He was on his way to a new artistic language.

In this task, Michael was helped by another Dominican in the community, the renowned Thomist scholar Father Lawrence Dewan.[32] He introduced Michael to the French Thomist philosopher Etienne Gilson, whose book *Painting and Reality* would play a key role in his understanding of his vocation as an artist. Michael was already familiar with another Thomist writing about art, Jacques Maritain, whose *Art and Scholasticism* was one of his favourite books, shaping his idea of what a "sacred artist" could be. For example, on the relation between faith and art, Maritain advises the artist:

> Do not make the absurd attempt to dissociate in yourself the artist and the Christian. They are one, if you *are* truly Christian, and if your art is not isolated from your soul by some system of aesthetics. But apply only the artist to the work; precisely because the artist and the Christian are one, the work will derive wholly from each of them.[33]

The combined impression of these writings on Christian art was a sense of recognition, that what he had been living and learning intuitively at the ground level they expressed on a theological and philosophical level. They were articulating his own experience, Michael thought.

In spring 1978, the pastor of the Ukrainian Orthodox Church phoned and asked Michael if he would like to have a show in June when their new church on Byron Avenue was to be blessed. Michael accepted, and the exhibition was a success. It generated enough income to keep them afloat for three to four months, their financial horizon stretching just up until the birth of their second child. The tendency was clear. Michael was having exhibitions in churches, thus preaching to believers, but not, as Kurelek had wanted, reaching out to nonbelievers as well.

In connection with the exhibition in the Orthodox church, Michael made a renewed resolution never to paint simply what is popular in order to pay the bills, but instead to continue to trust in the Lord for the sustenance of his family. A quick reply came the next day, when Canon James Winters of the Church of St. Barnabas,

Apostle and Martyr (an Anglican church), asked Michael to paint a triptych, a three-paneled work that would be installed in the reredos, the ornamental partition wall above and behind the altar. This was Michael's first church commission, and he set about to do sketches to be presented for approval. The pastor and the parish wanted a modern Christ, and for Michael this meant that they had asked him to paint a tame messiah, a football-hero Jesus. He thus felt totally unable to produce a sketch. This creative sterility went on for weeks.

Finally, it dawned on Michael that he had to paint the image of Christ that God desired to reveal to the congregation at St. Barnabas. He fell on his knees before the empty panel and begged that God's will would be done. A surge of certainty and inspiration immediately welled up. He saw before him the stern but loving image of Christ Pantokrator (Almighty); he knew that this was not what the pastor had wanted, but decided to trust in the inspiration.

From Michael's conversion, up until 1978, the Church had struggled during the chaotic period after the Second Vatican Council; the traditional Catholic world was more or less disintegrating in the face of the expectations of a radical aggiornamento with modernity. The intention was that the outer forms were to be updated in a positive attitude to the secular world, the other Christian denominations, and even other religions, but, at the same time, the universal message kept clear. It was bewildering for most Catholics, and as seen in Michael's extended family, the edifice seemed to crumble.

The pope elected during the Council, Paul VI, had—after his encyclical *Humanae Vitae* in 1968, which took a firm stance on the use of contraceptives—been faced with open resistance even from theologians and bishops' conferences. The problem was that the secular world was evolving, as seen in the student revolts of 1968 and the sexual revolution sweeping through the Western world. The Church could only go so far in its accommodation of modern ways, but where did the important line between the core message of faith and morals, and the outer forms of expression and mere customs, lie? The question was how the changes and process of renewal set in motion in the 1960s were to be handled. Who was to carry the flag of renewal forward, while remaining true to the Catholic tradition?

On August 6, 1978, Pope Paul VI died, and the process of electing a new pope began. It was a true crisis in the history of the Church, a turning point, with several avenues open. At the same time as the election of a pope was important in the Catholic Church, the new era belonged in a special way to the laypeople. Without the work and sacrifice of men and women such as Michael, who in a spirit of heroism took upon themselves to evangelize the modern world, the writings, talks, and exhortations of popes were doomed to be unfruitful. Clearly, it was the task of laypersons to evangelize modern culture at the ground level.

In August 1978, one could read in the *Ottawa Journal* about a bearded, "soft-spoken and serious" Catholic artist painting icons, who in the photo accompanying the article sits at his desk in front of an icon of St. George and the dragon. The article notes that

> his dream is to express the elements and meaning of icons in mod-
> ern terms. And he's firmly convinced modern man should heed their
> message. "They speak to modern man of realities he's begun to for-
> get. They call him to be silent and still before a mystery he doesn't
> understand."[34]

The question was whether modern man would heed the message of stillness and veneration.

On August 26, Albino Luciani was elected pope as John Paul I, with the intention of carrying the reforms of the Council forward.

In the middle of September, Michael's drawings for the Church of St. Barnabas were, contrary to his expectations, approved. Canon Winters said to Michael, "This is not what I expected; this is not what I wanted. I'm going to have a lot of trouble getting used to it. But we trusted that the Lord would give to you the word to be spoken to us."[35] The three panels were to portray Moses, Christ, and St. John the Baptist.

A week later, September 20, 1978, Michael and Sheila's second son, Joseph, was born after an easy labour and delivery. The same week, Michael had another exhibition, this time in the nave of St. Matthew's Church, on Glebe Avenue, during their St. Matthew's festival, and he sold several paintings and received private commissions.

This dramatic month ended with the new pope dying after only thirty-three days in office. The crisis of the Church had unexpectedly returned, and new directions opened up again. On October 22, Karol

Wojtyla was chosen as the next pope under the name of John Paul II, to honour his short-lived predecessor. Michael wrote in his diary, "A beautiful gift to the Church—a man for all seasons." For the next twenty-seven years, it was this pope who would formulate and live with vitality and energy the intentions of the Council.

A renewal was on its way, but, at the same time, the forces that had sucked the life force out of Catholicism in the extended family of Michael would continue unabated, undermining what had once been Catholic nations.

And the struggle was ongoing between those who saw the Council as merely the beginning of a radical renewal of the Church that they welcomed and supported, and, on the other hand, those who saw the Council as imbued with the spirit of revolution that previous popes had fought with such vigour and determination.[36] The John Paul II program of renewal built on the idea of the continuity of tradition in the middle of a process of reform. But to an impartial observer the changes looked radical, especially in the liturgy: the difficult question was what could be changed without tradition becoming broken.

At the beginning of November, Michael had a new exhibition, now at Thornloe College in Sudbury, which had commissioned an icon of St. Mark from him.[37] At the same time, plans were confirmed for his upcoming one-week exhibition at the Lonergan College of Concordia University. This was his eighth exhibition. Michael was obviously working at a very intense pace, and things were beginning to look, if not good, at least promising for his career as a painter of sacred art. The triptych for the Church of St. Barnabas was finished, and later he completed several new minor commissions.

On Friday, January 12, 1979, the triptych was blessed and dedicated by Bishop Robinson during Solemn Evensong and Benediction. Two Anglican bishops officiated, and to Michael they appeared more Catholic than the Catholics that he was used to. It was a magnificent celebration in the High Anglican or Anglo-Catholic tradition, with incense, many priests and altar boys, mediaeval banners, and beautiful sacred music. The church was full, and some parishioners came up to Michael afterwards and said, "This is quite an unusual image!" There was not a lot of enthusiasm for the paintings, and no "wows", as Michael put it.

But months went by and I would go back to the church from time to time and sit in the back row. Little by little people started seeing me there. They'd come up and say, "Mr. O'Brien, I hate to tell you this, but, when we first got your paintings, we hated them! But we love them now!"

That was said over and over again. The Anglican bishop of Ottawa said, "These are right on. This is what this church needs."[38]

To Michael this was a reminder to trust in the inspirations of the Holy Spirit.

7. Logos

Thinking about Art

It was seven o'clock in the morning, and Michael rose slowly, merely semiconscious, while Sheila was still in bed nursing baby Joseph, who had been born only two months earlier. Beside them lay two-year-old John sleeping. It had been a rather trying night for the young mother and father.[1] Michael dressed and went to the kitchen for tea, still only partly awake. To shake off sleep and enter the world of the living was for him a slow process, and strong tea was a necessity; you have to put on your own oxygen mask first, he used to say, before you help others. He then did his morning prayers with Sheila, who by now had joined him.

During breakfast, which consisted mainly of porridge, they talked about Michael's upcoming show and the needs of the two small boys. Their move into the city had proved to be a step forward in the development of his art, but Sheila did not find the city the place of her dreams; she longed for the rugged landscape of British Columbia and having her parents and relatives nearby.

Also for Michael, the idea of returning to Blue River was slowly becoming appealing, as they agreed that the city was not an ideal place in which to bring up children. But to abandon the momentum of Michael's artistic work, and to head for the isolation of a small village in the mountains, would be a challenge. On the other hand, Michael had abandoned a budding career ten years earlier in the same manner. But then he did not have a wife and children; this time a little shack with no running water and only an outhouse would be insufficient.

After breakfast, Michael walked for forty minutes to his studio in the Dominican monastery for which he merely paid a token rent. It was, as usual, peaceful and still—quite a contrast to the company of the lively boys at home. Today, he first had to finish writing a short text about icon painting.

After a short prayer, he sat down at his desk. His main idea was that the icon was deliberately nonrealistic; its task was not to live up to the Renaissance ideal and present lifelike representations, such as the depth of landscapes and the materiality of the naked human body.

Michael paused, and looking up, he gazed at the stylized, austere features of a Christ icon on the wall, which looked back at him in confirmation. The expression was so much deeper than the vague smiles of the sentimental, saccharine nineteenth-century Jesuses of Catholic devotional material, he thought.

He continued his writing—something had been broken in the cultural-spiritual fabric of the West with the great schism of the eleventh century, when Eastern Orthodoxy and Western Catholicism went separate ways. Later the idea of man as the measure of all things (the motto of Renaissance humanism) had led to dehumanization, in other words, to twentieth-century modernity, and even the horrors of Nazism and Communism.

The task of the icon painter, on the other hand, was to express the unity of the human and the divine, to create a symbol that reveals a holy presence to the viewer. The icon was not a mere aesthetic object; it was an instrument for establishing a spiritual relationship, and the appropriate attitude toward it was prayer and contemplation.

The vocation of the icon painter, as envisaged by Michael, was hence difficult and demanding; he was a prophet with a mission, but forced to live in a social desert. "The icon painter must learn then that to be free means a readiness to work on diligently without apparent success, to work out of love of God and love of mankind, with no bread and no praise. He must be willing to be a 'failure', just as Christ was a 'failure' and 'draws all men to the Father' (cf. Jn 12:32) through the Cross. By uniting his own temporal and spiritual struggles to the Cross of Christ, he participates in the redemption of mankind."[2]

Michael was obviously not merely an icon painter. In his diary, one can see that he was constantly reading and jotting down thoughts and reflections on art and Christian life. In the 1960s, he had been focused on the written word—the flow of visual artistic creativity began after his conversion. It was thus natural for him to carry on a sustained reflection on icon painting, creativity, and Christian art, to develop a theology of sacred art in a reflection on his own artistic practice—and also to express it in talks and writings. A famous quote from Goethe is "Create, artist! Do not talk!"[3] But for Michael these parallel streams of imagination and thinking were natural and founded on a prayerful interior life.

On that day, Michael was also beginning the painting of a new icon. After his writing session, he took the empty board with its smooth, white gesso surface in one hand and knelt on the linoleum floor before the crucifix in his studio. He felt his unworthiness deeply and with such sharpness that the desire not to make the icon surfaced. Who was he to attempt to create a picture that could mediate a relation to the divine? After a moment of struggle, he chose not to give up and entreated the Holy Spirit to fill his interior emptiness—so that he, in his turn, could fill the white emptiness of the board. Michael pleaded with God that this icon would become a holy image, and that he would have strength and guidance in matters of technique.

After these petitions, he put down the board and prayed the Rosary; then he became silent and went deeper into prayer, closed his eyes, and prostrated himself in front of the crucifix. As he lay on the floor, an image of Our Lady, the subject of the icon, appeared in his imagination. He prayed to Christ for a sense of "go ahead", an experience of peace about the icon. Shortly thereafter, a sweet overflow of tears began, and he prayed the following prayer:

> Lord Jesus Christ, One God, You who are infinite in the Holy Trinity, in the fullness of time You were born of the Holy Virgin, Mother of God, and thus clothed human nature in a manner which passes all understanding. You have revealed Yourself and imprinted the traits of Your very Holy Face on the Holy Shroud.
>
> You, the true God, have poured out the light of Your Holy Spirit on Your apostle and evangelist, Luke, so that he might reproduce the beauty of the Immaculate Mother carrying You, a child in her arms. Divine Master of the Universe, illuminate the soul, the heart, and the spirit of Your servant; guide his hand so that he might represent in a perfect and dignified manner Your created image, and the images of all the saints and of Your most pure Mother. Save him from all temptation of the evil one, and forgive the sins of all who venerate this image, rendering homage to the Model who is in heaven, by the intercession of the Most Holy Mother, the Blessed Apostle and evangelist, Luke, and of all the saints.

Holy God, Holy Mighty One, Holy and Immortal One, have pity on us. Amen.[4]

When the prayer was finished, he began to draw the image with diluted yellow ochre mixed with water, and the picture of Our Lady gently materialized through subtle, transparent strokes of the sable brush. Michael gradually became so absorbed in his work that he lost all consciousness of time, and the hours slipped away. As in sleeping, when he works (both with painting and writing), his consciousness leaves the world of time and space for an interior realm; and it is only slowly, and with some effort, that he comes back to what we call reality.

During the day, Sheila had taken the boys for a walk in the park and along the Ottawa River. At five o'clock, after lunch and some household chores, they went out again. Joseph was swaddled on Sheila's chest, and when John saw Michael coming around the corner of the block, he ran toward him and fell into his arms. This coming-home ritual was repeated almost every day.

After dinner, Michael played with the boys, before they put them to bed. They then prayed the Rosary together and afterwards picked up their copies of *The Lord of the Rings*, by J. R. R. Tolkien, and did some reading in bed with their backs against the slanting stucco ceiling before falling asleep. Sheila insisted that when she came to the scary parts Michael should read the same passage. When Sam was about to enter Shelob's lair, she asked Michael, "Where are you?" And she did not join Sam in his adventure, until Michael was there too.

A Novel

The beginning of November 1978 was, as we have seen, a very busy period for Michael: the large triptych had been finished; he had several exhibitions and wrote on the theme of icon painting. Amazingly, at the same time, through Michael's combination of reason, contemplation, and artistic imagination—in that particular inner creative world of his, where spiritual inspiration animates pictures and ideas—something new was born. A fictional story began to take form in his imagination, combining image and text. From the beginning, it was a mere idea, but it developed and became more complex. As with his writing on icon painting, it was based on a reflection on his own situation. In his diary, Michael summarized the plot as follows: "The simple man, an artist, reared in the bush of Northern Ontario, becomes crushed by the complexity of civilization, by its corruption, and travels through death to resurrection."[5]

He felt that this story was a novel in the making. The question was how to handle such an inspiration. He was, after all, in the middle of a very demanding painting period, combining shows and talks. Still, to let a new inspiration fall by the wayside is not natural for Michael. When he feels such strong creative impulses, he mostly sees them as coming from God, though the discernment process can be painful. His creative work is fundamentally intuitive: he sees pictures emerging in his imagination, and this creative flow is connected to his prayer life, particularly to the reception of the Eucharist. The pictures are scenes to be painted, but also narratives, divine words, and presences. There was, and still is, no clear dividing line between his spirituality and creativity, and to insert artificially such a neat compartmentalization would be to do violence to how his inspiration works.

Michael's decision was to put icon painting to the side for some months and instead write the emerging novel. It was, so to speak, showing itself to him. Despite this initial resolve, in December he experienced doubts again and felt that this new activity might be a distraction, drawing him away from his primary vocation of painting; but his emotional turmoil stabilized, and he became convinced that he was on the right track.

With this literary well springing up in his mind, the two main streams of his creative work had begun to flow. They alternate in a kind of crop rotation: when he writes a novel, he puts down the brushes; and when he begins to paint again, the writing of fiction is paused until the idea of a new novel emerges with overpowering energy and presence; then the brushes have to rest again for some months.

8. Purification

Discernment

In the spring of 1979, after five months of hard work, Michael finished his novel *A Crying of Stone* and began to paint again, but he and Sheila continued to feel restless. The idea of returning to Blue River was on their minds. Already during the previous year, when Sheila was out west visiting her parents in Oyama, she had learned that an old wooden house in Blue River was for sale; it was, despite its age, comfortable and had three bedrooms and some small barns. She phoned Michael to ask his opinion: "Should we buy the house and move west?" At first, he said no; but, during 1979, the idea continued to grow in power, and, by July, they were united in their intention to move back to Blue River. They experienced a common, quiet peacefulness about the decision, and Michael phoned the owners. One of the readings of that day was the exhortation to Abraham to leave his land (Gen 12:1–4), which Michael considered a sign. Their plan was to move after Michael's exhibition at Concordia University in November 1979.

For Sheila, the move fulfilled the vision of a rural homestead: a safe place to bring up the children. It would be easier to keep the faith that way also, she thought, and her family was not far away. The central gathering point in summers for her brothers and sisters was the house of their parents in Oyama, which was only a four-hour drive from Blue River. Moreover, the children would be able to meet their cousins more often. For Sheila, it was like going home, after being on an adventure out East; while for Michael it was more difficult, and despite the initial peacefulness, doubts and fears began to trouble him. He found refuge once again in the liturgy of the day that contained the psalm verse "the swallow finds a nest for her young" (Ps 84:3), which is a cornerstone psalm for Michael and Sheila in their marriage. Moreover, while praying, Michael opened the Bible at random and found passages about making the desert bloom, and about leaving and going to a new land. He remarked in his diary that they had always thought of British Columbia as "the desert" that was to bloom. Then they also received a letter from a nun containing a poem about God calling people out into the desert.

The will of God was seen by Michael as manifested in specific Bible passages and in providential "coincidences"; these built up a case, supporting the idea that moving west was indeed the will of God. The weakness with such a case, to use a legal metaphor, was that it was built on circumstantial evidence. On the one hand, the understanding of their choice as willed by God rested upon the interpretation of textual fragments, but the existential anxiety was directed toward whether God would also *provide* on the path laid out, despite the material conditions indicating the opposite.

I will not tire the reader with more details of this discernment process, but suffice it to say that Michael continued to experience doubts and find similar confirmations and signs of God's Providence. I think that the underlying cause of this vacillation was that he knew that supporting a family on Christian art in Blue River was going to be not only very difficult, but close to impossible.

Driving West

On December 12, 1979, it was time to move. Sheila and the children had flown to British Columbia while Michael and a friend shared driving. Once again, a battered old truck was supposed to do the job, but now with a trailer attached to it. As it pulled out of Ottawa, the truck groaned and wheezed, loaded as it was beyond all security limits. With his strong imagination, Michael saw the total collapse of the truck somewhere on the outskirts of town; his hands held the steering wheel in a tense, tight grip. While passing the first block, the muffler fell off, confirming his worst fears, and the truck let out a roar of disapproval: the old wreck had begun to disintegrate. Michael crawled in under the rear of the vehicle and lay there in the snow slush, feeling the cold numbing his fingers while trying to wire the muffler in its proper place. After the ordeal, they resumed driving, but the metallic tube fell off again after a couple of blocks. Michael lowered himself into slush once more in another attempt to tighten the bolts, and after that the muffler amazingly stayed on for the remainder of the long trip to Blue River.

On arriving safely at their destination five days later, Michael's co-driver said, "Only you could get away with this, O'Brien!"

Art in the Wild

Now the young family of four had a house adequate for their needs. Sheila also bought goats that occupied the barn and some chickens to live in the pen. The major unknown factor was how Michael's work with sacred art would develop: whether it could function as their main source of income, or whether they were too unrealistic, especially in moving to such a remote area.

Michael used the basement as his studio, where he began to paint in a more Western religious style, supplementing the icon painting. An example of this new style was a series called "Faces of the Warsaw Ghetto". A friend tried to encourage Michael to paint portraits of people in Blue River, but he was doubtful. His new painting style was merging the basic qualities of the icon with that of Western realist and symbolical painting. The outcome was a personal style of sacred art, with solemn, stylized figures filled with gravitas, painted alternatively in clear colors or in graduations of sepia and brown, the latter being mostly portraits.

Michael managed to support his family at this time mainly through commissions of icon painting and some exhibitions, but he also worked part-time as a janitor at the elementary school and helped out at the weather station.

In December 1980, he reread his discernment notes of the previous year regarding their move to Blue River. What struck him was that God had promised to support and guide them, to sustain Michael's vocation, "yet he did *not* do so in ways I would have expected or had counted on." During the winter, Michael was afflicted with viral meningitis, and together with the emotional stress coming from chronic lack of money and recognition, he felt that he was coming close to a burnout, both physically and psychologically. To return to Blue River had been for him the beginning of a process of purification; he continually had to press on with his art against all odds.

The situation became somewhat better toward the end of January 1981, and he began to work on a second novel, *The Sojourners*. It chronicled three generations, beginning with an Englishwoman and Irishman coming to Canada in the nineteenth century from Europe and settling in the valley of Valemount, which was given another name in the novel. At the same time, he submitted his first novel, *A Crying Out of Stone* (later renamed *A Cry of Stone*), to a Canadian publisher, but it was turned down. The same happened with a major art commission in a United church in Saskatoon and an art exhibition in Calgary.

In February, he found it impossible to paint and very difficult to write. Their economic situation was dire; Sheila was entering the final three months of her third pregnancy and felt exhausted. The family was growing, and Michael felt the pressure of supporting them. Luckily, he then received a grant of four thousand dollars for writing his second novel; and, in spring, his health was returning after he managed to complete the first part of the novel.

The Singing Baby and the Pope

After midnight, May 11, 1981, Sheila began to have contractions, so they got into the car for the one-hundred-kilometre drive to the hospital in Clearwater. It was a beautiful night with a full moon and northern lights flashing in the sky.

Early in the morning, after a long and difficult labour, their first daughter, Mary Theresa, was born. She managed to confuse the nursing staff with her unusual humming; they had never heard anything like that. At two in the morning, the concerned staff called the doctor, who after examining the baby, said that she was perfectly normal; she was just happy and singing.

The following day, May 12, on the square of St. Peter's in Rome, the new, energetic Polish pope, John Paul II, was shot with several bullets in the stomach and rushed to the hospital, bleeding profusely.

A few hours later, in another hospital, while walking down the corridor, Sheila met an older man and his wife. The man had a benign grandfatherly look, but when he learned that Mary was Sheila's third child and that she was Catholic, he coldly accused her of selfishness in bringing more than two children into the world. When leaving, he said to his wife, "That one's a Catholic and she just produced another one for the Vatican!" Sheila was astonished by this attack, as it was the first time she had experienced a direct anti-Catholic diatribe. Michael, naturally, became very upset by the incident, but later he rejoiced that John Paul II was recovering: "What a Christ figure—a man for all seasons he is; the first pope who captures my enthusiasm on all levels."[1]

The End of the Novel

After the birth of Mary, Michael continued the hard work on his second novel. At times, he was excited to see the main ideas becoming clearer, while at other times he had to struggle through periods of inner darkness, but when he sat down in June to write the final chapters, his mind was calm and focused.

The novel was partly based on real stories of the first people who had settled in the valley, but one of the main characters, Jan Tarnowski, was based on Michael's most interesting and eccentric neighbour. Bronislaw Katanakzsa, whom everyone called Bruno, was a Polish refugee from the Second World War who had survived the Katyn Massacre of 1940. Bruno, a humble man who could barely read and write, had the most fascinating theories of the world. He seriously believed, for example, that the earth was flat, and tried to convince Michael by showing him a map he had made. Another day, he phoned Michael almost screaming: "Mike! End of the world! Big monkey ... *big* monkey." When Michael came into Bruno's cabin to see what was happening, he had difficulty keeping a straight face when Bruno excitedly repeated, "See, Big Monkey break city, America," pointing toward the television set playing a black-and-white *King Kong* movie. Michael tried to reason with him, but it was difficult. In the novel, the portrait of Jan Tarnowski is clearly made with great love and appreciation for Bruno. In his backyard, Jan is building the *enduvdervorldkluk*, an end-time contraption made of junk that strikes a bell every day at three o'clock. Jan is clearly "a fool", but one who, in all his eccentricity and social marginalization, sees things that reasonable people do not see.

The focus of the novel is on interior personal development set in the wider theme of building a civilization in the wilderness. In a sense, Michael fulfilled what he had promised his father ten years earlier: that the move west would benefit his art through nature studies. Little did he know then that the medium of expression would be a novel.

Terry and the Bear

If Michael was struggling with emotional turmoil and existential vulnerability, so was his brother Terry. In the late summer of 1981, Terry headed west on his motorcycle to visit Michael and Sheila. After his recent divorce, he was tormented by loneliness and a lack of love in his life, and he even challenged God that if there were no solution—or at least an answer provided somehow—then on his return trip through the mountains of British Columbia, he would race full throttle to his death. Somewhat childishly, he then said to God, "And it will be all your fault."

When Terry arrived in Blue River, he was exhausted after days of driving and wanted just to rest and sleep. Michael, however, overjoyed to see his brother, said, "Great, Terry, you're here; we're going to shoot a bear tonight." Terry replied, "I'm too tired to go hunting." But Michael continued, "Oh, but we don't need to go hunting; the bear is going to come here, in my backyard." Terry was sceptical and asked, "How do you know a bear is coming into your backyard?" Michael explained, "It comes every night to break open my rabbit cages." Terry went to bed, hoping that the bear would decide to take a pause in his rabbit hunting, but at nine o'clock in the evening, there came a loud banging sound from outside. They went out onto the porch—Terry holding the flashlight and Michael an old World War I .303 rifle. The four-hundred-kilo black bear had torn the cage open and was ripping the leg off a little rabbit. Michael took aim and shot, but the bear just looked around perplexed and continued with its dinner. Michael fired four more bullets into the bear before it collapsed. He then walked toward it to poke it in the eye with the gun to see if it was really dead. It was dead all right, and as Michael was kneeling in front of the bear, Terry came up and said, "You should be more careful; it could still be alive." It was dark and Terry could not resist joking, so he roared and clamped his fingers fiercely around one of Michael's ankles. The proud hunter flew into the air, convinced that the animal was alive and had decided to switch from a rabbit to a human diet. Terry had a great laugh at his brother's leap of fear.[2]

Whether it was the joy of hunting, or pulling his brother's leg, or the little everyday chores Terry did in Blue River, when he rode his motorcycle back east, his suicidal thoughts abated, and all that was left was a mere mild depression, attenuated by the beauty of the prairies surrounding him. He slowly sensed more peace and joy each day and began to think about God in a new way; he already believed in God—racing with him in the mountains could be taken as a sign of that—but his life had little connection to his faith. However, healing had begun during the visit.[3] Eventually, Terry became a born-again Protestant. Despite one brother being a Catholic and the other a Protestant, and the seriousness with which each took his faith, they continued to have the same humorous teasing relation as seen in their common bear hunt. They agreed to pray for each other, I suppose both hoping that the other would see the light, but religion was also very much part of their ongoing sibling bantering.

Igor Khazanov

In October 1981, Michael made a trip to Vancouver. Though he wanted to, he had not been able to attend a recent exhibition of the Russian émigré painter Igor Khazanov (October 5–12), who two years earlier had arrived from Europe to live in Canada, with his wife, Olga. He was born in 1943, in Moscow, the capital of the Soviet Union, and his father, who was a painter, saw to it that his son received an excellent art education, enrolling him at the age of seven at the Moscow Central School of Art. Igor continued to excel in art schools, trained under the rigorous discipline of socialist realism. In 1968, at the age of twenty-five, he had his first exhibit in the Union of Soviet Artists, and, during the 1970s, his fame continued to grow with more exhibitions. As a result, he received a government grant to travel and paint the everyday life of workers along the Volga River. What he saw there was not the life of heroic Communist workers; instead, he caught a glimpse of intense poverty and inhumane working conditions. Embracing the truth of what he saw, Igor let it flow onto his canvases. There was outrage from the Communist critics: he had betrayed the working class, belittled their sacrifices in building the true Communist society. The result was complete ostracism: no more exhibitions or grants. He became poor and invisible; his exhibitions from then on were illegal, one-night, one-man shows at small cafés.[4]

Igor's thoughts naturally turned to the idea of exile, and, in 1979, he was allowed to leave with Olga, who was also a painter. First, they travelled to Austria and then to Italy, but continued to Vancouver in 1980. Fortunately, he quickly found a patron who made it possible for him to paint full-time. His first exhibition was in 1981, in Robson Square Media Centre, Vancouver—the show that Michael had just missed.[5] As the address of Igor Khazanov Fine Art Studio was marked on the advertisement for the exhibition, Michael went there for an improvised meeting.

Michael rang the bell and Igor opened it; he looked at Michael intensely. Quiet and cautious at first when Michael introduced himself, he gradually warmed up as they talked. The Fine Art Studio was in reality a tiny apartment crammed with hundreds of paintings, most of them huge, and the Khazanovs were obviously poor: Michael saw no expensive possessions, just a few books, and a bit of furniture.

Michael showed them slides of his paintings; and, after a while, Igor said, "In Russia, Michael, you would never be allowed to exhibit these paintings. In fact, you would be dead." He then took a book of modern Russian paintings from one of the shelves and said, "This is Socialist Realism, but the best work couldn't be published or shown in the Soviet Union." Some of the paintings were stylistically quite good, Michael thought, and a few depicted very moving human scenes brilliantly executed.

"Who painted these?" Michael asked.

"A friend of mine. He lived in our building in Moscow. *They* killed him. He painted a portrait of a forbidden poetess. And they killed him!" Igor answered with emphasis. He continued,

Everybody is dead here in the West. In Russia, we artists are starving, dying, persecuted, but we are *alive;* we are joyful. Here, art is dead. In Russia, we all help each other; the poets and writers and painters.

Igor and Olga had only been in Canada for one year, and they still acutely felt the particular loneliness and culture shock of the East European émigré—depicted by another Russian exile, the filmmaker Andrei Tarkovsky in his film *Nostalgia*. They were adjusting to a condition free of direct state repression, offering an abundance of freedom, but plagued by a superficial consumerism.

Michael told them how he had received an inspiration a year earlier to adopt spiritually an unknown "son" or "brother" living behind the Iron Curtain. They were moved, but Igor said,

You know, Michael, I believe in God, but I don't know how to pray. They took that all away from us as children. If you are religious in the Soviet Union, like my mother, your life and your future is finished. No job, no artist, no hope.

Michael mentioned that creating paintings could be a form of prayer, and Igor agreed, saying, "Art is a search for God, hidden in the truth of light." Then he continued, "Michael, I think you should pray for Canadian artists more than Russian ones. Here, they are dead. They are dead; their art is dead."[6]

When Michael was preparing to leave, Igor asked for his address and offered to introduce Michael to his art dealer next time he came to Vancouver. Finally, they shook hands warmly, lingering in the moment of goodbye before Michael left.

When Michael returned to Blue River, he wrote to Igor and Olga and invited them to visit; he also sent them the book *The Power of Light,* by Isaac Singer, containing Hanukkah tales, a gesture honouring Igor's Jewish descent.[7] A few days later, Michael received a reply letter together with an enormous book on Russian icons, a book that they had carried with them on their exodus from Russia. Michael was overwhelmed by their generosity and thanked God for the meeting and the oneness and brotherhood that he had known there.

Michael was impressed by the courage of Igor Khazanov and how he had faced persecution and exile: the consequences of his decision to portray truth—something the author Aleksandr Solzhenitsyn had suffered already in 1974. Both Khazanov and Solzhenitsyn did not merely direct their criticism against Communist Russia, but also toward the materialism of the spiritually dying West. With this Eastern European experience of intense suffering and the civilizational role of Christianity, Michael felt a spiritual kinship, as he had with William Kurelek previously. The painting of icons had intensified his gaze toward Eastern Europe. For Michael, the West, through its materialism, had an empty centre—the modern liberal democratic society was a splendid construction, one had to admit, but it was morally hollow. Eventually, this hollowness would show itself as a lack of resolve in the face of evil, as confusion, whenever what was at stake was more than pleasure and a comfortable life.

In the heroes living under Communism, in their willingness to suffer for holding fast to truth and life, Michael found inspiration to live through his own isolation and marginalization. There was a similarity between one-night shows at a café and displaying your paintings in church halls. Notwithstanding that the state and the guardians of public culture had decided that you were nonexistent, or at least invisible, you were alive, building a culture in the undergrowth of society.

9. The Winter of Our Discontent

The Crazy Curator and the Burning Gallery

In the early summer of 1981, Michael showed his art to the curator of a major art gallery in Calgary who, moved by what he saw, said, "I'm absolutely determined to have a show of your work here. If the board of directors refuses, I will resign." A couple of months later, when Michael phoned the gallery to see whether he had made any progress, and if there was a date for the show, a secretary told him that the man had been fired. Amazed, Michael wondered if it was due to his paintings. He drove to Calgary and visited a smaller art gallery, owned and managed by a married couple, and showed them some slides of his paintings. The gallery had a good reputation for high-quality art, and they offered him a show there later that summer. Even though the first gallery had failed, Michael thought, God had opened another door.

The day before the show was to open, Michael arrived in the city after a ten-hour drive with a truckload of his paintings. The man running the gallery came to meet him and said, "I am very sorry, but we have to cancel your show; my wife has just had a nervous breakdown and is in the hospital; we are actually closing down permanently." The explanation of God opening another door seemed not to apply anymore; if He had, then someone else had decisively closed it.

Nevertheless, Michael had another show scheduled in November at a gallery in Ontario. Just before he was to leave with his truck full of paintings for the long journey east, he made a phone call to make sure that everything was in order. After all, something of a curse seemed to hang over his attempts to show his paintings in art galleries. The person answering the phone said, "I'm *so* sorry, but we have to cancel your exhibition; we are closing down the gallery as it was struck by lightning last night."

The trend was not good, but Michael did not want to surrender and looked for another opportunity in Calgary. He walked down the main cultural street and found a new gallery, whose owner said that his paintings were good work and that she would be happy to give him a show late in 1981. Michael phoned in November, wiser by experience, and asked when the opening day was to be; she answered, evasively, "I'm not sure about this anymore; it's not really our type of painting." So, this attempt too came to nothing.

He also made a trip to the city of Victoria on Vancouver Island, hoping to interest gallery owners there. In meeting after meeting, the curators or owners told him that they liked his painting style very much and would be happy to exhibit his work, if he was willing to make changes in his subject matter. "The art-buying public is no longer interested in these themes," they explained.

"Do you mean because it's overtly Christian painting?" Michael bluntly asked.

"Yes," the curators admitted, embarrassed but immovable.

A clear pattern of closed doors was emerging when it came to the art world. The causes were various: insanity, lightning, or resistance to Christian art. But the result was the same.

When in Calgary, Michael usually stayed with some friends interested in art, and hearing about his misfortunes, they suggested to him that as he could not exhibit at art galleries, then there was still the possibility to show his art in churches or parish halls. After all, he painted mainly sacred art. They recommended that he contact the pastor of St. Luke's Catholic Church in Calgary, whom they knew personally. Michael talked to the priest, who was very welcoming and said that a show of Michael's art was an excellent idea. Here then was the open window, when all the doors had been closed—although this was what Kurelek had urged him not to do; he had tried his best to engage with secular galleries, but it seemed not meant to be.

Exhibition in Calgary

In early November 1981, Michael finished his second novel, *The Sojourners*, and sent the manuscript off for typing and then to the Seal Books First Novel Competition, which carried a prize of fifty thousand dollars. He could now focus wholeheartedly on his art again, and the upcoming exhibition in Calgary toward the end of the month, where he was to show both icons and his new style of sacred art.

Furthermore, Bishop Adam Exner of Kamloops had written and invited him to have a show in February 1982 at the Conference of Western Catholic Bishops in Edmonton. Michael considered it a breakthrough, and it filled him with renewed purpose: to be able to address the entire leadership of the Catholic Church in Western Canada. His mind was set on convincing them of the need for a renewal of Catholic culture. The bishops had to lead this process and support laypersons struggling in, at best, an indifferent secular society.

He thus had two exhibitions in front of him during the upcoming four months, but it was also wintertime, with darkness, snow, and cold, making living and travelling more difficult.

During the week leading up to the exhibition in late November, the whole family suffered from dreadful colds, fever, and endless coughing. This was, however, merely the beginning of the preexhibition trials. On his way to Calgary, Michael drove into a blizzard east of the Rocky Mountains and escaped a near-death experience on the highway as the car's signal light and one headlight burned out; finally, all power died outside Calgary, and with a stone-dead battery he rolled downhill into the first gas station. When the car was fixed, he continued his journey.

On the way to the opening of his exhibition, which was set for 7:30 in the evening of November 19, Michael was late. He drove with eyes glancing at the clock, when suddenly, he heard a metallic groaning sound and a loud bang, as the rear door of the station wagon fell off onto the street. He had no time to lose, so after he dragged the door to the side of the road, he drove on, clenching his teeth—he had to make it to the opening. However, someone was trying to get his attention, because a few moments later the car heaved a sigh and died in the middle lane of Crowchild Trial, one of the largest and busiest streets in Calgary. Michael sat devastated behind the wheel and thought, "This is my life! Unbelievable."

Then unexpected help came from some people driving by, who recognized him and saw that he was in trouble. One stayed with the car, while another drove him to the show with the paintings loaded in her vehicle. They had to open both back windows before driving, and Michael with both his arms stretched out of the windows (his left arm through the left window, and the right arm through the right window) held the large mural of *Nazareth* onto the roof of the car as they drove. It was so cold that his fingers began to freeze, and his arms were aching. He thought hopefully, "Maybe the little crucifixion before the resurrection?"

Somehow, Michael and cars did not go together well. Most probably because when he became their proud owner, they were into their declining years and in urgent need of retirement or substantial repairs. To then be recruited as the workhorse for a young artist father, braving snowstorms and late for exhibitions, was too much to ask.

The show was in the parish hall, and in the advertisement in the magazine *Artswest*, an icon face of Jesus looked straight at the reader with a solemn, piercing gaze, probing one's intentions—a face that brooked no compromise. The church was, on the other hand, one of those modernist buildings, a heavy, flat-roofed block of concrete, which did not even pretend to look like a church.

As Michael had suspected, the series *Faces from the Warsaw Ghetto* did not appeal to most people, though they liked the other paintings. One exception was a Polish man, who arrived with his wife and two adult children. In his teens, he had lived through the war in Warsaw, and he told Michael during the exhibition a story of the cruelty of the Nazis that he himself had witnessed.

> I was working in an orchard and a S.S. Lieutenant was playing Mozart on the piano in a house nearby. A little Jewish boy started to cross the orchard and the officer saw him. He called the boy over. The boy was terrified and wanted to flee. The officer gave him an apple, and as the child took it and turned to go, he drew his revolver and shot the boy on the spot. He put his gun back in his holster, turned back to the piano and nonchalantly began to play Mozart once again.[1]

The wife of the Polish man said with tears in her eyes when she saw the paintings, "This is *great*; great; unique!" while her husband added, "Canadian people don't understand! They don't see it can happen here."

Michael had struck a chord that resonated with the experiences of those who had suffered in Central and Eastern Europe (Poland then being behind the Iron Curtain), but which did not appeal to the tastes of a Western audience. Michael's underlying fear was that beneath the surface of the Western form of freedom and the sensual indulgences of a consumerist society, there was growing another form of totalitarianism. Without the upward gaze of religion, intent on seeing things eternal, soft materialism would bind the human spirit with bonds both intensely oppressive and, at the same time, seemingly empowering. He thought, "It could happen here; yes, it could happen here."

Deep Winter

Although Michael had spent several years in the Arctic, he found the long winters in Blue River a trying experience. In late January 1982, he was lying in bed due to pain in his back. Some days earlier, he had driven the four hours south to his show in a flower shop in Kelowna, but it had been a "dismal failure" due to record snowfall and a depressed economy: very few came and he only sold two paintings, one of them to a kindly relative. When at last he went to see his doctor, he was told that an enlarged, inflamed cyst on his tailbone (the coccyx) was causing the pain, and he had to have surgery soon.

When he came home, there was more record snowfall; the children were sick with the flu; and he had to stay in bed trying to shrink the cyst by resting, so that he would be able to sit and stand again. Sheila was tired and worn out, having done a lot of solitary parenting as Michael travelled back and forth promoting and trying to sell his art all over British Columbia and Alberta. The bills were piling up, and Michael's novel was returned from the Seal competition; it did not even make it to the finals, but that year there was no winner at all. On top of all this gloominess, John seriously sprained an arm, the sun had not shone for the past six weeks, the roof was badly leaking, and the snow was piling up high outside the windows, while Michael could not do any shovelling in his present condition.

Lying there in low spirits, he also felt afraid of God, because during prayer he had fallen into helpless crying, accusing God of being a failure as a Father: "You weren't there! You are not there when we need You! You are not a Father!" Michael entered into utter emptiness and struggled to stay afloat mentally, but eventually came to a condition of stillness, and a quiet acceptance of his inability to make a success of his art and to be a good father. At this depth of discouragement, he crawled out of bed with pain and effort and knelt to pray. And then he felt the gentle touch of God's kindness.

> It comes to me that my wounds concerning the poor fatherhood I received as a child have been transferred to God. I misread existence in the light of my wounds and the result is fear. A deep and beautiful stillness as I kneel before the Shrine of the Sacred Heart in our living room. I sit by the chair and imagine God as Father sitting on it, waiting, always waiting for me. I rest my head on the chair seat, on his invisible knees. There are no words, no thoughts, no emotions, just a profound stillness and peace. It heals me. Come, the presence says, come every day and rest by me, in me. And I will set you free.[2]

Meet the Bishops

In February, Michael continued his spiritual struggle with abandonment to God's will; he had not yet reached the end of the darkness, and the cyst was still causing him excruciating pain. The show of his paintings and the talk that he was to give at the meeting of the bishops was fast approaching. Michael convinced his doctor that it was extremely important for him to attend the meeting. The doctor eventually gave in, but said that if there was the slightest sign of trouble, he was to call a surgeon friend of his in Edmonton for emergency surgery.

With the aid of painkillers and some pillows, he managed to sit in Bishop Adam Exner's car as they drove from Blue River to Edmonton, the paintings stacked in the back seat and trunk. They prayed the Divine Office together during the trip, but the bishop seemed to Michael to be preoccupied and tired, and Michael held back talking to him about his own struggles and dreams.

In the evening, they arrived at the big Conference Centre of the Grey Nuns. The bishops' meeting was to begin the following evening, so Michael had plenty of time to set up the display of his paintings, but he was tense, as usual before a performance, and slept badly during the night.

The next day, there was a beautiful sun, and Tom de Paul, with whom Michael had shared a cabin in Blue River before marrying, and who was now living in Edmonton, came over to the centre in the afternoon and had supper with Michael in the sisters' dining room. Despite Bishop Exner's invitation to eat all his meals with the bishops, Michael was too shy to do so.

After supper, Michael and Tom went out for a walk on the icy streets, and Michael had to walk backwards to support Tom as his crutches were slipping a lot. Michael really appreciated Tom's presence, and, fortunately, Tom had little respect for men of position and authority. He made Michael imagine the bishops as little schoolchildren in their underwear, an old trick used in order to relax when addressing a respectable and exalted crowd. Michael laughed at the scene and thought that part of his problem was due to being lifted out of the isolation in Blue River and dropped into a wine reception with almost two dozen bishops—it was a clear case of culture shock.

The bishops had scheduled Michael's talk at 10:00 P.M. after their last meeting; so, supported both by his crutches and Michael, Tom listened as Michael tried to speak his address in a trial run. Michael considered it a real mess, all confused and garbled ideas; and he spoke, he thought, with a tiny little voice with no authority. Tom kept saying, "Don't worry, you'll do fine." When they arrived back at the centre, Bishop Exner and Archbishop Halpin rushed Michael into the hall. The bishops had already finished their meeting, one and a half hours early, and wanted Michael to speak right away.

They served Michael a drink as the bishops fixed theirs, and then gathered around in a circle of chairs arranged in the gymnasium. Archbishop Halpin invited Michael to sit in the middle of the ring of bishops, which made Michael feel like the child Jesus conversing with the doctors in the Temple, minus the wisdom on his part. Archbishop Halpin said, "Michael, we have worked hard, and now we are relaxing, and we're here to listen to you and see your work as kind of dessert, a treat." Michael stood up, took a deep breath, and prayed silently, "Come, Holy Spirit . . ." A stillness filled him, confusion fled, and all his jumbled thoughts arranged themselves into an order. He began, "I know you have gone up a large mountain this weekend, and I don't want to add any more rocks for you to climb, but I do want to tell you of my deep concern for the state of sacred art today."

As Michael began to speak, he saw Bishop Exner begin to smile, with a mixture of relief, encouragement, and pleasure. He suddenly looked, according to Michael, very fatherly, and there was constant attention and a sense of thought going on in the faces of the bishops, Michael remembered, although he spoke for close to half an hour. Among other things he said was:

> Art is the cry of a people and if our art is poor it says something about the spirit of our people....
> Just as you represent hundreds of thousands of Catholics, I stand here representing a small, a painfully small, group of religious artists.[3]

While he gave his talk, Michael was intensely aware that he was speaking for the creative souls of the West who were, he believed, in desperate need of spiritual direction, of vision. He felt keenly his own fatigue, foolishness, and smallness, yet there was also the worthiness of the dream, he thought. For a brief moment, he was not defending or promoting himself, but his dream—the dream of the flowering of a people, the vision of the Hidden Face of God, the light of the Kingdom made visible in art. For a time, as he put it in his diary, he felt that he was embodying in himself all artists crying out for nourishment and guidance, that he was carrying a mission on his back—despite his weariness and unworthiness—that what he was doing held meaning.

While Michael was trying to get his message across to the bishops, Sheila was handling their household in Blue River. John was six and Joseph four years old, while Mary was only a year old. Sheila had considered homeschooling John, inspired by her elementary school teacher who in the 1950s had homeschooled her own two sons. To Sheila, schooling in the home had a romantic aura; she was especially impressed by the way the teacher had been able to pass on her English cultural heritage to the boys, who spoke with a British accent. But, one day, the principal of the school in Blue River came by on his horse and asked why John was not registered for school; she, then, dutifully registered him.

Besides caring for three little children, which is enough to keep one busy, Sheila had to milk the goats and take care of the rabbits and chickens—and keep the fire of the wood furnace going during the cold winter. She was very busy and, besides Mass in the afternoon three times a week, her prayers were mostly said while working.

At the beginning of the bishops' meeting, the infected cyst on Michael's spine burst and began to drain internally. Arriving home, he was in bad shape after all the emotional tension and physical effort; his limbs shook, and he found it hard to focus and think. Filled with dread, he faced the question, "Am I physically poisoned by the draining cyst, or am I undergoing psychological disintegration? The latter fills me with absolute horror."[4]

He wondered whether they now needed to leave Blue River, as he did not know if he could psychologically survive another winter like this one. Still he thought that they should wait, that things were not yet clear. But worse was yet to come.

Near Death

In the first week of April, at the hospital in Kamloops, Michael underwent an operation removing his spinal cyst. When home in Blue River, he had to lie on his stomach for several weeks so as not to disturb the deep wound in his back. Sheila and the local nurse changed the packing every day, but after a week, the nurse tore out the packing so violently that the wound began to bleed again; nevertheless, she merely repacked it and left.

When Michael woke up an hour later, the whole bed was soaked in blood. Sheila called the nurse, who said, "What he needs is a very hot bath." Following the nurse's bad advice that the heat would cauterize the wound (and not open the blood vessels wider), Sheila poured a steaming hot bath for Michael, but as he lay there soaking, the water was turning increasingly red, and he felt dangerously drowsy. He called out to Sheila, who helped him out of the bath, but he could not stand anymore, as he had lost so much blood. Sheila phoned the nurse, who when seeing Michael's condition, said, not very helpfully, "Oh, we're going to lose him." In the middle of this, some friends from Calgary showed up to look at Michael's latest art. When they saw the bloody footprints from the bedroom to the bathroom and the blood-filled bathtub, they said, "Call the ambulance."

A half hour later the ambulance came; the attendants put Michael on a stretcher and carried him outside, while the nurse kept repeating pathetically, "We're going t'lose him; we're going t'lose him." Sheila was frightened, but Michael, who was close to clinical shock, felt suffused with an all-embracing peace and prayed, as the ambulance drove at top speed to the hospital in Kamloops:

Lord, if this is the time You are calling me to heaven, look after my family; or if I am to work more for You in the world, please help us get to the hospital. But whatever You decide is fine by me. Your will be done![5]

At the hospital, they managed to stop the bleeding and gave him blood transfusions. Michael had to stay a whole week in the hospital for his convalescence. On the last day, Holy Thursday, the sun was shining in through the window of his room. As he looked out at the towering hills of Kamloops, he felt peaceful, but wondered, "How will I survive Blue River and all its psychological negatives?" He opened the Bible for guidance and read, "He will supply all your needs according to His riches in Christ Jesus" (Phil 4:19). "*All* your needs?" Michael asked rhetorically.[6]

Artists' Retreat

In 1882, a group of Benedictine monks from the Swiss Engelberg Abbey founded a new monastery on a hilltop in Oregon, United States. They named the hill and the monastery, appropriately, Mount Angel (a direct translation of "Engelberg"). It developed into a centre of culture and learning: a college was opened in 1887; a seminary in 1889. They also began publishing books. Sadly, in 1892, all the buildings were destroyed in a fire, and the monks had to collect funds to rebuild the entire monastery and seminary. Somehow, the monks did not handle fire very well, and the whole monastery burned down again in 1926. For the second time, a rebuilding process began that continued through the 1930s.

Besides education, and rebuilding, the Mount Angel monastic community took an interest in art. In the late 1970s, a group of young Benedictine monks who were poets, artists, potters, wood craftsmen, and calligraphers began to meet and reflect on their artistic practice. They called themselves "The Fort". In 1979, Leonardo Defilippis, an actor in the Oregon Shakespeare Company, read about the Fort in a newspaper article and immediately bought a bus ticket to the abbey. He longed for a community who could relate to his love for both the Church and the arts. Three years earlier, Leonardo had had a life-changing conversion experience, and, since then, he had tried to bring his newfound faith and acting into some kind of synthesis. At Mount Angel, he found friends and fertile soil for his desire and ideas.

A year later, he decided to use his talent as an apostolate and founded the company St. Luke Productions. At the same time, he wrote to Mother Teresa of Calcutta (the future St. Teresa of Calcutta) asking for guidance. She replied with a personal letter, encouraging him and gave him the mandate "Do something beautiful for God." As a token of gratitude, the first show he put on was based on Mother Teresa's Nobel Prize speech, while the next project was a dramatization of St. Luke's Gospel.[7]

In 1982 Leonardo went to the guestmaster of Mount Angel, Father Bernard Sander, a sixty-five-year-old, mild-mannered monk with a reputation of holiness, to present his idea of an artists' retreat, open to all forms of artistic vocations. The monk loved the idea and gave his support, though Leonardo, together with his future wife, Patti, also an actor, would have to organize it.

It so happened that Father Sander had a brother who also was a monk, but in British Columbia. Father Sander mentioned the artists' retreat to his brother, who in his turn passed the news on to the Poor Clares in Mission, British Columbia, who knew Michael and Sheila, and who saw this as a great opportunity to connect with other Christian artists.

In the end of April 1982, merely a month after almost bleeding to death, Michael drove the thousand kilometres south to Mount Angel. He had a few free days before the actual retreat began and walked on the beaches of the Oregon coast, not far from the abbey, picking up stones, listening to the waves, and wondering what the retreat would be like.

The abbey became like a refuge to Michael, after so much struggle in Blue River. In the blooming fruit trees, he saw nesting songbirds, while in the abbey church, a choir of young monks sang the Divine Office. To him it was as if a sense of holiness pervaded the whole environment, both nature and culture.

The structure of the retreat was built on the Divine Office, and in between Lauds, Sext, Vespers, and Compline there were talks by different monks and by Leonardo, who was the only layman to do presentations. His task was to encourage and inspire the artists participating.

There were painters, poets, sculptors, actors, liturgical artists, writers, architects, singers, and calligraphers. Many friendships were formed, and one of those was between Leonardo and Michael, who conversed and found common ground.[8]

Afterwards, Michael summed up the themes for those attending the retreat as a thirst for deeper prayer as the source of their work, and a loneliness that pointed to the need for spiritual direction and a community of fellow artists.

The latter theme was vital for Michael. By meeting other creative persons, he had gained a sense of something larger than his one-man quest to revive sacred art in the wilderness. Also important, he realized that in order to find a critical mass of laypersons who wanted to revive traditional Catholicism, he had to transcend the limits of Canada and connect to the larger North American Catholic world. Equally interesting was the crucial supportive role of a monastery, whose institutional strength relied on a distance from the world made possible by the pledge of celibacy and poverty. A struggling large family is much more vulnerable as a social unit. It is a story that we will see repeated many times in Michael's life: a family living a Christian, countercultural life while depending on institutions of religious life.

Comparably, Leonardo, like Michael, experienced a radical conversion, a rediscovery of his faith. In a sense, this Catholic subculture was a reformulation, a revitalization of the Catholic faith, after the shock of modernization in the 1960s and early 1970s. Just as Michael had decided to paint Christian art, Leonardo decided to perform Christian theater and film. And they were of one mind in seeing their art as an apostolate.

Poor Clares

In the week before Pentecost, only a week after the artists' retreat, Michael arrived at St. Clare's Monastery in Mission, British Columbia, to paint an icon of St. Francis of Assisi for their chapel. Sheila had friends in the monastery, and in her youth, she had even thought of entering herself.

At the time of Michael's visit, there were sixteen nuns, and their spiritual life of material simplicity drew many people to lay before them different kinds of problems, asking for the sisters' prayers. They tried to the best of their capacities to help visitors to find faith, but sometimes years of intercessory prayer were necessary for certain problems, they said.

In an article from 1982, "Prayer at Hatzic Monastery: The Poor Clares; At Work in Mission", it is obvious that the reporter had been impressed by the common spirituality of the sisters but also by their individuality.

> An inner warmth of "cleanness" seemed to radiate from the sisters as they talked. One nun's eyes sparkled as she talked, another was very restful and spoke from a deeper assurance. Each nun is different, but all stressed the reality of their contact with God.[9]

The first morning in the guesthouse, Michael woke up very early, about four in the morning. Not long after, the sun rose like a brilliant red flower through the mountain pass in the east; the leaves of the trees surrounding the convent were trembling in a light breeze, and birds were singing. To Michael, it seemed as if nature was coming to life, the whole earth pulsating with fresh energy—it was like a divine revelation, he thought, but then the notoriously noisy crows, known to rise early as well, broke his reverie with their hoarse imitation of Lauds.

During the week that Michael painted the icon of St. Francis at the monastery, he also gave a talk to the sisters on "The Spirituality of the Artist", which was taped and transcribed.[10] In it, some glimmers of his humorous side come forth with the sisters bursting out in laughter and engaging occasionally in a teasing dialogue with Michael. But his main points were serious, focusing on, besides the consolations of nature that he had experienced at the monastery, the purgatory that is necessary for an artist to go through—"It is a fearful thing to fall into the hands of the living God" (Heb 10:31).

Michael experienced this purgatory intensively when he was to begin the painting of St. Francis. As at previous times, he felt completely empty of inspiration. For several days, he just sat in the guest room, or prayed in the chapel for divine illumination, but the interior wells of creativity were dry. At one point, he was so overwhelmed with a sense of defeat and unworthiness that he prostrated himself on the floor of the chapel and cried to God that it was impossible for him to make an icon of St. Francis. It would have to be painted by someone else! As if in reply, there flashed onto the screen of his imagination an image of the saint holding an empty, cracked bowl, representing the poverty of our humanity, dipping his fingers into the bowl.

He then rose to his feet and went to find the abbess, to tell her about what had happened. They met in the hallway between the guest room and the enclosure, as she was just coming to see him. Before he could say a word, she said, "I don't want to interfere, Michael, but as I was praying for you just now, I saw in my mind an image of St. Francis holding an empty, cracked bowl and dipping his fingers into it."[11]

This is typical for how Michael's creative process works, at least at critical junctures of his artistic development (both in painting and in writing). First, there is an absolute emptiness in which his human strength and willpower are completely inadequate; he prays and waits, and when the impossibility overwhelms him, a revelation of the image unexpectedly appears. When it comes to novel writing, such sudden materializations in the imagination are also common.

In the finished painting, the elongated, dark triangular form of St. Francis, shrouded in a bulky brown habit, is silhouetted against a kaleidoscopic background: a mélange of gold, orange, and green metallic leaf. Around his head there is a golden leaf halo accompanied by two smaller circles in each upper corner: one golden and one silvery—that is, symbols of the sun and the moon. St. Francis looks straight at the beholder with intense eyes, while a smile is playing on his lips. In his right hand, which carries the stigmata wound, he holds a cracked, empty bowl, a symbol of human poverty. The mood of the picture is one of intense seriousness, and the basic pictorial language is that of the icon, but the form is freer. The volcanic background, the anatomically impossible position of the hands, form of the head, and size of the body, gives it a touch of expressionist inner tension, which, however, is balanced by the recollected facial features, especially the large dark eyes and the elongated icon nose. In the painting, Michael combined the message of poverty as an ideal with that of religious intensity and authenticity, realized through a style in which tradition is influenced by modern developments in art, even as it challenges modernity.

A month later, he weighed in his mind whether he henceforth should refuse all icon commissions in order to concentrate on his dammed-up list of inner ideas and inspirations on which he longed to work. It was not an easy choice as the commissions were critical to the family income.

10. Valemount

The retreat into the desert had proved to be very difficult for Michael and his growing family. By 1982, he had lived through a three-year purgatory in which his resolve to labour full-time with sacred art and not to shy away from poverty—that is, if his apostolate did not prove to be profitable—had been sorely tested. Besides material scarcity, the social isolation and the lack of confirmation from the art system (the galleries and curators) was hard on his psyche. Despite the best of intentions, the situation in Blue River became at a certain point too isolated.

Maybe it was time, they began to wonder, to leave the desert for a more public and active role. One solution was to accept an offer to move ninety-one kilometres to the north, to Valemount, which was not precisely a big and bustling city, but at least it was a larger village with close to a thousand inhabitants, four times the size of Blue River. In Valemount there were also a few Catholic families with a similar outlook on life as Michael and Sheila's, so they would have a larger social network.

At the invitation of the resident priest, Father Anthony Vella, they had been offered the apartment on the ground floor of the small Catholic centre, while the priest lived in the finished basement. This was not the realization of a home of one's own with space for numerous children, a playground, some goats, rabbits, and a kitchen garden, plus an airy studio with a cool northern light streaming down from skylights, and Handel on the stereo, as Michael used to say.

It was instead, once again, the awkward fit of being a layperson and literally living in the church, as in Ottawa when Michael had his studio in the Dominican monastery. Through his dedication to sacred art and writing on themes of importance for the Catholic Church, he was closely serving the Church. He was not living in the secular society according to its rules, being a witness to the Christian faith in the world, but he was, without realizing it, becoming a kind of a prophet for the Church—and for the world, if it would listen, of course.

Church residences are not built for families. Nevertheless, Michael and Sheila decided that this was better than their present situation; and, in November 1982, they moved from the isolation of Blue River to a place with a constant stream of people coming and going. They did not see it as a permanent solution, but as a temporary measure.

There was no place for a studio in the parish centre, so Michael rented a cabin about an hour's walk from town. It was heated by a woodstove and situated in a birch woods, overlooking a mountain stream. The beautiful mountainous landscape provided an inspiring and contemplative milieu for his painting.

Michael and Sheila were responsible for certain church activities and for receiving guests, which, together with the small space, made it difficult to make a separation between family and parish life, something that Michael one day experienced after a night of poor sleep.

Mary and Joseph had been sick the whole night, and, in the afternoon, Michael felt tired and worn out. He took a bath and lay down to get a nap before he was to make a four hours' drive to Kamloops. However, his head had barely touched the pillow, when Mary, who was napping in the crib beside Michael, woke with an agonizing cry. He picked her up and sat her on his lap, ready to do his fatherly duty, and then, hopefully, he thought, be able to get a few minutes of rest before dressing and starting the drive. This was not meant to be, because suddenly Mary vomited copiously all over him and the bed—several times. So much for bathing and sleeping. Michael managed to wriggle out of his sopping wet clothes, and wearing only his underwear, his body dripping with vomit, he made a dash for the bathroom with Mary in his arms, who naturally screamed for all she was worth. In the meantime, a catechism class finished downstairs, and the students, a couple of teenage girls, entered the O'Briens' apartment without knocking. The shock was mutual. As Michael wrote in his diary, "A seminaked man covered in vomit trying to placate a hysterical baby ... a truly inspiring sight."[1]

The sale of their house in Blue River was taking its time due to legal machinations, which meant that they were temporarily without money and had over a thousand dollars in bills. Their economic situation was also aggravated because several persons had not paid for their paintings. For the first time in their married life, Michael would have to tell the landlord (that is, the priest) that they could not pay the rent; it was a new form of humiliation, and a blow to his natural pride of being the breadwinner of the family.

On December 4, a month after they moved into Valemount, Michael underwent a severe test of faith, doubting the value of the whole period of seven years that he had dedicated to sacred art; now it all seemed like vain self-delusion. It was merely, he believed, a road to exile and discouragement.

That night he took off the large cross he had been wearing under his shirt, as he felt deep sorrow for his anger, mistrust, and lack of faith and considered himself no longer worthy of carrying it. He was face-to-face with his own failure in being a spiritual hero. The following evening, he decided that in the morning he would put on the cross again, but "with a humble awareness that I am not worthy of it, and for that precise reason must not reject it, but learn, step by step, beginning with my own poverty and spiritual shallowness".[2]

Michael was going through an interior struggle that gradually chiselled away at his confidence in himself. In taking off the cross, he was fighting with the tangled nexus of despair and pride, while, on the day after Christmas Day, he experienced, as in his conversion in 1969, intense hatred from an invisible evil presence.

He was having a peaceful time of quiet prayer in church before going to bed, but as he left and walked through the sacristy to their apartment, he suddenly felt attacked by what he called "horror". It caught him off guard, but he took his rosary with him to bed and felt some relief. Nevertheless, when he had finished, the attacks returned and so strongly that his hair almost stood on end.

When Sheila came to bed, he asked her to pray over him, and this drove away the terror somewhat. As during his conversion experience, Michael felt as if an oppressive presence had tried to tear him open, to enter and possess him. Naturally, he felt frightened and kept repeating acts of faith and love of God.

Finally, he drifted into a very troubled sleep, but kept waking up the whole night, dreaming one nightmare after the other. The next morning, he was exhausted and shaken after fighting desperately and weakly against evil in each of the dreams, and he heard in his mind, "I have you; I've got you; I'm in you ...."

When walking to his studio after breakfast, he felt painful doubts: "Could this be true?" he wondered. "Had evil taken root in me?"

Then he saw a vivid interior image of two angels with drawn swords walking to the left and right of him. He felt physically and emotionally strengthened by the sight, and a surge of joy and confidence filled him. The image of the two angels faded in his mind when he approached the studio.

Michael's spiritual life, as we have seen, was marked by stark contrasts. He was thrown into the blackest night of near despair, self-contempt, and attacks of terror and evil, but he also rose to intense feelings of peace and joy, of images of angels and Christ.

I would like to give you one more example of the second category from January 1983 to balance the scale, and, in this way, illustrate his intimate love of the Eucharist and his emotionally strong relationship to Jesus. In his diary, Michael wrote that it was with some hesitation that he committed the following to paper as it definitely placed him in the "lunatic fringe", as he expressed it. Nevertheless, it was so deeply peaceful and joyful that he did not mind such lunacy, "and if this is madness, then thank God for madness."[3]

Michael had been thinking a lot about Gethsemane lately, and because Christ is outside of time, he wondered if it would be possible to go back in spirit to the moment of fear and solitude that Jesus had experienced in Gethsemane, and somehow console Him in an invisible way. Being a man of action, Michael knelt in front of the tabernacle and embraced the box and held it as a symbol of Christ's body—as it was, he believed, encasing the living and actual presence of Jesus in the Eucharist. He even stroked the box as if he was consoling one of his own children. All sense of strangeness in doing this fled from his mind as he went deeper into prayer.

> Silence and an unspeakable fondness seemed to flow through me and into a communion with Jesus. I felt really with him in the garden of Gethsemane. I felt his anguish, his terrible fear, his aloneness. I spoke words of consolation to him, words of gratitude for what he endured (endures). Yet conscious too that had I actually been there in history I would probably have run away or slept. Yet here and now, as an offspring of his "yes" to the Father's cup, I was empowered through his merits (not my own) to remain awake.[4]

While embracing the tabernacle, Michael began to cry tears of compassion for the suffering Jesus. It was a gentle and quiet experience, in stark contrast to the attacks of terror a month before.

The interior turmoil and trials, however, continued during late winter as Michael came closer to his talks and exhibits in March: the first was at Newman Theological College in Edmonton and the second at the Fourth Annual Diocesan Conference "Ministries in the 80's" in Winnipeg.

A New Style of Art

Michael had not slept much the night before he was to give his talk at Newman Theological College. Despite this, he felt such a high rush of adrenalin when he arrived in Edmonton and began preparing, that he first ran a few times around the college to burn off some of the extra energy. Then he prayed in his room with outstretched arms and felt a peacefulness fill him, and began to pray in tongues. He also went to the tabernacle in the church and lay face down before it and prayed: "Behold the *empty* man, Lord! I thank you for all that will be." The following words came into his mind: "Take your emptiness up there with you—it is a gift to be empty."[5]

Michael felt recollected when he began his talk "The Sacred Arts: Ministry and Prophecy".[6] The last word in the title was important; Michael saw the artist, especially those dedicated to sacred art, as fulfilling the task of the prophet in relation to the contemporary West. Beginning in the Renaissance, materialism and the principle of man as the measure of all things had led to the modern fragmented individual and a particular form of soft totalitarianism. In this development, even sacred art became commercialized: the junk food of art, with sentimental holy-card images of saints and Jesus. Michael told the audience that the merchants in the Temple had constructed an idolatrously tame God.

It was thus time for artists, as Pope Paul VI had said at the closing of Vatican II, to leave their exile and come back to their true home, the Church.[7] Michael's dream was a renewal of sacred art, but, at the same time, this was dependent on a renewal of Christianity itself. The task was thus not merely to raise the standard of art in churches; his focus was on a larger spiritual renewal of which art was part. Michael was taking an unusually strong stand against modernity, against both the Communist system in the East and the commodification of human life and hedonism in the West. This combination of seriousness, critique, and a call for religious purity and sincerity was that of a prophet.

In a newspaper article commenting on the talk, the journalist Glen Argan writes:

> Mr. O'Brien himself gives the appearance of an Old Testament prophet. At Newman, the 35-year old bearded artist stood at the front of the room making his points in a firm, uncompromising style. His paintings reflect that style. There is no trace of sentimentality in his images of Jesus and Mary.
>
> And his work is harshly critical of contemporary culture. One painting entitled "Prophet in the Wilderness" shows a white-haired, bearded man holding up a cloth with a picture of the suffering Christ on it. In the background is a modern skyline.[8]

There was much enthusiasm among the audience over the talk. He sold several paintings and received commissions and a substantial honorarium from the college. Despite this confirmation, he felt deflated, his energy spent, as he began the long drive to Saskatoon and Winnipeg. He was clearly looking for affirmations of his calling, a sense that he was on the right path—that what he was doing was not merely a crazy dream. This meant that his whole organism, physically and psychologically, was in a state of high stress each time he was to perform or be evaluated. His whole project was up for review with every show or talk.

Michael's main fear in Winnipeg was that he would be boring and too lengthy. The risk was high, as the talk was scheduled to begin as late as 9:30 in the evening, and the audience was going to be tired, and Michael too for that matter. He was also worried that his painting *Woman from Auschwitz* would offend Archbishop Exner, who the previous year had said that it was best to let the past be and not needlessly bring it up.[9] Michael was thus contemplating whether to shorten his talk and remove that painting. However, he saw it as a temptation to please other people, even the archbishop whom he greatly respected, and decided that he was to tell the truth and not try to soften it. That meant a long talk and that the painting would stay.

The archbishop began with a very warm and thoughtful introduction, but Michael's exhaustion and the lateness of the hour (the talk began actually at 9:45) made it a difficult task. Nevertheless, some people came up afterwards and seemed touched by the talk. For him, however, it was a Gethsemane experience, compared to the acclamation he had received at Newman College.

In connection with the talk, Beatrice Fines from the *National Catholic Register* interviewed Michael, and, in the photo, he stands beside a large painting called *Christian Mandala*, painted according to a wheel design divided into triangular slices illustrating different phases of human life. In the middle is an image of Jesus with the earth globe in his hands. This was an example of Michael's modern style. Fines writes:

> More recently he has developed his own style while still retaining the strong messages of icon painting. The results are sober figures in brown hues against dark, often black backgrounds, many incorporating images of the modern world. One of the most striking displayed at the conference was "Woman of Auschwitz". The central figure of the Virgin is surrounded by scenes of horror and atrocity.[10]

When she asked Michael about the lack of joy in his paintings, he answered,

> Though I am myself a happy man, I am concerned with suffering and evil. Our culture, being materialistic and pleasure-seeking, denies suffering and does not face the reality of death. Therefore, I feel a call to bring the message of the Cross to people.[11]

Quite right, in the photo Michael looks at the camera without smiling, and one can see that his beard has become longer, and that his unruly, curly, dark hair, though not long, bears no obvious evidence of a haircut. There is nothing frivolous about him. What did Michael then mean by being a happy man?

In his diary, we can see how his mental state oscillated between, on the one hand, the darkness of the temptation to despair and anger at his situation, and, on the other hand, elevated conditions of spiritual peace and intense joy. This is, however, a somewhat one-sided picture, due to the format of the diary. What largely went unrecorded were the support and joy he found in the ordinary life of his family. Nevertheless, in another interview that spring, the reporter touches on the same question.

The dominant mood of most of O'Brien's work is suffering and pain. Though he describes himself as "not a depressed person" he feels these themes should be inherent in his art. "You cannot have Resurrection without the reality of the Cross," he said. "Today's culture tends to deny suffering. We distract ourselves from reality through our constant search for pleasure. We can't live fully until we realize the realities of death and suffering."[12]

This preoccupation with suffering can create the impression of Michael as a deadly serious prophet constantly tormented by existential angst. My own impression is that he has made a wholehearted dedication to God and the Church in combination with a strong will to spiritual purity, but that at the same time he is a man with a warm sense of humour. It could be that the prophet has mellowed with age, but his sister, Patti, tells me how he had an uncanny ability to tell a joke with a completely straight face when they were younger. Michael's brother Terry has this same tendency of mock seriousness and playing with words.

Based on the description of David, their father, this sense of humour seems to be a paternal inheritance, while Christian devotion comes from their mother. It is a lightheartedness very much connected to the imagination, and the play of words. We thus have to imagine a serious, bearded prophet with a sense of humour. However, I think we must also acknowledge that this was a very difficult period in Michael's life, when he had to carve out a niche for his creative work, against overwhelming odds. It is, therefore, not surprising that this struggle is also reflected in his art.

Later in the 1980s, he began to paint in a style inspired by Kurelek, where the gruesome aspects of the Cross are not palpable in the same way. There are both colourful landscapes and religious themes in this category.

I would like to focus on one called *A Place Where We All Could Live* from 1988, which exists in two versions. In one of these, we see ten houses clustered around a church in a rural wintry scene with high, snow-covered mountains in the background. Smoke is curling from the chimneys, and a family with six children has just come out from one of the houses and is walking on the only road (actually, only tracks in the deep snow) to the village church, whose pitch-black spire with a dark green highlight stretches vertically almost to the same height as the mountains. The houses are painted with strong colours: clear red and blue, combined with pale yellow and apricot. The image captures the ideal that Sheila and Michael carried with them, but which was so difficult to achieve.

In 1982, Michael had begun to feel restlessness with icon painting as he was developing his new style of sacred art. A year later, this sense had developed into a conviction. While he maintained a profound reverence for icons, more and more he came to see his own iconography, and especially commissions, as something that kept him rooted in copying, as exercises in technique, while his creativity tended toward a freer form. He was again thinking of refusing all icon commissions except those from churches. If he began to turn down private icon commissions, it would be another heroic decision, because they brought in vital survival money for the family. However, Michael seldom chose safety when his inspiration and moral sense of mission pointed in another direction.

As he worked on an icon of the Transfiguration in late May, many images came to him in his imagination, which he thought were beautiful, but they were combined with a very strong aversion to icons. He thought that icons were important and had taught him much, but that the seven-year apprenticeship was now over, and that he was free to begin painting modern "icons" guided by this new inspiration. His hope was to make a painting of the Transfiguration in the new style as a beginning of the next seven years.

We have seen this before, a new start leads to a creative block; thus, in the middle of June, Michael could not paint at all, and in July, he made the momentous decision to destroy some of his old paintings—not icons, but rather some of his neo-modern experiments.

> Today I burned several of my old paintings. Dead ends, false starts and mimicries. Part of me had held onto them in the hopes of someday selling them and regaining some of the lost time.
>
> It was not lost time in reality, because it was all a lesson in internal geography. Where and when not to go. Meanwhile this somehow has a mysterious effect of sharpening my sense of focus creatively. Leave the dead to bury the dead.[13]

Four days later, he began to paint again, but in September the block returned; he was clearly in a transitional stage in the development of his art. The year 1983 was otherwise a very busy period; he had six exhibitions and completed several commissions. Besides the talks in Edmonton and Winnipeg in the spring, he spoke at Marylhurst College in Portland, Oregon.

He also went to another artists' retreat at Mount Angel Abbey that deepened his friendship with Leonardo Defilippis, who in 1983 was touring with two plays, *St. Francis* and *The Gospel of St. Luke*. The icon of the Transfiguration Michael painted was for the wedding in August of Leonardo and Patti. As a gesture of thanks, they were to bring the two plays to Valemount in October.

In May, Michael wrote in his diary:

Until we form communities of creative people, living and prophetic communities, I'm afraid the renewal of the sacred arts (especially the visual arts) will remain limited to those wild-ass types, who somehow manage to survive in the desert and from time to time stumble into civilization with their latest creation.[14]

The Catholic world of Canada and the United States was in this sense borderless, forming a larger North American Catholic context with English as the common language, as seen in the artists' retreats and workshops in Oregon. Still, the work of bringing those with a creative talent together to initiate a renewal required communication on a broader scale.

Michael's idea of prophetic communities was a vision of the 1970s, when there was a strong urge to form small religious communities on the model of the village, based on physical proximity with a local outreach. With modernity, effective communication had developed that could form communities over larger distances: the printing press, airplanes, telephone, television, and, in the middle of the 1980s, the computer revolution, which was beginning to gain momentum. Due to his and Sheila's aversion to modernity and their preference for the natural world and small-scale communities, they were resisting this development.

Michael's paintings were originals made in solitude and sold to individuals and churches, and he had to travel to hold exhibitions and talks. There was a need for a way to reach out more effectively, something that modern mass media had already accomplished, and, earlier, the printing press. Michael had not published any books at this point, neither fiction nor books with his artwork. He had, however, continued to write essays and articles about the renewal of sacred art—for example, "Art—The Cry of a People", published in April 1983 in *Our Family Magazine*.[15] The problem for his novels, as for his art, was that secular publishers, like galleries, did not accept the explicit "conservative" Christian message of Michael's writing and art. So, what was a prophet to do? Merely labour on in solitude and trust in the Providence of God, or bond together with other entrepreneurs and establish printing presses and television channels transmitting their message?

An example of the latter in the United States was EWTN (Eternal Word Television Network), a Catholic television channel founded by Mother Mary Angelica in 1980. She began broadcasting in 1981 from a garage studio in her convent in Alabama, and today EWTN has a global outreach, reaching 250 million television households in 140 countries.[16] In 1983, this development had merely begun.

Another such pioneering venture was Ignatius Press, founded in 1978 by the Jesuit Father Joseph Fessio, in San Francisco, California.[17] It similarly presently has a global outreach due to the position of English as the lingua franca of the twenty-first century. We can see how in the beginning of the 1980s, during the pontificate of John Paul II, a Catholic "orthodox" subculture was established that wanted to uphold the teachings of the Catholic Church, both its dogmas and moral principles, even when they clashed with the direction taken by the postmodern West. Through pioneers such as Mother Angelica and Father Fessio, this subculture acquired institutional form in television channels and publishing, but also in new Catholic liberal arts colleges, which were formed in reaction to the crumbling of the Catholic "identity" at older Catholic universities and colleges. An example is Christendom College, established in 1977, in Virginia, United States, by Warren H. Carroll, a lay convert to the Catholic faith. On their homepage in 2015, one could read the following statement:

> The purpose of Catholic education is therefore to learn and to live by the truth revealed by Our Lord and Saviour Jesus Christ, "the Way, the Truth and the Life," as preserved in the deposit of faith and authentically interpreted in the Magisterium of the Roman Catholic

Church, founded by Christ, of which the Pope is the visible head. That central body of divine truth illumines all other truth and shows us its essential unity in every area of thought and life. Only an education which integrates the truths of the Catholic Faith throughout the curriculum is a fully Catholic education.[18]

This part of the mission statement of Christendom College provides a clear picture of the ethos of the Catholic subculture that had formed in the late 1970s and gained momentum in 1980s. This was also the final decade of the Cold War with the election of Ronald Reagan in 1981 as president of the United States and the rise of what has been called the Christian Right.[19]

But the pioneering institutionalization of Catholic culture was tilted in North America toward the United States; there was no similar growth of publishing houses, television channels, and Catholic liberal arts colleges during the 1980s in Canada. Michael was a pioneer and united with the spirit of this subculture, but he was not an organizer. His talent lay in his art and imagination, in the written word and pictures, but in Canada at that time there was not a publisher in the mode or calibre of Ignatius Press. There was therefore no natural channel in Canada for Michael's two novels, and he continued to exhibit his paintings in churches and to accept commissions, struggling with the self-questioning that follows from an artistic life on the margins of society.

St. Francis Comes to the Village

In October 4, 1983, Leonardo and Patti Defilippis came as promised to Valemount, to perform the play *Francis, the Troubadour of Peace* at Valemount Elementary School. This was, fittingly, the feast day of St. Francis; however, Michael could not attend, because that day Sheila gave birth to their fourth child, Elizabeth Rose. The baby's head appeared ten seconds to midnight, but she was born the next day, October 5, a few minutes later. The official papers say that Elizabeth was born on the fifth, but Michael maintained that the fourth was more accurate, and, according to "Kingdom standards, she is a Franciscan!" It was a difficult birth; Sheila became so exhausted that

Michael was afraid for her. The doctor and the nurse were, according to Michael, "stumbling all over themselves to have the baby born without damage, but she was stuck at the shoulders and without oxygen for a few minutes. It felt longer."[20] The doctor was anxious, as he had lost his own child only a few months earlier.

Finally, Elizabeth came forth and turned from indigo to red as oxygen burst in, and then she cried. Michael and Sheila wept with joy and gave thanks to God for their fourth child. As for Sheila, the birth had been so difficult that she had to stay in the hospital for seven days to recuperate.

The next evening, Michael attended the second performance by Leonardo and Patti: the dramatization of the Gospel of St. Luke, performed in Valemount's community hall. Between trips to McBride Hospital to see Sheila and the baby, Michael took Leonardo and Patti on a hike in the mountains around Valemount. Three days later, they joined Michael in a trip to the mountains near Blue River. It was a day of friendship, full of laughter and prayer; they prayed the Rosary together after Leonardo had read poetry written by his friend Father Jeremy, a monk of Mount Angel Abbey. The sun gave a strong autumn light, illuminating the yellow leaves falling all around them. As they gazed at the river below and at the peaks above, they sensed the sweet smell of cottonwood trees. The scene was one of perfect peace and made Michael long for simplicity of living. Leonardo and Patti then told Michael that Mount Angel Abbey was considering having an artist in residence. Michael wondered:

> Could it be a married artist? Could it be a tired, sick, self-doubting, sometimes inspired artist, who preaches poverty and radical trust, but trembles in terror that he might be left out in the desert to die? (Or thrive ☺)
>
> How I yearn for a year in a Catholic town surrounding a dynamic prayerful monastery. How I yearn to create great images, life-giving images.[21]

Once again, we can see how a longing for community was moving Michael. But was it necessary to leave Canada to achieve this? Even if the border to the United States was not far away, for Sheila the cultural difference was too big; she did not want to leave Canada.

The Dream of a Home

The living situation in Valemount was not sustainable; it was hard both on Michael and Sheila, especially now with four children.

> The centre is so small. I built a little bed of spruce for the new baby—a side-car bed which will fit beside ours. So now we are four in one little bedroom. Cozy! Hope we can sleep. Dreams almost every night of searching through old broken houses, which are always too isolated or too expensive, no place to shelter my family. Pain. We are pilgrims, Sojourners.[22]

Sheila was weak and in low spirits after the difficult birth of Elizabeth; furthermore, later in October, the baby developed colic, so they got little sleep. Michael had also sprained his lower back and was tired due to flu, and the car engine was completely dead. On top of this bundle of troubles, there were many visitors in the Catholic centre and a crisis was brewing in the other half of the building. In September, Father Emile Sasges had been appointed vicar in Valemount again and was now living in the basement, and there were personality clashes between parishioners. Michael and Sheila were not involved, but the situation contributed to the tensions under which they lived.

John and Joseph had begun school in September, and Sheila reacted:

> How universal the anti-life, anti-child comments were on the first day of school—mothers glad to get rid of the kids. Our loathsome culture again. People have so many interests, expenses and entertainments. They find their children are exhausting and distracting.... If children were our culture, they wouldn't be experienced as a burden.[23]

This worry for the education and formation of their children on the part of Sheila was combined with her dream of a spacious, stable home, where the children could be given an alternative upbringing to what the consumerist society surrounding them had to offer. Unlike the 1970s, the 1980s were not appreciative of farming and a life close to nature. With the new decade, the hero was the yuppie, the young urban professional, indulging in senseless materialism. The human ideal was becoming synthetic rather than natural.

In 1981, the German pioneering electronic music band Kraftwerk released the LP *Computer World*, the follow-up to their 1978 *The Man-Machine*, and in 1984 Apple introduced the first Macintosh computer. The digitalization of human culture and the human person was beginning in earnest, and the cyborg represented this coming together of machine and human person. I have difficulty envisioning a more antithetical ideal to what has inspired Michael and Sheila throughout their life. However, in this vision of cyborgs, androids, and artificial intelligence there is a paradoxical, dystopic streak, a fear of totalitarianism, besides the enthusiasm for technotopia. This can be seen in 1984 movie *The Terminator*, featuring Arnold Schwarzenegger as a cyborg assassin from the future. This anticipation of the inhumanity of technological civilization had a natural link to a Christian eschatological critique of late modernity.

Besides the steady march toward the digital future, there was a growing unease of what a thoroughly man-made future would do to humanity, especially when coupled with a totalitarian machinelike ideology. But was it possible to leave the system? Was it possible to establish radically alternative structures?

In their attempts at discernment of where and how to live, Michael and Sheila prayed a novena to St. Joseph to intercede for them; they prayed for the gift of wisdom, discernment, and knowledge of the direction of their lives. At this time, a friend offered them five acres in McBride, rent-free for thirty years; they only had to pay the taxes. Although they felt overwhelmed by the generosity of the gift, they thought it was better to pray and wait for more clarity. During that year, they also had an offer to move to Ontario to help with a retreat centre. Another possible place was Mission, close to Vancouver, where the convent of the Poor Clares was located.

During this period, Michael wondered whether his call was leading him not on to "success", but to more instability—that they would have to remain pilgrims, open and flexible. Sheila replied that this was not God's way for families, that they needed roots, stability, and a measure of security—and, also, a piece of land of their own. Michael was, in a sense, proposing a Franciscan spirituality of mendicant friars, while Sheila was more attracted to the model of a traditional monastic life based on the principles of stability and self-sustainability at a location withdrawn from the busy life of the city.

In June, Michael had prayed,

I will dare to ask of the Lord in his Providence to show us a home and studio we can afford. A large house, three bedrooms, spacious and sound, outside of town bordering on woods with a studio nearby that is also large and has power. Near enough to schools and church and store to make it practical.

In his mind, he heard the following: "Michael, you do not have to worry. It is all going to be provided.... Doubt no longer but believe!" Michael continued to pray, trying to wring definitive answers from what he called "the Silence". In the midst of a state of inner calm came a sense of being held by Jesus in His arms; and Michael said aloud, "Someday I will embrace You as Your real friend." He heard the answer (in his diary he describes it as a realization of interior meaning not as concrete words):

—You are already embracing Me as My friend.
—But Lord, I am so poor in faith, so poor in Love.
—Follow Me.
—Where to, Lord? Mission, Ontario, elsewhere ...?
—It is not necessary for you to know where; it is only necessary for you to believe and to follow.

In Michael's mind, there were still doubts, but in his heart, he felt at peace. Still, he could not let go of the question "Are these words my own imagination?" He therefore said aloud, "This is unusual, this dialogue, Lord, so I am going to accept on faith that it *is* You speaking to me."[24]

One night in late November, Michael and Sheila discussed once again where they were to live and how. The conversation, how-ever, degenerated into discouraged thoughts. Sheila cried that they would never have a proper home—a place to call their own. It struck Michael as a knife thrust, and left him with a feeling of discour-agement about their life, his vocation—a sense of hopelessness. He wrote in his diary that he realized that this was an illusion, but that nonetheless the feeling of hopelessness was real, and it did not go away easily.[25]

In December, Michael was confined to bed for six days with a severe cold, and mostly read books. Sheila was still recuperating from childbirth and had little strength; she was unhappy with the living accommodations in the centre, but even more, she told Michael, she felt overwhelmed with powerlessness—an inability to protect their children from the pressure of society, particularly of its values, or rather its nonvalues, and omnipresent materialism.

The day before Christmas Eve 1983, Michael wrote, "Praying for a sign where we should be—where to live!"

11. Mission

A constant theme in Michael's fiction is that of the sojourner, which provided the title for his second novel, *Strangers and Sojourners*. The central character is mostly an individual, battered by life, stumbling from place to place, never allowed to set down roots and merge with a place, a landscape, or a particular culture. There is a modern restlessness afflicting these persons, and at the same time they are looking for a true home, a place of stability and security. They are not cynics who have embraced despair as a lifestyle; they have hope, even when such hope seems unfounded, or foolish. However, when they do find a homelike place, it is mostly a temporary consolation, a place of rest before the sojourner continues on his journey.

Since his conversion in 1969, Michael's eyes had been set on the permanent stability of Heaven, the final destination that is hidden, seen "through a glass darkly", and mostly experienced in interior, spiritual states. From such a perspective, the things of the earth, its possessions and riches, appear to be burdens. To him, the freedom inherent in Franciscan poverty held a powerful attraction. However, if a bearded, youthful, artistic soul can make do with a shack in the mountains and some potatoes to keep his body alive, he also knew that a family needs stability and a supportive social context. The wanderer or pilgrim as an ideal is hard on a family—that is, if one is not a hunter-gatherer. Sheila and Michael were thus united in their search for a home, a base where they could bring up their children and where Michael's work as an artist would flourish. At the same time, they were haunted by the spirit of the sojourner. No sooner than they moved their family and their few belongings to a new place, something conspired against them, making Michael burst out, "My life is impossible!" And the search for a new home had to begin again.

Valemount had proved to be little better than Blue River; but in 1983, they were once more praying for a sign, entreating God to direct them where to go. Both parents were worn down by financial insecurity, sickness, and the care of four small children. Sheila had not yet recovered physically and emotionally from the difficult birth of Elizabeth, and a move could mean leaving the part of the country that she loved and where her parents and three of her four siblings lived. To settle in a city would be the antithesis of her dreams of a homestead in a rural surrounding. So, when the sign came, would they accept it?

On New Year's Eve 1983, they received the news that an acquaintance in Mission, British Columbia, was interested in renting his house to them; he had actually tried to phone them the week before, when they were away. Such a telephone call was one of the signs for which they had prayed, so it seemed to be a clear signal to start packing.

Mission is a district municipality on the north bank of the Fraser River, an hour's drive from Vancouver. It stretches in an almost rectangular form from the more settled, urban area in the South, close to the river, to the mountains and lakes in the North. To the east of the main urban area, five kilometres along the Fraser River, is the village of Hatzic, and one kilometre to the north of the village centre is St. Clare's Monastery—where Michael had painted the icon of St. Francis in 1982.[1]

Two kilometres by car west from Hatzic toward Mission (as a bird flies eight hundred metres), one comes to the Benedictine Westminster Abbey (officially, the Abbey of Saint Joseph of Westminster) and the Seminary of Christ the King, which are beautifully located on a hill with surrounding farmland and woods. It was here that Michael had come in the 1970s to discern whether he had a calling to the priesthood.

The tolling of the bells in the high bell tower, which was completed only in 1982, could be heard over a long distance, even to the prospective house of Michael and Sheila. The abbey had grown from a priory established in 1939, when a few monks had been sent from Mount Angel Abbey in Oregon (where Michael went for artists' retreats) to manage a seminary in Ladner outside Vancouver.[2]

St. Clare's Monastery in Mission was established in 1962, when a handful of Poor Clare sisters moved from Vancouver to be in the vicinity of Westminster Abbey, which had agreed to take care of their spiritual needs (that is, daily Mass and Confession) if they lived close to the abbey. In 1984, Sister Mary Barbara Collins, one of the founders of the community and a nun since 1933, had been the Mother Superior for a year.[3]

Michael and Sheila's new home on Ewert Avenue was a big, blue house, full of light, as Michael described it, located on a park near a school, a mere five minutes' walk away from the Poor Clares and with a view of the Benedictine abbey on the mountain. Their oldest son, John, remembers how much richer everything seemed in comparison to Valemount; to him it was like a verdant paradise, where everything grew greener and taller.

It was only a twenty-minute walk between the two monasteries, and they were to live in between them. Once again, we can see how Michael, together with his family, in his service to the Church gravitated toward close contact with institutions of celibate life. The shadow of the monasteries seemed to promise stability and a good soil to cultivate a vibrant Catholic culture.

To try to live as Michael and Sheila did in accordance with the moral teachings of the Catholic Church was to be decisively counter-cultural. The problem was on a basic level a very practical question—namely, the consequences of having more children than the average two. Even a lot more. To have a large family with one income, in a society and economy that rewarded families with two incomes and no more than one or two children, created enormous disparities.

In the Western world since the Second Vatican Council, much of the Catholic support structure had crumbled, and a majority of Catholic families had opted for a lifestyle in harmony with the ideal of the secular (or at least not intensively religious) middle class. In the 1980s, a large family was an anomaly also in the Church. However, in some small ways, the situation was changing.

Two new ecumenical movements were born in the 1970s, due to the dechristianization of the North American societies: the pro-life and the homeschooling movements. The first put value on the openness to life that Michael and Sheila were concretely living.[4] With the homeschooling movement, Christian families seized the opportunity to form their children according to their own values and not according to those prevalent in the surrounding culture or imposed by the secular state. Because homeschooling was from the beginning built upon the hard work of especially mothers teaching their children in their homes, it was a natural development to seek the company of other homeschooling families and to share certain activities together. A process of institutionalization began and led to new forms of schools and programs designed for homeschooling.[5] In Canada, homeschooling was pioneered in the 1970s and began to be organized from 1979 onward.[6]

What we can see in these two examples is, as I have said, signs of a Christian resistance to the development of the increasingly secular Western societies. At the same time, new divisions between and within Christian denominations were created. Affinities began, for example, to be forged in the pro-life and homeschooling movements between families who resisted late modern moral ideals, but were part of different churches.

For Michael and Sheila in 1984, the Catholic form of this subculture had merely begun to be formed. In a sense, their own life was part of the stumbling attempts to find ways, solutions, and formulations to move forward without compromise to the deposit of faith. To seek shelter in the shadow of a monastery or two, or even three, was one such way.

But the spiritual and cultural benefits afforded to a Catholic family by the vicinity of celibate institutions did not solve the basic problem of income. Michael considered the rent for the house in Mission to be expensive, while it was reasonable according to the standards of ordinary Canadian society. Still, Michael wrote in his diary, "Yes, we will go, Lord willing."

The Poor Clare Food Program

The move to Mission had not helped their strained economy. Rather the opposite was true; their living costs went up as they had to pay a higher rent. Poverty as an ideal can be hard in practice, but often help comes in unexpected ways. In late February 1984, Sister Barbara, the abbess of the Poor Clares, phoned Michael. She asked whether he could come up to the monastery, as she wished to discuss something with him.

Michael walked the five-minute distance to the monastery somewhat puzzled. When he arrived, the abbess told him that the sisters wanted to share their extra food with them, as donors often gave the sisters far beyond their needs. Even the poorest of their friends refused to take it, she said, but they hoped Michael and Sheila would give them the joy of sharing their surplus. It meant, for example, nine litres of milk per week. Michael accepted gladly, but he made her promise that the sisters would never deprive themselves in order to give to the O'Brien family. The abbess protested that it would give them great joy to deprive themselves, but Michael made her promise anyway. And the arrangement would be in the strictest of confidence.

The family car had broken down once again, this time with a blown head gasket; the machine was a veritable black hole into which they poured their hard-earned money as an offering to the mechanization of human life. This meant that when Michael for the first time went to the Poor Clares, he had to use a wheelbarrow to transport the three boxes of foodstuffs the sisters were giving as part of the secret support program of the O'Brien clan. Joseph happily helped Michael push the wheelbarrow up the long hill to the convent. At Mass in the chapel, Michael felt a presence before him as he prayed; it was an interior image without form, as if a messenger were waiting to bring something from him and deliver it to the Father. Michael wondered if this was an "angel"—anyway, he placed in the hands of the messenger the promise that with all his being, he would serve only God and not mammon. He also promised once again to go all the way, to the very last penny and last ounce of energy in serving God. The Gospel of the day was appropriately, "No one can serve two masters"—it was either "God" or "mammon" (Mt 6:24).

In the readings of the day was also the passage about the lilies in the field, that one should not worry about clothes and possessions (Mt 6:28–34). Strengthened in his resolve to dedicate an undivided heart to God, Michael left by the back gate together with little Joseph. As Michael pushed the wheelbarrow loaded with the boxes down the driveway, an expensive, shining sports car drove up beside them. Inside sat a beautiful couple with a likewise beautiful baby on their laps. Joseph was not quite looking like a lily as he was wearing his most ragged coat, but he was in a jolly mood, oblivious to the difference in standard of living of the family in the sports car. He waved to the baby, trying to catch its attention. As the picturesque couple looked his way, the tarpaulin covering the wheelbarrow blew off and exposed its contents: oranges, eggs, and potatoes. The couple stared at the scene with raised eyebrows.

Michael felt a shot of embarrassment and his face turned red, but was startled when he interiorly heard the following words: "Today, you enter paradise." Later that night while reading a book, his eyes fell on a passage that said, "On the day you are poor and humiliated, that is the day you enter paradise." He took this as confirmation of the mysterious words. They did not seem to mean that he was to die, to his relief, and the family continued to benefit from the now-exposed secret food program.

Michael told me that at this time he also experienced a third and final attack of the evil spirit that had afflicted him during his conversion. When it assaulted him by surprise in the middle of one night, he addressed the malevolent presence with the words, "It may be that you will attack me again throughout my life. But from now on, whenever you do, I will pray an entire Rosary for the most hardened sinner I know." Michael felt the presence back off to the corner of the room, and he sighed with relief, thinking that he could now go to sleep. But the attack immediately resumed. Now Michael got out of bed and knelt on the floor and prayed the entire Rosary, which, he remembers, took almost superhuman effort on his part. By the time he had completed it, he sensed that the evil presence had not only withdrawn, but disappeared altogether.[7] During the more than thirty years since then, it has never returned.

Mount Angel Abbey

In May 1984, Sheila and the children joined Michael in the now-annual trip to the artists' retreat at Mount Angel Abbey. This was also a sort of vacation, so they went to the beach in Oregon together with Leonardo and Patti, and made a little pilgrimage to the Trappist Abbey in Carlton, Oregon, and the Carmel Monastery in Seattle, Washington State, where one of the former superiors had just died. Her body was laid out in the chapel, barefooted with roses, and eight-month-old Elizabeth kept calling, "Hi, hi!" to the body, gleefully.

Toward the end of June, Michael was back in Oregon with the boys, as Sheila was at her parents' place with the girls. This was an opportunity for some more vacation time on the Pacific shore. Michael, John, and Joseph beachcombed together and plunged into the water, delighted by the large waves. Michael also had a show of his paintings in the Alvar Aalto library of the monastery (Mount Angel Abbey Library), and the boys helped him to the best of their abilities.

In August, for the third time that year, Michael returned to Mount Angel, now as teacher in the annual artists' summer workshop, an event that had grown from the artists' retreat. Michael spoke on writing prose, while Father Jeremy talked about poetry. The monk and the artist had long discussions, looking out over the agrarian landscape surrounding the monastery. Michael read part of his unpublished novel *Strangers and Sojourners* to Father Jeremy, who was moved as the content the book seemed to come alive. Father Jeremy said, "Never give up looking for a publisher." And Michael thought, inspired by the light of the summer, "Someday I will take my family to paint in Italy."

The Pope in Canada

On September 9, 1984, Pope John Paul II arrived in Quebec, the first pope to set foot on Canadian soil, and, in front of him, he had a twelve-day intensive journey across the whole of Canada.[8]

After nine days, it was time for the papal Mass at Abbotsford Airport outside Vancouver. Two hundred thousand people had gathered, and among them were Michael and Sheila with their children. The morning had been cloudy, and there had been some rain, but as the pope arrived in a helicopter, the sky cleared, and when it touched down, the sun was shining.[9] In prayer before the Mass, Michael and Sheila offered their whole lives, work, and children to God's will. At that moment, they felt a strong sense of praying with the universal Church.

As the popemobile passed along the aisles in the immense crowd, the O'Brien children were seated on the grass by the edge of the aisle, their shining eyes eagerly waiting for him to come. But as the vehicle approached they saw that he was turned away, facing the crowd on the other side. Just at the last moment, however, he turned to the other side, saw the O'Brien children, smiled, and blessed them.

The homily during the papal Mass was on the theme of the Sacred Heart of Jesus, and as he listened Michael thought, "The Holy Father is a true prophet, a great prophet." Michael also attended another papal Mass in a stadium in Vancouver, which confirmed his understanding of the pope as a prophet. The pope's homily now addressed the crucial moral issues facing the Church in Canada. At one point, Michael remembers, he raised his voice and said, "The unspeakable crime of abortion must stop!" Michael was disappointed, however, when he watched the television news coverage of the event at a neighbour's home. All the networks had deleted this and only gave short extracts from his gentler statements.

John Paul II was really the itinerant pope; through his travels, he established a direct contact between the person of the pope and large gatherings of lay Catholics. In a sense, one can describe this as a hierarchical relationship, as the pope after all is the supreme leader of the Catholic Church. But at the same time, this was an emotional, charismatic contact, as seen in Michael's reaction, or in this report of a First Nations couple, James and Freda (Alfreda) Nahanee, who

> were "awestruck," he [James] said, when they were asked to be one of eight couples presenting gifts to the Holy Father. Their present was a sheep's wool blanket and, as the Pope held out his hands to receive it, he told them, "You are the First People."
>
> "I can still remember the warmth of his hands," said Alfreda. "We felt that this was a tremendous thing to happen to us and one of the greatest things we could give from the First Nations people. We were in awe."[10]

This new type of "democratic", omnipresent papacy set, however, a precedent that would be difficult to follow. The faithful could be led to believe (at least implicitly) that the authority of the pope depended on his personality, on the charisma of the man holding the office. It is not easy to draw the line between the person and the office of the pope in an age of global communications. How is a layperson to know when the pope is speaking and acting as an individual and when as the incumbent of the chair of St. Peter, when his every word and gesture are being recorded and spread globally almost instantaneously? This is an important question, as not all popes have been paragons of virtue and wisdom. Also, the affective relationship to John Paul II as a father figure did not automatically translate into obedience to Catholic precepts and teachings of morality. Authority, through this direct charismatic relationship to the pope, could then become more a question of emotional identity, than the beacon for a disciplined life aimed at sanctity.

Novels and Essays

Michael wrote his novels and essays on a manual Halda typewriter from the 1950s, a Swedish brand that Hemingway also turned to in later age.[11] For the 1984 July/August issue of *Artswest*, Michael used it to write a short piece titled "Spiritual Visions", and for the November issue of the *Canadian Catholic Review*, the article "Fire in Our Darkness: The Artist as Minister and Prophet". In the first piece, Michael laments the loss of the spiritual in modern society and art, while in the second he formulates a program for the renewal of Christian sacred art. His analysis of the art of our times as despiritualized is coupled with his view of modern life as dehumanized. The loss of spiritual vision leads inevitably, by an ideological logic, to a similar loss of human dignity—close on the heels of the death of God comes the death of man. With the death of El Greco in 1614, Michael states, the great age of sacred art ended. Thereafter, fine art became increasingly secularized, and the religious "market niche" was flooded by commercialized holy images of poor artistic quality and shallow religious depth. Artists working with sacred art have since then been marginalized figures, and "they tend to be solitary by nature, watchers, thinkers, contemplatives."[12]

The consequence is that in the twentieth century, if the artist embraces the sacred, he must go through a painful desert, a process of emptying out, in which false securities are lost. "It is here that the artist will discover miraculous glimpses of fire, signs of the country he is being led toward, still beyond his horizon. Here he will be taught to trust in things that 'no eye has seen' (1 Cor 2:9), and will conceive the signs and promises of love to carry back to his people. It is a place of fearful beauty, and as Dostoevsky wrote, 'The world will be saved by beauty.'"[13]

In his article "Fire in Our Darkness", Michael highlights the artists Georges Rouault and William Kurelek, and he puts forward some concrete suggestions such as creating institutes of sacred art, and scholarships, and lists of Catholic artists. However, there is an almost tangible tension between the solitary artist—who like a prophet ventures into the desert to hear the voice of God and then returns to his people to give form to what he has heard and seen—and, on the other hand, the school of sacred art and similar structures of instruction and support. Is a school for prophets really possible?

Earlier in the article, Michael proposes another solution, a revival of the master-apprentice relationship. In other contexts, the relation between the prophets Elijah and Elisha is central to Michael's thinking; this form of instruction seems more compatible with his view of the artist as a modern-day prophet proclaiming divine beauty and redemption.

However, there is also a risk (or opportunity if one is so inclined) that when the artist is modelled so closely on the prophet, then he will not easily stay within the limits of art. He will think his message is so urgent that the forms of art will not be sufficient. Perhaps modernity in this way has undermined the contemplative mission of the Christian artist and forced him to become a teacher of morality, a defender of a Christian way of life. There is no Christendom anymore to support the artist; he may come to feel that he must carry a whole civilization within himself in order to create sacred art.

In October 1984, Michael was also working on a revision of *Sojourners*; it was mostly concerned with questions of style and not content. Michael's eldest son, John, remembers that Michael was constantly reworking the novel over the years. In November, an earlier version of the novel was returned from a publisher, after they had thought it over for two years. They had delayed the answer, the editor in chief explained in the letter, because two assistant editors wanted to publish it, but in the end, he had made the decision that the reading public was no longer interested in the novel's worldview. However, he added, "If you could rewrite the novel with a more realist view of religion and human relationships, we would be very happy to reconsider our decision." This was, of course, not even an option for Michael; he considered the supernatural as part of a realist description of human life: reality was larger than the secularist worldview maintained. Despite his unwillingness to compromise the spiritual core of his novel, he was still hoping that a Canadian publisher would decide to publish his writing without diluting or warping the religious content. He was in for a long wait.

Homesick

For Sheila, to live in suburbia was like giving up her personality. She was, she thought, a village and mountain girl, and not meant to live in or near a larger city. She felt like a fish on dry land and longed for a home, but did not really know where home was. One day when praying in front of the Blessed Sacrament in the Benedictine abbey in Mission, this feeling of alienation increased to a critical point; she then made a decisive abandonment of her will. From now on she would go where God's will directed her.

In October, when the property owner notified them that he wanted to move into the house as soon as possible, the search for a new home became not merely an ideal, but an urgent reality once again.

In late November, Michael and Sheila decided to pray the Rosary in front of the family's image of Our Lady of Guadalupe, petitioning for guidance and a home. In the middle of their prayers, a friend of the Poor Clares arrived at the door and asked if they would like to live in an empty house she owned, which was only five minutes' walk from the Poor Clares. It was a small and rundown farmhouse, but it was on five acres, and on the same hill as the Benedictine abbey, which was a mere ten minutes' walk away. The rent was only as much as would be needed to cover taxes and renovation. This was happy news to the strained finances of the O'Brien family.

At the beginning of December, Michael went to see the house. He considered it to be in very poor shape, with a mountain of garbage lying around, but the five-acre property and view were beautiful. The house had three small bedrooms, a kitchen, living room, and bathroom. It was not large, but sufficient, and after driving several truckloads to the dump, he decided that the place would be fine.

12. The Enchanted Garden

The signs were auspicious: the skies had opened up, providing the moving family with a brilliantly sunny day—and when the move was complete, the clouds closed in again. The same happened when Michael set about building a studio on the hill behind the house (the funds were provided by a gift from Sheila's parents). The sunshine held until the roof was in place, and then it rained for a few days. When the building was completed, the sun returned and Michael painted his studio. As soon as he was finished, there was heavy snowfall. Maybe this was the true home, of which they had dreamt so long. Could it at least be a very long pause in the sojourn before the next departure?

In early January, the garden was covered by a thick carpet of white snow, but when it melted in spring, and the leaves were sprouting, the beauty of the property became apparent. Holly trees flanked the white house, and beside Michael's studio, two horses were grazing in a lush pasture. Later a neighbour gave them an old Shetland pony, which they named Rusty, or "Rusticus Ponicus". The children were allowed to ride her at pleasure, but frequently she was not in the mood. Then she would charge straight toward a tree with low-hanging branches to scrape the boys off and leave them hanging.

The coastal climate made for bountiful gardens; parents and children alike relished the fruit provided by a pair of magnificent pear and apple trees that stood on the hill beside Michael's studio. The blackberry bushes grew as if they had been planted with some kind of magic spell. Michael cut tunnels in the tangled, thorny net of branches through which the children could creep and feel the excitement of fairy-tale danger as they picked the juicy fruit. Michael and Sheila, who had few material resources to offer their children, always endeavoured to give them food for the imagination, reading aloud to them in the evenings, surrounded by the family's ever-growing collection of books bought at different secondhand bookshops.

Beside fruit from the trees, the O'Briens got eggs from their chickens, who retired to the chicken coop during the evening. The proud rooster crowed every morning as Michael and Sheila rose early to go to Mass at the Benedictine abbey with the children. They walked for ten minutes through the woods that separated their five acres from the monastery. On the way, they heard the croaks of early-rising frogs in the dark, the chirping from the ubiquitous crickets, and the clear tolling of the monastery bells. During Mass, the monks sang beautifully the old melodies of Gregorian plainchant.

After coming home, Michael and Sheila had breakfast with the children, and then he went to his newly built studio on the hill, a place he loved very much. It consisted of one room, four metres wide and seven metres long. The view up the Fraser River was inspiring, and some days a mist lay over the river that the rising sun gradually dispelled. Despite the chill in the mornings, it was not necessary anymore to use the electric heater.

The children remember the studio as a sanctuary of the imagination. It was the place where the full power of Michael's thoughts, dreams, and visions were unleashed: there were knights with drawn swords, imposing angels, the solemn face of Jesus as He was on the way to His Passion, brightly coloured scenes on flat wooden boards, brushes in different sizes and shapes, and the old typewriter. At the heart of this place of creativity stood a statue of St. Joseph, on whose feast day Michael had dedicated himself to the difficult mission of Christian art.

In the house thirty metres away, Sheila was homeschooling the children. This was their first semester—she was trying it out to see if it was possible and worth the effort. It was exhausting for Sheila, but the children clearly loved it. In Canada, education is a provincial responsibility and not a federal one. There are thus differences between provinces such as Ontario and British Columbia. In the latter, the Catholic schools at most received 50 percent of funding from the province, and they therefore had to charge tuition fees. In Ontario, the Catholic schools were fully financed by taxes. In British Columbia, a Catholic school was not an alternative for the O'Briens, due to the cost.[1]

One day, Michael To, the father of a Vietnamese family, who had just been reunited after fleeing Vietnam, appeared at the doorstep and asked if his two daughters could join "Sheila's school". Like the O'Briens, the Tos were sincere Catholics and poor. At the time, they lived in a small mobile home that they rented and in which they said their Rosary every evening in the typical Vietnamese melodious, singsong way. To survive, they formed a musical band and played at weddings and picked and sold berries. Eventually, their strong work ethic paid off, and a few years later, the To children managed to buy a home for their parents in Mission.[2]

Sheila accepted the addition to her homeschool, and a friendship was formed between the two families. Like John and Joseph, the three To boys loved fishing and music, and when the sixth To child was baptized, the first one born on Canadian soil, Michael and Sheila were the godparents. In two of Michael's novels, *Eclipse of the Sun* and *Plague Journal*, there are fictionalized portrayals of the To family, with numerous significant details borrowed from their life.

Meanwhile, in the studio, after his customary morning Rosary, Michael was thinking about the pain and disruption caused by severed relationships for the children if they were to move again. For the children, Mission was a safe and delightful place. In March, during one of his many visits to Mount Angel, two women had spoken with him together with two of the monks during lunch one day. They had put forward an offer to sponsor him as artist in residence in the monastery. He would give occasional talks, paint, and simply be there. It was a very tempting offer—the symbiosis between the stability of a monastery and being a married Christian artist would then be complete. In a way, it seemed the perfect solution to their problems. For Sheila, however, this was not so easy; after having just settled in their new home in Mission, they would move again, and now to a new country. And once again the children would have to get used to a new environment.

Abraham's sacrifice came to Michael's mind. However, Abraham was not compelled to follow through with his offer, and on May 17, Michael heard in his mind the words, "You will not go to Oregon, but you will move closer to Me." Michael wondered, "Are these the Lord's words? Or are they a deception?" In a week from now, the whole family would be going to Oregon, as Michael was to attend the annual artists' retreat at Mount Angel Abbey. They also would go to the ocean for recreation, which was a mere two-hour drive from the abbey.

When the children had time free from homeschooling, they played in Joseph's little playhouse in the garden and with the family dog, a collie named Foxglove. Michael, having a break from painting on an icon commission, was writing in his studio, this time in his diary, when Mary came back from a walk with Sheila. He asked her, "What did you see on your walk, Mary?" "Slugs!" the little girl replied excitedly. "We poke them, but not too hard!" Then she asked, "What are you writing?" and Michael answered, "Thoughts." She gazed with a serious look at the organized scribbling in Michael's diary and said with a fascinated expression, "Ah, thoughts!"[3]

John enjoyed swinging baby Elizabeth around, and she laughed with delight; Joseph, on the other hand, when not playing with the dog, was focused on inventing Lego spaceships with a dignified, self-possessed expression on his face.

The house, studio, and garden in Mission was a small and safe world for the children, with cousins and relatives only a three-to-four-hour drive away in the Okanagan Valley. Clearly, it was not necessary to move for their sake, and in the end, Michael decided that moving to Oregon was not a viable option for his family.

Fatherhood and Motherhood

As the children grew older, Michael wondered in his diary at their unique personalities: the childish innocence of the small ones and the growing maturity of the older ones. In 1985, John was nine years old, while Elizabeth was a mere two years old. They were still children; the period of parenting teenagers had not yet begun.

Michael began to reflect on his own role as father and on fatherhood in general. As usual, he was hard on himself. In the background was the existential pain of trying to provide for the needs of the family, and his need for affirmation of his work. The lack of both of these gnawed at the heart of the father.

In the beginning of July 1985, Michael took Elizabeth in the stroller to the Poor Clares; she sang all the way in a happy singsong voice, "Daddy-ride, daddy, moo (cows); daddy, daddy, daddy." When Michael went to the graveyard to say a prayer at the grave of the founder of the Poor Clares, Mother Agnes, Elizabeth danced around on the graves. After some time, Michael found the headstone of the foundress, and he knelt beside it and asked for her intercession. Wave after wave of sadness filled him, as he saw his whole life as simply impossible. They were eight thousand dollars in debt, which weighed heavily on his trust in Providence. He thought, "I cannot paint fast enough or well enough to survive financially." To his mind the simplicity of poverty seemed like a key, a gateway to freedom, although it appeared to be the very opposite of freedom. "If I can only persist," he thought, "then the darkness may fall back." This picture of the troubled artist kneeling in the graveyard immersed in heavy thoughts, while his little two-year-old girl was dancing besides him, captured nicely the two opposite poles: the carefree child and the troubled, middle-aged man burdened with heavy responsibilities.[4]

In September, their economic situation was strained to the limit, this time amplified by the fact that earlier Michael had refused to take a cheque as payment because a buyer of a commissioned icon had expressed reservations about the painting. Instead, he had insisted that the buyer take the painting home and think about it before paying. This was, of course, delaying important income, when every penny counted. Michael came to see this as an act of pride on his own part. As a result, in the middle of the month, he had to take the coins that John had saved in his piggy bank, so that they could buy milk, tea, and potatoes. When John came home from school that day, Michael told him that his savings, all thirty dollars, had been used for groceries. Before his father could explain, the child burst into tears and cried, "Now I have no money." Michael felt deeply distressed, but managed to make John happy by promising full reimbursement.[5]

When, in 2016, Michael looked back to this period, he told me that all of this took place in the midst of several comments made to him by well-meaning wealthy Catholics in Oregon and Vancouver, saying he would do far better financially if he stopped painting the Cross and focused instead on the Resurrection. "I paint both," he invariably replied. "And there is no Resurrection without the Cross." Nevertheless, in his private thoughts he continued to wrestle with the question of his responsibility to provide adequately for his family.

At one point, a person who had commissioned a painting called him by phone to tell him she was rejecting the completed work, because (she angrily told him) she did not like the colours he had chosen; then she hung up on him. Hurt and dazed, he sat there struggling with the ongoing dilemmas, and thought to himself, "Maybe I *am* too overfocused on the crosses in life. The way of the dark night is for saints like St. John of the Cross." He was in the middle of these very thoughts when the phone rang. It was another person from Vancouver, asking him, out of the blue, if he would take on a commission to paint an image of St. John of the Cross. Michael remembers that he was astonished by the timing, and what it implied. Once again, he thought, a seeming coincidence had reassured him that the hand of Divine Providence was on him, and that he was on the right track, regardless of how dark the track looked at times.

During October to November 1985, Michael engaged in a period of intense activity. He drove thousands of kilometres, gave fifteen talks, held six exhibits, and helped conduct a crucial retreat, all within two months, and he was sick with the flu or had a cold the whole time. In the middle of this marathon, he felt like a bad father, having so little time with his children. He shed tears of sadness and thought,

> I love each of them so very, very deeply, and I would give my life for them. But, in the actual day-by-day living out of a life, I have been a poor father. So little time, so little energy. They get only table-scraps from me. The ache of this is so deep.[6]

He came to think of his own father and the distance there had been between child and father, and how much David in his turn had suffered in relation to his father, Stephen. It was like a wound of fatherhood transmitted throughout three generations, Michael thought. In a way, his wrestling with fatherhood resembled his struggling with God, the Father, and with his own ideal of sanctity. He had high ideals and felt it very sharply when he did not manage to live up to them—for example, when he lost patience with the children.

Being a father is a task placed in the midst of managing a whole life; there is no separate family life, parallel to other "lives" such as work life and hobbies lined up nicely with their own criteria of success—at least not when one has four children and counting. Added to this acute sense of not being the father he wanted to be, Michael felt anxious about external threats to their children's safety.

After the period of intense activity and travel, Michael had a series of three dreams. On the first night, he dreamt of black wolves circling the house and how his gun was useless against them. The second night he dreamt of an alligator coming up from a swamp close to the house and grabbing a child in its jaws. The third night he dreamt of being in priestly robes and receiving Communion from another priest; he was among a crowd of seminarians who were joking and jostling toward the Eucharist, which was a bowl of potato chips. In this dream, the spiritual threat against the children was combined in his mind with a sense of decay in the Church.

In 1986, two dramatic episodes increased the pressure on Michael's understanding of fatherhood, both divine and human.

On the night of January 15, 1986, he drove the boys to catechism; he was plagued by thoughts of financial insecurity, the recent infestation of rats, and the flooding of the basement. Arriving at the high school where the parish rented classrooms for catechism classes, he met the young wife and five children of a family that to Michael seemed to have it so much better in many respects, living comfortably off their farm. The husband was the ideal man: handsome, strong, faith-filled, and gentle, though somewhat shy. Michael thought, "It's easy for you, Paul. It's easy for you to be noble and virtuous! Nothing ever goes wrong for you!" Michael managed to control this brief moment of inner resentment and said hello to the wife and children. Strangely, he had forgotten that a year before, Paul and Marie had lost a child who had died of leukemia. And if Michael had known the real situation of the family at that moment, his attitude would have been completely different.

While they were exchanging greetings at church, Paul was in the barn feeding the cows, but when he looked up he saw that their house was on fire. He knew that his wife was with the children at catechism class, but sometimes she left the baby sleeping in the house; he was not sure, so he ran into the house and upstairs to the bedroom. The baby was not there, but Paul was overcome with the heat and the poisonous gases and fell to the floor.[7] This was a heroic death; he was a truly good man, Michael thought the next day, ashamed of himself and in a shock of disbelief, when he heard what had happened.

His emotional reaction came on Friday, six days later, when he was alone in the house, and Sheila was visiting relatives with the children. He spent two hours yelling at God the Father, "Where are You? What kind of father are You?" and he threw things in his desperation.

"If You are a father, then *be* here. If You want me to be a son, then You be a father."[8]

There was only a ringing silence; Michael had cried out like Job, but no answer was forthcoming. On Tuesday morning, a funeral Mass was celebrated for the heroic father. Several hundreds of people came, and Michael had a sense of inner healing. There was a sense of light overcoming darkness.

If this was a story of self-sacrificing fatherhood, of giving up one's life for the children and the heroism of the wife managing after such a blow, on Holy Thursday (March 27), the dark counterpart of father-hood manifested itself. While Sheila was preparing the Passover meal, they heard four loud bangs. They did not think too much of it, but at midnight, having attended the Mass of the Last Supper, they were woken up by a police officer who asked them if they had heard sounds of gunfire earlier. They remembered the bangs, and the police officer explained that three houses away a man had killed his two children and then turned the shotgun on himself. Michael thought, "The horror, the horror."

Toward the end of 1986, Michael and Sheila knew that next year they would have a new child, and in June 1987, Sheila "heard" the name of the baby during Mass: "He is Benjamin Michael." She heard interiorly also: "What do you most wish for your children?" To which she replied, "Lord, I do not wish for health or happiness for them, but that they would love You and always be faithful to You." Again, she heard the voice: "Because you have asked for the better part, it will not be taken away from you."[9]

On July 14, Benjamin Michael was born in perfect health, weighing nine pounds and seven ounces. July 16 was Sheila's first day home after the birth of Benjamin, and when they prayed the Rosary a magnificent doe bounded out of the field and stood in the lane gazing in through their living room window.

The Cosmic Christ

Michael's decision for sacred art in 1976 had given birth to a reflection on icon painting in the place of sacred images in the secular West. The step from art to culture in general was not long in coming, and his writing repeatedly dealt with the secularization of the West and the need for a rediscovery of the sacred and of Christ. In his critique of modernity, he came to focus on the danger of a soft, secular total-itarianism. In this way, Michael emerged as a cultural critic speaking from an "orthodox" Catholic position. He was neither a neoliberal nor a spokesman for conservatism, but lived a Franciscan ideal of poverty and dedication. He was zealous for the flowering of a faithful Catholic cultural renewal, and his understanding of culture and soci-ety was marked by a clear opposition and struggle against what he saw as sinister forms of modernity.

In October 6, 1985, Father Ian Boyd, editor of the *Chesterton Review*, invited Michael to submit book reviews on any book dealing with "the culture war". Gilbert Keith Chesterton (1874–1936) was a true role model for Michael, a man of legendary wit and zest who had fought a similar fight in the early twentieth century in a diverse set of genres from crime short stories, novels, and newspaper columns to Christian apologetics. Chesterton had tried to expose the ideas of modernism, for example, in debates with George Bernard Shaw, a socialist who admired both Stalin and Mussolini, promoted eugenics, and stated his atheism clearly.[10]

Closely connected to Michael's thoughts on culture was a reflec-tion on his role as father, leading a growing family. The challenge was to sustain the small world of the family in the context of a radically secular environment and lax Catholic praxis.

A new development came when Michael took the culture war to a general theological plane in the summer of 1987. He had decided to write for the *Canadian Catholic Review* a critique of the ideas of the Dominican theologian Matthew Fox, who was conducting seminars on his "creation-centred spirituality" at Catholic col-leges and seminaries.[11] Fox's books were also being advertised in the Canadian Church's national monthly missal, effectively putting promotion of his writings in every pew in the country. Fox was clearly on the outskirts of Catholic orthodoxy, weaving together a syncretic web of mystics such as Meister Eckhart, the gnostic ideas of psychologist Carl Jung and Native American rituals, and various neo-pagan spiritualties. He worked with modern witches and self-proclaimed Luciferians such as David Spangler, in what he called "deep ecumenism".[12]

As his promotion of a kind of cosmic New Age consciousness was gaining momentum in the Church, Michael decided to counteract it to the best of his ability. His article was published in April 1988, the same year as Fox wrote an open letter to the prefect of the Congregation for the Doctrine of the Faith, Joseph Cardinal Ratzinger (the future Pope Benedict XVI), with the heading "Is the Catholic Church Today a Dysfunctional Family?" According to an article sympathetic to Fox in *National Catholic Reporter*, he invited Ratzinger "to take a year off and join him". He continued, "Why not step down from your isolated and privileged life at the Vatican to do circle dances with women and men, old and young, in search for authentic spirituality?"[13]

Michael wrote individually to the ninety bishops in Canada, enclosing copies of his article. He attended a "Cosmic Mass" at the Victoria cathedral and was shocked; Fox at the time had undertaken a deconstruction of the Catholic Mass and with the help of "witches, Nigerian drummers and American Indian shamans" created a kind of syncretic liturgical dance.[14] Michael also handed out copies of his article at a workshop which Fox was leading at the University of British Columbia, even though Michael was threatened with arrest by the event's organizers.

Soon after, Fox was forbidden to teach and lecture for a year, and in 1993, he was expelled from the Dominican Order, left the Catholic Church, and became a member of the Episcopal Church. In 2005, he nailed ninety-five theses to the door in Wittenberg, where Martin Luther had done likewise in 1517. Fox was calling for a new neo-pagan Reformation.[15]

In this way, Michael expanded his concerns from sacred art to theology and spirituality in general, especially as it concerned syncretic influences. Through his articles and talks, he was trying to raise awareness of the erosion of traditional Catholic faith and theology. In this way, his prophetic role extended beyond the realm of aesthetics.

Alex Colville

Alex Colville (1920–2013) was a Canadian realist painter who began his career as a war artist during World War II, illustrating, among other themes, his impressions from the newly liberated Bergen–Belsen concentration camp. After returning to Canada, Colville settled in Sackville, New Brunswick; painted and taught fine arts at Mount Allison University until the 1960s.

In his realist paintings, human persons are often depicted as static and soulless; they very seldom express feelings. Their silent materiality is unsettling; they show a hard surface with an ominous undercurrent of loneliness or sterility. Even in a painting from the 1950s that depicts a soldier and girl kissing at a railway station, the faces are hidden, and the arms of the soldier seem stiff and slightly hovering around the almost abstract form of the girl's back. The background, including the train, is reduced to geometrical forms stretching in uninterrupted lines to the horizon. The general feeling, despite the kiss, is that of a place haunted by impersonal modernity.

On the other hand, when Colville painted animals, they were usually portrayed in lively and energetic movement. The most famous of those paintings is that of a dark horse running at dusk along a railway track toward an oncoming train, the symbol of modernity. The spectator can feel the coming clash of biological life and mechanical force.

In 1988, Alex Colville was sixty-eight years old and an internationally established artist. During 1984–1985, he had exhibited in Beijing, Hong Kong, Tokyo, and London. Michael had had an ongoing correspondence with him since writing an article for the *Canadian Catholic Review* about Colville's work in which Michael sensed a spiritual, or at least symbolical, dimension. Colville sent a letter to the journal to which Michael responded in April 1988. A conversation began that led to Michael, together with a young artist friend, Matthew Wheeler, visiting Alex Colville's home in Wolfville, Nova Scotia, in early October.

Colville received them in a very relaxed and friendly manner, and they sat in his studio for about three hours discussing art. They exchanged ideas on the necessity of knowing the heritage of art history: a foundation on which to build one's art.

Michael showed Colville some slides of his own paintings; he was appreciative of them and was enthusiastic about Michael writing another article about his work. He had been impressed, he said, by the way Michael in his first article had considered aspects of the implicit religious sense in art.

For his part, Colville showed them his latest painting, *French Cross* (acrylic on Masonite), which was based on a photo. It depicts a girl on a horse, turning in her saddle, looking back at a large five-metre-high cross standing on a three-tiered stone pedestal. The black form of the cross is silhouetted against a grey, cloudy sky and conveys an ominous message, perhaps a warning or merely a sad reminder of a lost civilization. Michael wrote in his diary, "The painting is loaded with meaning—perhaps not intended by Colville, but definitely *there.*"

Finally, they had a lovely tea and scones with Mr. and Mrs. Colville, talking about art, philosophy, and the writings of Thomas Mann.

There was a warm farewell and wishes that they might meet again someday. It never came about, but they continued to correspond through letters.

Madonna House

On his way home from the East, Michael made a side trip to Ottawa and stopped at Madonna House in Combermere. There he talked with his spiritual advisor, who encouraged him to meet Don and Posie McPhee. The McPhees were running a retreat centre, to which families came for one-week retreats during the summer months. To Michael, the couple seemed to be very perceptive, evangelical Catholics. Unlike the monasteries in Western Canada, their apostolate was run by laypersons and directed toward ministry to families. Still, Madonna House contributed with priests for the retreats, and though not officially involved, it constituted a supporting background context.

Don and Posie told Michael that the rectory of an old church in the region was available for rent, and they went together to see the house. It was a large, old stone building with six bedrooms, a parlour, a dining room, and an immense kitchen, plus an office and three big, enclosed upstairs porches. It had at least quadruple the floor space of the house in Mission. The pastor of the parish, who had read an article on Michael in *Our Family*, offered to let the rectory to the O'Briens for fifty dollars per month, a phenomenally low rent.

Across the road was Our Lady of the Angels parish church, with a cemetery on the left side that continued in a field on the side of the road where the large house was situated. Surrounding the church and the rectory was an endless forest, with a house here and there, some inhabited and some abandoned and left to decompose. The most densely populated area was the cemetery.

The landscape was visually very beautiful, but Michael had his doubts, wondering, "Yes, but does one move three thousand miles for a house? What would life be here for the children? And for Sheila would it be too isolated?"[16]

Michael was not easily deterred by things that made other people take another road; material and social poverty was not in itself an argument—the important part was God's will. They were struggling to make ends meet in Mission. Here the rent was a mere token. They had to fast and pray for discernment, Michael thought. He considered the doors opened wide in Ontario, but were they really closed in British Columbia? Though he told the McPhees that he and Sheila would be sending their answer to the pastor within three weeks, he thought the answer would be an unambiguous no.

On October 27, 1988, after a painful discernment process and a novena to St. Joseph, it was, contrary to their expectations, very clear to them that they were to move to Brudenell, to the rectory of Our Lady of the Angels Church. They were moving away from the shadows of the walls of the monasteries to the more insecure world of a lay family apostolate run by the McPhee family and supported by Madonna House. In a sense, Michael was moving back to his origins, closer to Ottawa, where he had been born. Ottawa was a two-hour drive away, while it was four hours to Toronto and a half hour to Combermere. Though Brudenell was remote and isolated—a mere handful of souls with a church—a person looking on the bright side could say that it was less isolated than Blue River.

If you now, despite my description above, picture Brudenell as a cozy, little village, small but thriving, I must disappoint you. Its decline had already begun in 1893, when a new railway bypassed it. Before that it was something of a Wild West town with three hundred inhabitants and three hotels, where gambling, alcohol, and other vices were indulged; it was known as the "sin-bucket".[17] At the time Michael looked at the church and the rectory, those days were long gone; there was no resident priest, and most of the inhabitants had left or died—just a few were still hanging on. If the Internet had been in place in the 1980s and the children O'Brien had surfed to the website Ontario Ghost Towns, then they would probably have questioned the wisdom of moving to the outer rim of the social periphery.[18] In comparison, Mission appeared as a piece of heaven on earth.

13. Angels and Divine Humour

The announcement to the children that the family was moving to Ontario, the mythical province of Michael's ancestors, came without warning. John was calm, even a little excited to embark on such a grand adventure, but the parting with his friends was not easy. At the age of twelve, he was leaving the land of his childhood, and before him lay the teenage years in unknown territory. Also for Joseph, then ten, Mary seven, and Elizabeth five years old, the period in Mission had been a happy one. To go east was for the children to leave the supportive extended family behind and settle in the semiwilderness of rural Ontario with all its charms and drawbacks. Benjamin (Ben), on the other hand, was a mere one and a half years old, so for him Brudenell became his first real home.

The two older boys and Foxy, the collie, had the privilege of riding with Michael in the large moving van on the epic eight-day drive across the country; Sheila was instead to fly with the baby and the two girls in a few weeks. As the boys and Foxy looked through the windows, they saw rushing past them a landscape covered with snow, punctuated here and there by colourful placards entreating them to vote for the right candidate in the upcoming parliamentary election. Little disturbed by politics, John instead collected hockey cards that came with the sale of gas at the countless fuel stops along the way, and the boys found it exciting to smuggle Foxy into a new motel room every night.

On the evening they arrived in Brudenell, their first impression was that of an enormous, empty house dimly lit by the full moon. They could see no other houses, but on the opposite side of the road, the dark silhouette of the church steeple added to the eerie atmosphere. The wintry scene was, indeed, a contrast to the more temperate climate and suburban character of Mission.

After Michael had familiarized himself with the many rooms of the large rectory and prepared to retire for the night, the boys came running excitedly up to him, shouting, "Look! Look! An angel!" Michael peered out of the window and saw an oblong shape brightly lit up by the moonlight in the field beside the house. It certainly looked almost supernatural, angelic, but they did not go out and explore the phenomenon, as it was dark and cold, and they were tired after the long journey.

In the morning, they saw that the field beside the house was a graveyard covered with gravestones and memorials seemingly randomly placed, many of them inclining in different directions as if they were on the verge of falling over. Michael went straight to a red granite obelisk, which was the one that had been lit up by moonlight the previous night, and to his amazement, there was chiselled on the base—"O'Brien". When looking up, his astonishment increased as he read the full dedication: "Michael O'Brien; Died; May 31, 1890; Age 76 YRS; R.I.P."

As they got to know the house better during the coming months, the children discovered a large basement full of old artifacts and in the attic a colony of bats that would fly out in the summer evenings—occasionally a bat or two took a wrong turn and flew into the house. There were also rumours of a resident ghost; perhaps it was a priest who had died in the house many years ago and could not leave his old parish.

Because Ontario, unlike British Columbia, had a fully funded Catholic school system, Michael and Sheila enrolled their three oldest children in St. Andrew's Catholic School in Killaloe, fourteen kilometres away.[1] Arriving in the middle of the school year, and after having been homeschooled, they were unsure about the academic level of their children. They reenrolled John for grade six, which was one year behind his age, but this was unnecessary as after a short time it became obvious that he was well ahead of his fellow students. John had prayed privately that the transition to the new school would go all right, and after a few peaceful weeks, he put a ten-dollar bill as thanksgiving into the collection basket at Sunday Mass.

During the first months, Michael was happy about their new situation; they had in a sense their own church just across the road and plenty of space in the new house. One other benefit was the outdoor life. The whole family did cross-country skiing and canoeing, exploring the wilderness. One of the children, when looking back, said that Michael in Mission had been like a badger in his studio, almost hibernating in there, while in Brudenell he could explore his great love of unbounded nature. For the children, this freedom was the main advantage of their new home.

When doing creative work, Michael became so intensely absorbed that he fell, like Alice in Wonderland, down the rabbit hole; he became oblivious to his surroundings, even to the needs of his own body; there are tales of him wandering into the kitchen and absent-mindedly eating something without realizing what it actually was. Dinner and Rosary in the evening was transition time, the period when Michael's soul returned to his body, and he came up from the hole to the world of the family. One of the children, describing a typical situation when he was in the middle of a writing project, said that he would come down to dinner with a faraway look, and Sheila would ask, "In the middle of your book, dear?" And Michael would answer enthusiastically, "Oh, yeah, it's like the inspiration is flowing, just flowing."

The children were often fidgety and distracted during the Rosary when praying all the Hail Marys, but they knew that afterwards it was story time. They did not have television, so Michael read to them imaginative books like the *Chronicles of Narnia* and the Arthur Ransome novels. Michael and Sheila were constantly looking for new stories in secondhand bookshops or garage sales. Searching, selecting, and reading required a lot more discernment and work than to switch on the TV set and tune in to a children's channel. They were trying to build an alternative family culture and were struggling to preserve its integrity from the increasing breadth and intensity of the products of the modern entertainment industry. They wanted their home to be a minisociety in which certain Christian values, traditions, and stories were fundamental. It was thus necessary for them to evaluate carefully all cultural materials entering the home. The weak link in that project was the school; even if it was a Catholic school, the question was whether it really did uphold the same values and made the same discernments as those of the O'Brien family.

When playing with the children, Michael used his power of imagination to build up theme worlds. One winter he read Tolkien's *The Lord of the Rings* to the two oldest boys and made large maps, and each night they traced Frodo's journey across Middle Earth by marking his progress with a coloured pen. Over the years, as the younger children grew older, Michael reread the trilogy aloud three times.

Music was also an important part of the upbringing. Sheila enrolled the children in piano lessons with a local teacher. Seeing the O'Brien family's low income and simple lifestyle, she insisted on teaching the children for free, year after year. By way of thanks, Michael gave her one of his best paintings.

Michael continued to paint religious commissions, moving increasingly away from icon painting, and in this way developing his new style of sacred art. It was also here that he began to paint more colourful works, clearly inspired by Kurelek.

It was fitting that the church that Michael and Sheila were caretakers of was named Our Lady of the Angels. Both Michael and Sheila had experienced help at various points in their life, help that they attributed to angelic interventions.[2] Michael was convinced that angels were of vital importance for human life, and that one should accordingly acknowledge their existence and ask for their assistance. On Easter Monday 1989, they, therefore, made an act of preparation for a later more solemn consecration to the angels.[3]

Why Do the Wicked Prosper?

In early May 1989, Sheila got bursitis in the elbow and shoulder, which made it difficult for her to do household chores; and, to make things worse, after taking too much bee pollen (as an energy supplement), she had a severe allergic reaction. She developed a fever; her face quickly became swollen; her throat closed; her breathing stopped; and she collapsed on the floor. Michael prayed over her, calling out, "Jesus, save her!" and to his relief, she began breathing again. Then he rushed her to the emergency ward at St. Francis Hospital in Barry's Bay.

After coming home, Sheila continued to suffer from bursitis, and in the beginning of June, she developed a severe cold. Michael felt his old exhaustion and inner darkness coming back and, one day, sitting in church, he asked God, "Why do the wicked prosper?" As so often, the O'Brien family was short of money, and the house was old and in need of serious repairs. For Michael, the spiritual situation of the Catholic Church in Canada, and more locally, was also weighing on his mind. He asked God, "How do You create things of beauty, expressing divine order, when all within and around You are in disorder?" He lamented, "Our shepherds are weak; they are blind; they are asleep."

During this period, he had begun a large painting of the baptism of the Lord for St. Peter's parish in Woodbridge, a suburb of Toronto. Besides painting, Michael also continued to write articles and thought about new book projects. One that was particularly dear to him was to write a biography of his mentor William Kurelek. His idea was to give Kurelek's Catholicism and his sense of being a prophet in the secular age their proper place. The idea was born when he read Dr. Patricia Morley's biography of Kurelek, which he considered a failure in this respect.

While Morley, since they met in the 1970s at his first show of sacred art, admired what Michael was doing and from time to time would purchase a painting from him, she was critical of the Catholic faith. Michael had grown increasingly concerned during the period when Morley was writing the biography, since she told Michael that she strongly disliked the now-deceased artist as a person and disagreed with many of his moral stands.

In many respects, she was, according to Michael, his very opposite when it came to religion: a liberal Anglican, a radical feminist, and a pro-abortion advocate. Yet, mysteriously, she was drawn to Kurelek and collected Michael's paintings, and even wanted to write a biography of him.

According to Morley, Michael recalls, Kurelek was a "fundamentalist", and she argued forcefully against Michael becoming one too. Over the years, he patiently continued the discussions, attempting to show her that orthodoxy was not simplistic fundamentalism. Despite the pressure, he grew steadily in the path he had begun. Thinking that the true story of William Kurelek was in danger of being distorted by biographers such as Morley, he resolved to write it himself.

In the beginning of June 1989, Michael was preparing to drive to Toronto to meet William Kurelek's widow, Jean, to talk about the biography project,[4] but the car would not start. Michael flew into a rage against the noncooperative vehicle. "Why do the wicked prosper?" he yelled, at the car and God: "Why do those who wish to do a little good in this world have such uphill battles? The wicked jump into their Cadillacs and Mercedes and roar off to do their evil without a hitch!" He then kicked the car, which, shocked by the rough treatment, started. On the road to Toronto, Michael was passed by several Cadillacs and Mercedes, and he conceded that God had a sense of humour, but perhaps a little on the dark side.

The story has human and humorous qualities; moreover, and perhaps more importantly, I think it illustrates that the story of Michael's life is not uplifting in the manner of a prosperity gospel—that is, the idea that if you sincerely believe and trust, then all things (material) will come to you. Social success thus becomes the sign of the depth of your faith: if you do not have what you need—for example, a functioning car—then, obviously, your faith is not strong enough.

On the contrary, the poverty and social marginalization following upon Michael and Sheila's choice of Christian art was not a short passing tribulation on the way to resounding success and an easy life on Parnassus. For Michael, to embrace the cross was not easy; at the age of forty-one, he had not achieved a complete stoic mastery of his emotions; simply put, he became angry, argued with God, and kicked the car. He was struggling hard to make ends meet for the family, but also to make a difference in the Church—alerting people to the dangers of compromise, and of tribulations to come. He felt a prophetic urgency to get the message across.

For most Christian artists, driving old cars and being passed by modern ones is part of everyday life, but adding a significant number of children increases the level of difficulty. Children do not behave as one would like; they upset the plans that middle-aged stressed parents make. Little Ben was a child with an extra dose of energy, equipped with a desire to test the limits of things. One day in June, Michael laid his now-completed painting of the baptism of Jesus on a large plastic sheet with its edges curled up, making a kind of trough, allowing the painting to sit for a day or so as its paint completely dried. The painting was composed of layers of thin acrylic applied to a Masonite board, which was standard for Michael's paintings. He had worked on it for six weeks. After locking the door to the dining room, he left for other tasks.

Meanwhile, Ben was in the bathroom on the floor above, testing the pressure in the hose, and clearly excited to see so much water streaming out. Unfortunately, the water became a deluge and went through the floor down to the room below, filling the plastic trough and leaving the painting soaked in water for several hours. The painting of Jesus' baptism was baptized, so to speak, by Ben. It is definitely not good for Masonite to swell in that way, and Michael, naturally, became very upset. In five minutes, he went from anger to depression; six weeks of work had been spoiled; it was a real disaster! But, he collected himself, and he and his little son hugged each other, prayed, and went for a walk together. A month later, Michael was surprised to find that the painting had suffered no harm. To him this was nothing short of a miracle. Once again, he saw a glimmer of divine humour in the middle of what appeared to be a catastrophe.[5]

Joachim

In October, half a year after their special prayer to the angels, Michael came to believe that his guardian angel's name was Joachim, "God prepares". He had fallen asleep one night, asking his guardian angel to reveal himself more fully, and on awakening the next morning, the first word he heard interiorly was "Joachim", spoken with great strength.

A week later, Michael was sick with a bad cough; it had been raining for days—and, as so often, they were in a financially difficult situation. In the middle of the night, Michael awoke and began to pray to his guardian angel to guide, protect, and strengthen his family. Then he sensed the possibility of a mutual dialogue. In his diary, he describes it as similar to mental prayer, but with the difference that the voice that answered him was full of assurance, firmness, and knowledge, which he did not consider himself to possess.

After sensing the possibility of dialogue, Michael began by saying, "I am very ashamed of my poor love, my sins, and weaknesses. My love is so small and broken."

Then he heard a reply: "Yes, your love is imperfect, but you will grow in love."

"How? I am so weak. My sins must wound God."

"Your sins do not wound God, but they offend Him. But your greatest fault is that you do not believe in the fatherhood of God. You are not sufficiently grateful for His love."

"How can I become what He wants me to be?"

"Believe. Believe in the Love of the Father and the Father's love will flow through you to others."

"Is this really Joachim?"

"Yes. You doubt everything."

"It is wise to be cautious."

"Cautious, yes."

"How much of this dialogue is me and how much is you?"

"Some of it is from yourself, some from me."

"Is your name really Joachim?"

"Yes. 'God Prepares.' God prepares a way for all those who seek to love Him. He is always preparing the way for you."

"If you are an angel of God, tell me that Jesus is Lord."

"Jesus is the Lord and Saviour of all creation. He is the Light of Lights, the Lord of Lords, the Everlasting Father, the King of Kings. It is He whom I serve, the God of Abraham, Isaac, and Jacob. The God of Peter and Paul."

"Why do I sense darkness around us?" [Michael felt that the place had suddenly been invaded by an evil presence hovering at the edges of the dialogue.]

"The evil one does not wish us to converse this way. He would disrupt it if he could. You see darkness because your eyes are full of darkness. Your eyes are turned to the things of the earth. I see only light. You must pray the Rosary very often. Pray fervently."

"It grieves you when I sin?"

"It grieves me."

"Can you give me a sign to prove that you are a true angel of light?"

"Look up to the skies and you will see signs of light."

It was about four thirty in the morning and, according to his diary, Michael was lying in the dark by the window. He pulled back the curtains; the sky was completely covered and the clouds were thick with rain. He half-smiled, thinking, "You see, this is all just imagination." Suddenly, a hole appeared in the clouds over the moon, and it burst out with a brilliant light for a few seconds, then it was darkness again. A few moments later, the same thing happened; only this time, the moonlight shining through the glass of the window appeared as a brilliant Host surrounded by a cross. Stars also came out. Then, fantastic swirling shapes flitted with great rapidity through the night sky. No one looking at the aforementioned events would suspect them of being supernatural, Michael thought; yet, they were, according to him, suffused with a power, presence, and uniqueness. He had never seen a sky like this—strong words coming from a former weather observer. After feeling an inner prompting to open the Bible to Ezekiel 15, he went downstairs and read the passage about the destruction of Jerusalem by fire because of its sins (vv. 4–8). It made him recall recent prophecies about a coming day of fire and three days of darkness. Then he read some passages that included angels, and his final thoughts were that the Day of the Lord was probably not far away—perhaps only a decade—and that perseverance could be achieved through the intercession of angels.[6]

14. Family Matters

Nazareth Retreat Centre

In 1978, while living in the United States, Don and Posie McPhee converted from Evangelical Protestantism to Catholicism, though they had not yet been formally received into the Church. As their visas had by then expired, their spiritual director at the Trappist Monastery of Gethsemani suggested to them that Madonna House in Combermere would be the perfect place to nurture their newfound faith. Said and done; after loading their car with all their belongings, they drove the whole day to Madonna House in Canada. Upon arrival, Don walked over to the first person he saw, an old woman with a cane, and asked her where he could find the priest whom they were supposed to meet. He did not realize it then, but the woman was Catherine Doherty, the founder of Madonna House. She inquired why they had come to Combermere, and quickly found out that they came from a background of alternative living and that they nurtured the dream of building a community for Catholic families. In the spirit of the 1970s, their idea was to found an intentional community—that is, a minisociety of Christians—a religious village separated from the larger secular society. She looked at them intently for several moments and then said with her characteristic deep voice coloured by a Russian accent,

> God may be calling you to become Catholic, and He may even be calling you to Combermere; but forget this business about community. Your family is a community—a beautiful reflection of the Holy Trinity. Trust God. Trust Our Lady of Combermere.

Don then asked her name. She smiled and said,

> Folks around here just call me the "B". And remember, all this spiritual stuff is fine, but if God really wants you to settle here in Combermere, He will provide a place to live and a job. Don't move here without both.[1]

177

Within a week, Don had found a job and they had a place to live. Moreover, a few months later, they were received into the Catholic Church, and their three daughters were baptized in the Madonna House Chapel.

During several of the following summers, they attended Cana Colony, a weeklong family retreat arranged by Madonna House. These retreats had begun in 1952, after Pope Pius XII had expressed his wish to Catherine Doherty that her apostolate should extend also to families.[2]

In 1980, Don began to work in Ottawa with the pro-life organization Coalition for Life; it meant that he had to travel a great deal, and after some time it began to take its toll on the family. One day in spring 1982, as he was lying in bed, worn out and sick, the idea of a community of families took a new form in his mind. Modelled on the Cana Colony, he began to write a proposal for a Catholic Family Life Centre. Despite his weakness, it developed into a twenty-page typewritten proposal, which he later presented to the bishop.[3]

On the first page, Don wrote that the proposal was prepared as a response to *Familiaris Consortio*, the post-synodal exhortation promulgated by Pope John Paul II in November 1981, which in its turn was the outcome of the 1980 Synod on the Family. *Familiaris Consortio* forcefully affirmed the teaching that Pope Paul VI had put forth in his encyclical *Humanae Vitae* in 1968.[4]

When Don McPhee based his proposal for a retreat centre on *Familiaris Consortio*, he was giving an institutional form to the papal appeal of reinvigorating traditional Catholic morality for modern families.

Most of the families coming to the summer retreats at the Nazareth Retreat Centre were using artificial contraceptives, and some had been sterilized. According to Posie McPhee, what repeatedly happened during the retreats was that the couples experienced a conversion and stopped using contraceptives, and many sought to reverse their sterilization surgery. This was part of the forming of what later would be called the John Paul II generation. They were, and still are, a minority within the larger mass of mainstream Canadian and Western Catholicism, but they made up for that through enthusiasm and willingness to sacrifice their time and energy.

In his research during the 1980s on the pro-life movement in Toronto, Michael Cuneo named the lay movement protesting against the submissive attitude of the Canadian bishops toward trends in the

secular society "Revivalist Catholics". Unlike traditionalists rejecting the reforms of the Second Vatican Council, they interpreted the
Council documents according to a hermeneutic of continuity with
the preceding Catholic tradition—a position greatly reinforced by
John Paul II as pope and Joseph Ratzinger as head of the Congregation for the Doctrine of the Faith. This was of course in strong
opposition to those who saw the Council as merely the beginning of
a more radical modernization of the Catholic Church, especially in
the realm of sexual morality and structures of authority.

After the collapse of the social structures of preconciliar Catholicism in the 1970s, movements looking to the pope for guidance took
the lead in reviving Catholicism (for example, through the pro-life
movement).[5] But this subculture was living in tension with many of
the national bishops, who were more inclined toward accommodation with the secularizing Canadian society.

Catholic revivalism developed in a particular form of ultramontanism relying on the bountiful teachings of the pope. It reached
its highpoint in 1992 with the promulgation of the *Catechism of the
Catholic Church*. In 1982, the formation of this alliance of Catholic
revivalism and papal teaching had only just begun.

Having read Don's proposal for the centre, the local bishop
expressed his support and said that he would put in a word with the
other bishops, but added that his diocese was poor. Don continued
to promote the proposal and look for funding; finally, he managed to
collect a start-up sum of fifty thousand dollars.

One day when Don and Posie drove past St. Mary's, an empty
high school in Combermere, Posie said, "Why don't we find out
what it costs?" They learned that the Loreto Sisters, who owned the
school, were selling it for one and a half million dollars, which was
altogether too expensive. Nevertheless, Don went to them with the
twenty-page proposal and spoke of his dream. The sisters said that
they really wanted to help and offered to rent the building to them,
including twelve acres by the Madawaska River.

In the summer of 1982, family retreats began in the old school.
They were not officially connected to Madonna House, but it sent
a priest who came during the week of the retreat to offer daily Mass
and give talks. Madonna House also gave Nazareth Retreat Centre access to the mailing list for the Cana Colony, as it was mostly

overbooked, and thus in its inaugural summer the Nazareth retreats were fully booked.

The families arrived on a Sunday and began the week with a day of reconciliation, reflecting on their family life: how they were living as fathers and mothers. They were encouraged to see where they needed to forgive and to be forgiven. The daily teaching sessions, beside summer activities such as fishing, sports, and barbecues, were focused on areas in which people had gone astray from Church teaching, such as the Real Presence in the Eucharist, the role of Our Lady, and *Humanae Vitae*. According to Posie McPhee, many experienced healing and began a deeper surrender to Catholic family life.[6] An important element of the retreats was families sharing their joys and sorrows with each other during discussions; it was not a top-down approach where the priest would be talking most of the time and the laypersons merely listening. It was rather families speaking to families.

Don and Posie had five children at the time, and three more arrived during the following years. During Nazareth's first year, they did most of the work themselves, but the next year young people helped as volunteers for the whole summer. From this, teen conferences grew, in which they were taught the same things as their parents, though geared to their appropriate age group. The summer retreats continued in the old school until 1987, when they found a new building that was also located by the river. Madonna House bought the property and let Nazareth use the house. Don and Posie again raised funds and enlarged the house, which became both their home and the place of retreats and other family activities.

In 1985, Don became a permanent deacon, and in the new building they had a chapel with the Eucharist present. Catherine Doherty's admonition about giving up the idea of an intentional community, that the family itself was their primary community, comes to mind. The McPhees lived this principle for most of the year, but during the summers, that distinction became blurred by the continual influx of families living under one roof with Don and Posie and their children. Such an arrangement puts great pressure on a family, especially a large one, as it is difficult to preserve the private zone of the home when the apostolate is everywhere.

When Michael and Sheila moved to Brudenell, the new site of Nazareth had been in use for a year, and the retreats had been running for six years. In 1989, Don invited Michael to become editor of the Nazareth newsletter. He was not involved with the actual management of the centre. The editor job was an unpaid one, which for the O'Briens was possible, as the rent of the Brudenell rectory was phenomenally low; they continued to live on the income from painting commissions.

The newsletter built up a community larger than had been created by the intense *communitas* at the summer retreats. Accordingly, Don and Michael began to think about developing the newsletter into a full-fledged Catholic family magazine. The idea merely was not to sustain the community created by the summer retreat experiences, as with the newsletter, but to create an apostolate of its own—a magazine that could reach people who did not have the time or resources to come to Combermere. Such a venture was a bold step; even if Michael was not paid for his editing, in those pre-Internet days, the costs of printing and distribution were still high.

In November 1989, Don and Posie went on a pilgrimage to Medugorje in Bosnia-Hercegovina. There they put before God the idea of a Catholic family magazine: the retreat centre would have to fund it, at least in the beginning, and they were not sure if this was the right thing. Would the magazine drain the resources necessary to keep the retreats running? Were they spreading their energy over too many projects?

In the middle of November, Don and Posie returned from Medugorje, and to Michael they seemed filled with peace and new motivation. While praying before the large concrete cross on the mountain called Križevac (Cross Mountain), Don had realized that he must develop a faithful (doctrinally orthodox) magazine for Catholic families. The words "Truth and Love" had come into his mind.

Private Revelations

In the Catholic world during the 1980s, in parallel with the slow dying of the European model of national churches, there was an explosion of private revelations with exhortations of returning to God, but also with a clear eschatological message. They were more or less all of them saying, we are now entering the end-time. As early as April 1984, Michael had observed: "Many prophecies from various corners of the Church, from Charismatic to Marian, are saying that the tribulation and Apocalypse is about to break upon us. I do not doubt that this is true."[7]

In 1981, six children reported that they had seen the Virgin Mary in the village of Međugorje in Bosnia-Hercegovina, then part of Communist Yugoslavia. The children claimed to receive visions every day; the volume of the messages became thus decidedly larger compared with the brief messages of the classical Marian apparitions in Lourdes and Fatima. Another difference was that the visionaries did not enter convents, but married and had ordinary professions. Međugorje became perhaps the most important centre and pilgrimage site of a Charismatic Catholic subculture. It was nourished by the increasing number of private revelations being circulated.[8]

Many of the revelations of the late twentieth century were not connected to a particular place such as Lourdes, Fatima, and Međugorje, but to a single visionary who recorded and published visions and locutions. Such texts became quite voluminous, similar to the revelatory writings of mediaeval saints such as St. Brigid of Sweden. In the 1990s, with the help of the Internet, new messages were spread with an ease and speed previously unthinkable.[9]

One of the most important private revelations of this type during the 1980s was that of the Italian priest Father Stefano Gobbi (1930–2011), who claimed to have received locutions from the Virgin Mary from 1972 until 1997. Among many other themes, the messages contain interpretations of the Book of Revelation as unfolding in our times, and promising that the events predicted would come to a climax within ten to fifteen years.[10]

In the mid-1980s, Michael read Father Gobbi's messages and came to believe that the 1990s would be a decisive decade. In June 1989, Michael sketched a likely scenario in his diary. He began with stating that the great apostasy was well underway; the Church had entered a condition of confusion, and, especially in North American and Western European nations, it was weak and indecisive. He speculated that toward the end of the decade, the philosophy of the Antichrist would be in control of the world and a totalitarian anti-Christian state engaged in full-scale persecution of Christians and Jews. According to Michael's thoughts at the time, the end-time scenario would be completed with the return of Christ, probably at the millennium. For those who took private revelations seriously, the 1990s was lived in intense expectation.

A Catholic Family Journal

In November 1989, Michael and Don had their first meeting to discuss launching the magazine. They settled on the name *Nazareth Journal*. Michael would be editor and Don the publisher. Still, in December, Michael worried about scattering his energies. He wondered if he should focus on painting or creative writing—that is, his novels or essays? Being editor was a new task, and it was also time-consuming. "Will it drain my creativity?" he asked in prayer for discernment. It was a critical decision, as the task of editing would inevitably push his emphasis away from painting. Even though he did not perceive it at the time, he was preparing for a shift toward making writing his primary creative activity.

By this time, the children had been in school for a year, and in November, there was a meeting in Pembroke of parents who were concerned about the new sex-education program, *Fully Alive*, which in its pilot stage was proposing to introduce explicit sexual information at grade-one level and up. Michael knew that this contradicted several documents from various popes and Vatican congregations on education. Yet, the local ordinary supported the program, mainly out of loyalty to the bishops in Ontario who had originated it. Don McPhee pointed out to Michael that more valuable than protest was building a viable alternative to modernist Catholicism: to be islands of light in a darkening world. But Michael felt a calling to speak up when he saw something he considered wrong; it was not natural for him to be strategically silent on such issues. He had a habit of sticking out his neck, when most people withdrew out of prudence, or fear. In December, he was praying regarding the upcoming confrontation with the local Catholic school board.

In a meeting with the board of trustees, Michael and other Catholic laypeople made presentations citing the teachings of the Catholic Church on sex education and her guidelines on education, demonstrating that these were at odds with the new program. The trustees listened with, as Michael recalls, stony faces, made no comment, and nothing ever came of the efforts at resistance. In the province at large, however, there was sufficient parental protest to convince the creators of the program to delay the introduction of details of sexual intercourse until later grade levels. In May the following year, Michael had the opportunity to go one step further and become involved in politics, when a friend at the Chesterton Society in Ottawa asked if he would consider running as a candidate for the Family Coalition Party of Ontario (later renamed the New Reform Party of Ontario).[11] He did not see it as realistic at the time, as he had to reject the temptation to do too many good things, spreading his energy too thinly. He had to put the family first—it was his primary duty—and in second place came his creative work.

Missing the Boys

In May 1990, two priests from the organization Legion of Christ (founded in Mexico in 1941 by Marcial Maciel Degollado, better known as Father Maciel, a Mexican Catholic priest) came to Brudenell to take John and some other local boys on a four-day tour of the Immaculate Conception Apostolic School they ran in New Hampshire, USA. It was a Catholic boarding school for boys from grades seven through twelve, and the education was on the liberal arts model, with plenty of opportunity for outdoor activities and sports.

After the days in New Hampshire, John was enthusiastic and begged his parents' permission to attend the school. To Michael it seemed good, as the movement had a reputation for faithfulness. John began in the fall of 1990. Little did Michael and Sheila know at that time, but behind the pious façade of the movement, Maciel lived a double life, and it later surfaced that he had abused numerous young boys in the movement, had relations with women, and had fathered children. The organization was structured by him according to a principle of secrecy and shaming of those who dared to speak up, enabling him to protect his double life as outwardly a celibate, doctrinally orthodox priest, and in secret a sexual predator.[12]

Fortunately, John did not encounter any of the dark side of the movement at the school in New Hampshire. In fact, there were many excellent priests and brothers in the order, whom the boys considered heroes and role models. For them, of course, it was very hard to be betrayed by their own leader and founder of their organization.

It is difficult for a parent to discern correctly such things. How does one know if the teacher at one's children's school is not living a double life? When they lived in the Arctic, Michael's parents did not know of the secret life of Martin Houston. Nevertheless, one important point (and signal of trouble) in the Legion's methodology was the very restricted contact with the children that parents were allowed, extending to even censured correspondence. Strict discipline combined with very little or no contact with parents makes it easy for an abusive person to take advantage of children. Michael later discovered that during the recruiting stage, parents were being misled about the degree to which the Legion would assume total control over their children's lives.

Even Pope John Paul II was fooled by Maciel, while Cardinal Ratzinger was suspicious. Later, it would be Ratzinger as prefect of the Congregation for the Doctrine of the Faith who reopened the investigations that eventually led to the full exposure of Maciel's crimes, his forced resignation from headship of the order, and his exile to a life of silence and penance, which continued until his death.[13]

In 1991 and 1992, Michael made trips to New Hampshire to meet with the Legion's American director, Father Anthony Bannon, to talk about the issues of lack of respect for parental rights, limited access to their children, and the deceptive recruitment methodology. In these meetings and also in subsequent telephone calls, Michael received reassurances and a vague promise that the situation would soon be corrected, but the situation did not change.

In March of the following year, Benjamin, then four years old, suddenly looked up from the supper table and declared, "John-Boy is missing! He's part of us!"

The next year in April, when visiting the school for John's Confirmation, Sheila was quite upset about what she feared was a rigid and brainwashing regime. To Michael, John seemed to flourish, and he thought that brainwashing was depersonalizing and would look different. A bishop said to Sheila that the order had the strengths and the weaknesses of a new foundation, but that it was beloved of the Holy Father. Here, the particular form of ultramontanism espoused by Catholic revivalism showed itself to be a problem. Obviously, the papal charism of infallibility regarding dogma and doctrine does not extend to his personal opinions about, for example, different organizations; even a pope can be deceived. Sheila's motherly intuition saw something that eluded John Paul II; she considered John too young to be so far away from the family and the style of the school too rigorous.

The First Issue

During the whole of 1990, Michael and Don worked hard putting together the first issue of *Nazareth Journal*. Simultaneously, a new life was being formed; and, in April, Michael noted in his diary, "I am full of joy and hope—we are expecting a baby!" The new baby and the first issue of the journal were gestating in parallel.

In September, they consecrated the magazine to God with a little ceremony in the chapel of the Nazareth Retreat Centre. Before the common Rosary, Michael prayed alone for a moment and felt an inner light and assurance that they were to go forward in confidence, and that doubt impeded the flow of grace. Then he was amazed as he interiorly saw the image of a solemn angel come forth from the tabernacle and slowly inscribe a cross on his forehead. Nevertheless, throughout October, both Michael and Don experienced great trials and temptations. Don had pneumonia, bills were stacking up, and there was no income of which to speak. Despite these trials, the magazine was coming together, and Michael was happy with the result.

On November 30, Angela, a healthy baby girl, the sixth child of Michael and Sheila, was born at the local St. Francis Hospital. At the same time, *Nazareth Journal* launched its first Advent issue; the gestation period of both baby and magazine was over. Don had driven to Toronto with the digital file in the middle of the night, as the printing cost was cheaper there. He returned the next day with flat sheets of paper that they folded and stapled. The one thousand copies were mailed out to people in the middle of November.

In his editorial for the first issue, Michael wrote that the purpose of the magazine was not to focus on all the problems and decay within the Catholic Church. The magazine would highlight healthy Catholic family life, give inspiration and examples, and share stories of struggles and joys, but also provide sound theological teaching. Nevertheless, later that year, Michael penned an article on his childhood experience of abuse in Inuvik. It was a story that needed to be told, he thought, but Don did not want to print it, as he considered it too negative for the journal. It was only later, after a series of articles in the *Boston Globe* in 2002, that a new awareness arose that such things needed to be dealt with in the open.[14] Michael's article eventually appeared in the June 2002 edition of *Catholic World Report* magazine.[15]

After Michael's editorial, there was an essay by Father David May on the spirituality of *Nazareth*, and under the heading "Mother's Diary" a piece called "Cat Trauma", where one could read among other things:

> I'm pretty tired tonight. It's my eight month of pregnancy. I sit down to write in the midst of the start of school, the scramble for supplies, the arrival of out of town guests, two kids' birthdays, a new niece just born, laundry backed up, the fall fruit harvest waiting to be processed (even as I write three big sacks of plums are breeding fruit flies in the kitchen). I am thinking of a phrase that puzzles me more and more as the years go by: "God never sends you more than you can handle."[16]

Michael also wrote "The Flight into Egypt" under the heading "A Father's Diary". It told the tale of the hard winter of early 1982, "the winter of our discontent", as Michael and Sheila used to call it. In the middle of snow shovelling, Michael had developed a cyst on his spine that later would prove to be life-threatening. One night when the snow was piling up outside the windows, and all the financial and health problems were weighing on his soul, he sat in the rocking chair trying in vain to console their sick baby, Mary. In typical Michael O'Brien style, it was a story about life being emptied out and the impact of the Cross inducing a feeling of complete powerlessness, of poverty both spiritual and material, but then a light is lit. In this case, it came through the singing of a piece of poetry that calmed the baby. Michael interpreted it in the light of his relation to God.

> I had thought that God was silent. I discovered that I was deaf. I am still learning to hear, but on that night in the darkness I first learned to listen. I heard a music which I had not suspected was there: the song of holy poverty, a child breathing easily at last, the cry of a night bird, the poetry of wind, and the whispering of snow.[17]

During 1989 and 1990, while Don and Michael were busy creating the new family journal, the Iron Curtain fell, the Soviet Union was dissolving, and Marxism seemed bankrupt; the Cold War was over, and the West had won. In the summer of 1989, Francis Fukuyama published the article "The End of History?" which successfully captured the sense that something fundamental was happening. He wrote, "The triumph of the West, of the Western *idea*, is evident first of all in the total exhaustion of viable systematic alternatives to Western liberalism."[18] He continued,

> What we may be witnessing is not just the end of the Cold War, or the passing of a particular period of postwar history, but the end of history as such: that is, the end point of mankind's ideological evolution and the universalization of Western liberal democracy as the final form of human government.[19]

In the article, he dismissed religious fundamentalism as a serious political alternative, but acknowledged "the impersonality and spiritual vacuity of liberal consumerist societies".[20] Fukuyama thought that most religious groups were satisfied with the conditions provided by capitalist liberal democracy.

Though Michael and Don, and the Catholic subculture they made themselves spokespersons for in their journal, were grateful for the collapse of the Soviet Empire, they were not overwhelmed with joy. For them, the threat of what Fukuyama called "the emptiness at the core of liberalism"[21] was as potent an enemy as materialist Marxism; for them, the end of history was not a complete victory of liberalism, but the return of Jesus Christ. It is in this light we need to understand Michael's insistence on a Christian eschatological understanding of history. The empty core of liberalism was not merely a threat of ennui, as indicated by Fukuyama at the end of his article, where he writes,

> The end of history will be a very sad time.... In the post-historical period there will be neither art nor philosophy, just the perpetual caretaking of the museum of human history.... Perhaps this very prospect of centuries of boredom at the end of history will serve to get history started once more.[22]

For Michael, who believed that human history was the theatre of war between titanic spiritual forces of evil and goodness, boredom was not the big threat, but rather evil disguised as morally neutral niceness. According to Michael, the shift in the late 1980s in favour of the West was a mere temporary lull in the larger battle: to be satisfied with a consumerist lifestyle, focusing on pleasure and self-fulfilment, was to misunderstand history as management instead of spiritual warfare.

In January, Michael noted in his diary that Angela, only six weeks old, was smiling copiously, which gave him great joy. At the same time, he was wondering if they were now seeing World War III breaking out in the Middle East. When the United States and United Nations' attack on Iraq began on January 16 (Canadian time), the children and Michael knelt and prayed at the little altar in their home, while Sheila was in church for choir practice.

The war developed into a devastating loss for Saddam Hussein's large but outdated military; the technologically advanced West showed its supreme power. Perhaps Fukuyama was right after all, as the old Marxist powers were not involved. However, that war had sown a seed that during the next decades would emerge as the new threat toward the hegemony of the liberal West, a conflict in which religion would play a most decisive role, and also the question of good and evil. Interestingly, terror, the goal of terrorism, is the direct opposite of boredom caused by the technological management of a world society, which Fukuyama envisaged as the sad fate of mankind.

As Michael continued to work on the first issue of *Nazareth Journal*, he began to think more about the novels he had written up to then. None of them had been published. The first was *A Cry of Stone*, now about a young native Canadian artist; the second, *Strangers and Sojourners*, about three generations of a family in British Columbia. But he also mentioned two more novels, *House of Dreams* and *Eclipse of the Sun*, which were taking shape in his imagination but were not yet written. They were to be part of a series he intended to call either Children of the Last Days or perhaps Children of the Season of Darkness. He begged God for freedom to write and publish these stories and thought to himself: "This is impossible, so if it occurs I will know it is perfectly, completely a gift from God."[23]

Kurelek Mountain

During his visit in June 1989 to William Kurelek's widow, Jean, in Toronto, Michael had become convinced that he should write a biography of her husband. As the project progressed, he became increasingly preoccupied with, and fascinated by, Kurelek's farm in Combermere. It was as if Michael felt the spirit of his old mentor lingering in the contemplative stillness of the isolated house. They had not spent much time together, as Kurelek had died only seven months after their first meeting in 1977. Michael had benefitted from a brief moment of both spiritual and artistic fatherhood, before it was gone, as he had with his own father only two years earlier.[24]

Kurelek's words to Michael still reverberated in his soul: "Put your light on the hilltop!" This had proved to be extremely difficult. The gatekeepers of the secular hilltops had consistently denied him access to their elevated places. He had been forced to exhibit in church basements and halls, and his novels lay unpublished in a cardboard box in his studio. Symbolically, and perhaps by a turn of divine humour, there was a little mountain behind Kurelek's farmhouse, a hilltop for Michael to climb, so to speak. It was only a hundred metres high, and on the rock face Kurelek had painted a white Byzantine cross. Moreover, it was here that he had built his apocalyptic bomb shelter, which he did not get a permit to construct in Toronto.

When visiting in October 1989, Michael saw that the white cross had begun to fade, and that the shelter was in ruins. After asking permission from Madonna House, who now owned the house and property, he repainted the cross as a symbolic gesture, connecting his own witnessing to that of Kurelek's. After climbing to the top of the mountain, Michael stood still and looked out over the Madawaska Valley. The famous colour spectacle of the Canadian forests was at its height; it went from yellow and golden nuances, through intensive red, to purple. Michael was overcome with the tranquillity and beauty of the place and the far-reaching view of the whole area, where Madonna House was the spiritual centre attracting like-minded people and projects.

In November 1990, Michael spent an hour at the farm on the anniversary of Kurelek's death. As he prayed for the biography and his novels, he wondered if Catholic literature could be an instrument to draw souls back to Truth and Love, and he implored, "Oh Lord, I beg You to let it happen. It is utterly impossible for me to make it happen!"[25]

In February 1991, Michael returned to the farm for three days to work on the biography; he was focusing on the relation between Kurelek and Madonna House, and Kurelek's understanding of the apocalypse. In the midst of alternating between writing and praying, he looked up at the mountain with its painted white cross and became immersed in a feeling of peace.

On the crest of the mountain, he saw, with his inner eye, a stone chapel with a blue onion-top dome. Twelve gold stars were painted all over the dome, which was surmounted by a gold cross. Inside the chapel, he saw a large central icon of Christ the Saviour, flanked by two tall icons of St. Joseph and the Mother of God. On the hillside, he saw a trail zigzagging up the side of the cliff-face, and along it were Stations of the Cross, made of simple wooden crosses. The shrine was dedicated to "Jesus Christ the Saviour of the World".

The vision moved Michael profoundly, and he began to wonder if it would be possible for his family to move to the farm. Since it was owned by Madonna House, he sat down to write a letter asking them to sell the farm to him; Sheila had received a small inheritance, which could be used as down payment. In the letter, he wrote about his vision, but also about the difficulty of knowing what was divine inspiration and what was merely his own imagination.

> All of the above may merely be the fruit of a well-intentioned but rather strong imagination. I am, after all, an artist and an Irishman. I have never been able to distinguish with absolute certainty between inspiration and imagination. But perhaps there is room to consider the way God sometimes works through a consecrated imagination. I would not dare to call this a "vision" in the classical sense, but an interior image that seemed to be "given." I also know that there exists a gap between a vision that is given and the interpretation that the one who sees it can give to the experience. There can be distortion or jumping to conclusions.[26]

If Michael thought and prayed with the help of strong images, Sheila on the contrary found it difficult to do mental prayer; she liked to just sit in God's presence and pray the Rosary. She began also to

do eucharistic adoration regularly at the parish church in Combermere, where there was perpetual adoration, day and night without
interruption. Once every week, she took an hour of adoration in the
middle of the night, usually between three and four in the morning.

At the end of April 1991, Michael climbed Kurelek Mountain once
more to take photos for the biography. He prayed at the top and, as
he recorded later in his diary, received a powerful interior consolation. He thought, "I could have stayed forever; it was so beautiful."
When he came down to the valley bottom, he received a telephone
call from Madonna House telling him that they could not sell the
farm, as it was clearly stipulated in Catherine Doherty's will that no
property of Madonna House was to be sold. Nevertheless, Michael
learned that the mountaintop was not owned by Madonna House,
and his dream of building the onion-dome church remained alive.

A month later, he put the final touches to the rewriting of his
novel *Strangers and Sojourners* and managed to complete the Kurelek
biography. He sent the manuscript of the biography to Ignatius Press,
who later decided not to publish it because the publisher felt there
would not be enough interest in it to make it worthwhile; they also
had a long backlog of other titles to publish.

Later, as Michael was praying in the church, a priest called, and
Sheila took the telephone. During the conversation, the priest said, "I
have a word for Michael: Courage. The book will one day be published, but it will take persistence. Tell him not to be discouraged,
even if the book is turned down sixteen times by publishers." The
priest was right; Michael's persistence was truly to be tried; it would
take twenty-two years before it was published.[27]

Homeschooling Again

Since the Catholic school system of Ontario had not proved to be
what Michael and Sheila expected, they decided to try homeschooling again in 1991, for a year at least. There were other homeschooling
families in the area, and within a few years their numbers grew and
a local homeschool organization was founded, Our Lady of the
Valley Home School Association, with about twenty-five families
participating.

It was a major undertaking: Angela was not yet one year old; Ben was four years old and always up to something, such as incursions into Michael's studio. One day he managed to roll-paint part of the floor and track small white footprints everywhere. At the same time, John, fifteen years old, left for high school in New Hampshire, while Joseph, thirteen years old, was homeschooled for one year, but then he also left for the same high school. It was thus Mary, ten years old, and Elizabeth, eight years old, who were the real focus of home-schooling for Sheila in the beginning. At the same time, she had to manage the needs of the smaller ones, and she worried about the well-being of the boys now living in another country. And then, of course, though Michael helped her, there was the large house and the everyday duties of cooking and washing clothes. Some days of home-schooling were difficult, while others were wonderful, but Sheila naturally felt overwhelmed. The pressure and workload made her tired, and during that first semester, Michael worried that she would become burned-out. Nevertheless, the homeschooling proceeded well, and they decided to continue after the first year.

Sheila integrated the surrounding nature into her teaching; they would go out for long walks in the woods, using the trails made by local hunters and snowmobiles. They found, for example, a beaver dam in a swamp in the forest behind the house, and sometimes they watched the beavers swimming along with tree branches in their mouths. They collected flowers, tree bark, and mushrooms and then brought home the new additions to their collection and began the work of drawing and identifying them. To the amazement of the children, Sheila one day brought home the tiny eggs of a monarch butterfly, which they saw grow to fat, yellow-white, and black-striped caterpillars, then transforming into immovable green chrysalises; and finally there appeared the beautiful butterfly.

The White Horse Press

As the idea of using the small inheritance from Sheila's aunt to buy the Kurelek farm had come to nothing, Sheila thought that the money had to be used for another good purpose; just to pour it into the black hole of everyday expenses seemed too tame. She came up with a new idea, and to Michael's surprise, she said one day, "I would like to hire you for a year to paint the Mysteries of the Holy Rosary." Michael was deeply moved, because their practical needs were so many and urgent—to him it was a clear indication of her faith in his vocation as a Christian artist.

It was a bold venture. The idea was to make a book, using the paintings as illustrations, and include a short text for each mystery. However, funds to cover the cost of printing were also needed. The director of Madonna House Publications, Linda Lambeth, came to their help and managed to collect ten thousand dollars during the end of 1991, which would cover the entire printing cost.

The fifteen paintings that Michael made for *The Mysteries of the Most Holy Rosary* show clearly that he was still in the transition stage of his style. Some of the paintings like the first, *The Annunciation*, were in a Byzantine iconographic style, with clear colours, stylized figures, and no attempt to create an illusion of depth, or materiality of, for example, the clothes.

The five paintings of the Sorrowful Mysteries, on the other hand, are half figures of Christ in shades of brown and sepia with a black background; the only colour is an addition of some red, representing blood, and a thin blue outline of the Christ figure on the Cross. A characteristic of this style is the tilted, oblong head, which in combination with closed eyes creates an existential feeling of interiority.

Other paintings seem to have taken only one step away from the iconographic style; the forms are looser and the colours slightly more subdued than in the icons, but the images are still mainly arranged in a two-dimensional pattern. For example, the striped tunics of the doctors in the Temple do not indicate the volume of the bodies, but create an abstract surface pattern.

In *The Assumption of the Virgin Mary*, all the pieces have come together, and the result is an image of striking beauty. There is a strong depth perspective, but it is slightly strange, as if the scene is seen through a distorting lens. The body of the Virgin flows from the open coffin—and hovers over a pair of houses clustered on a hill in the foreground—toward a semicircular hole in the night sky. Out of the opening in the sky, which is rimmed by wavy lines of purple and nuances of blue, Jesus leans out and gently takes Mary by the shoulder, while an angel on the left reaches down to support the back of her head and the other shoulder. They direct Mary upward, toward the opening in the sky, as if she is weightless. On the earth below, it is night, but one can see a red road zigzagging toward a mountainscape running along the horizon. Beside the little village, a glowing, pink onion-domed church with a golden cross on the top is shooting up like a skyscraper filled with vibrant energy. Through the open doors can be seen a tiny radiant monstrance with the Eucharist. The faces of Jesus and Mary have delicate features that display tenderness. While the white robes of Mary have flowing ochre shades, that of Jesus is made up of swirling blue lines and small red crosses that give it an ethereal, cosmic materiality.

My impression is that in this painting Michael has achieved a very personal synthesis of West and East, which is narrative—that is, tells a story—and, at the same time, is lyrically contemplative.

In March 1992, Michael and Sheila decided that for *The Mysteries of the Most Holy Rosary* they would have to start their own publishing house. Michael made a sketch for a logo for Sophia House Press with the motto "Veritas et Caritas". However, they settled on the name White Horse Press, an allusion to G. K. Chesterton's *Ballad of the White Horse*, an epic poem about the battle between King Alfred the Great and the Danish Vikings in 878. To Michael this was a prototypical Christian victory against all odds. It was a perfect symbol for the humble little press, which was, indeed, low in human and material resources.

The Watchman

In April 1992, Michael asked in prayer, "So many, many doors are open before me: novels, a publishing house, articles for other journals, *Nazareth*, a mural in Montreal, etc., etc. Which of them do I pursue, Lord?"[28] Soon after, the answer came through a decisive interior struggle. Don rejected a couple of articles proposed by Michael; he also said that Michael's editorial "An Enemy of the People" in the Lent issue of that year was scaring people away, and probably the cause of the lack of new subscriptions. This was a question of principle. Should a family magazine only give inspiration through good examples, or should it also contain warnings and highlight what was problematic or dangerous to families? In the editorial, Michael had strongly expressed his worry about the Church and the surrounding

Western culture; it was an impassioned plea not to surrender to the mainstream.

> If people simply assume that they inhabit a sort of sane centre, then they will find no reason to reflect upon radical notions such as the suggestion that their society is collapsing into dehumanization and that their local churches are under pressure to degenerate into neo-paganism, and that both are awash in deadly half-truths and untruths. Such proposals seem outlandish, inconceivable, and indeed too pain-ful for the average person to consider. They must dismiss the idea as "extremism", or perhaps as "alarmism" because the moderate Western Catholic trusts implicitly in the collective good sense of the majority, the safe middle.[29]

Michael's reaction to the conflict at *Nazareth* was to try to keep his temper, which was not easy; but, at the same time, he was con-sidering resigning as editor. He had the natural instinct of a prophet to warn people when he believed that they needed to repent, open their eyes, and change course. The present situation in the West was, according to Michael, spiritually unhealthy; people needed to be warned. Nevertheless, he thought, "Maybe it is art after all that is my vocation, not copy editing."

On the night of Easter Sunday, the question of speaking up or not made Michael unable to sleep; he prayed and begged God for guid-ance regarding *Nazareth Journal*. As so often in situations as this, he turned to guidance from Sacred Scripture, and when he opened it, his eyes fell on Ezekiel 3:17–18:

> Son of man, I have made you a watchman for the house of Israel; whenever you hear a word FROM my mouth, you shall give them warning from me. If I say to the wicked, "You shall surely die," and you give him no warning, nor speak to warn the wicked from his wicked way, in order to save his life, that wicked man shall die in his iniquity; but his blood I will require at your hand.

And then Isaiah 62:6–7:

> Upon your walls, O Jerusalem, I have set watchmen; all the day and all the night they shall never be silent. You who put the LORD in remembrance, take no rest, and give him no rest until he establishes Jerusalem and makes it a praise in the earth.

As he continued to read, the confirmations continued—for example, "Zeal for your house has consumed me" (Ps 69:9; cf. Jn 2:17), undergirding his understanding of himself as a watchman; that he had a moral obligation to speak up about the spiritual situation in the Church and society. However, in May he sighed, "My heart is longing for freedom from *Nazareth Journal*."[30]

In June, on the feast of the Immaculate Heart of Mary, Michael consecrated the White Horse Press to the glorification of Jesus through the Heart of Mary, with a special Rosary and the offering of the Mass at Our Lady of the Angels, Brudenell. The Mysteries of the Rosary was underway, and Michael was working on his new novel *Sophia House* (The House of Wisdom) set in Warsaw during the Second World War. Michael and Sheila were also happy that they were expecting their seventh child.

On July 26, 1992, Michael and Don went out for supper during which they came to a new understanding regarding their cooperation; Michael saw it as a rebirth of the journal. The same day, Sheila, who was visiting her family in British Columbia, phoned and said she was bleeding, that they might be losing the baby. Two days later, she had to go the hospital, bleeding heavily after having a miscarriage; Michael wept and prayed after Mass; he felt the distance hard, although they were telephoning back and forth. They named the baby Anna.

They also lost another child the following year, the baby miscarrying at home on December 26. They conditionally baptized the three-month-old child, naming him Stephen, and buried him in a corner of the cemetery beside their house.

In September 1992, Michael's existential crisis deepened.

During the past few weeks everything in me has been tempted, shaken and tested with an unusual ferocity. Sickness, thousands of dollars of unpaid bills; Sheila very sick and anxious, myself unable to paint except with excruciating slowness. Endless grinding fatigue. Insomnia. Betrayals by our bishops, and the anger of my spiritual director when I asked if I could raise a voice in protest.[31]

Michael had posed the question to his spiritual director whether he should speak up and criticize *Fully Alive*, the new Family Life Education Program sponsored by the Ontario Conference of Catholic Bishops.[32] Michael told his spiritual advisor about the scriptural confirmations that he had received during the night—that perhaps his vocation was to be a watchman, a sentinel, who would see far and deep and sound the alarm when danger was approaching. His spiritual advisor responded, as Michael experienced it, angrily, "You are really mistaken about thinking yourself the watchman of the Church in Ontario, *you are the watchman of your family*—but not of anything else. *You cannot save this situation*—you can only suffer with it. The public media is not the place to discuss the wounds of the Church." He concluded, "If you must say something to the media, make it simple and only speak in peace and truth."[33]

Through an act of obedience, Michael accepted and did not speak up; he cancelled an interview with the local paper, but emotionally, on the inside, it was different:

> I weep and scream and hit back continuously in my mind. Everything is shaken. I am judged and judged ... not by the Pharisees but by the truly good little brothers and sisters of Jesus. Does He too reject me?[34]

Underlying the admonition that Michael received was the idea that it was not the task of laypersons to voice opposition toward Church authority, and, in this way, openly challenge the hierarchy of the Church. However, that principle proved to be very dangerous when it came to the sexual abuse crisis, which had not yet exploded with full force—that would take another ten years. Were laypersons not supposed to speak up in media if the bishop was covering it all up? This was the reason that Michael's article on the abuse in Inuvik was not published, and we must not forget that the perpetrator Martin Houston had been ordained a priest in the Catholic Church as recently as 1990, even though the bishop knew of his history of sexual abuse of young adolescent boys and his imprisonment as a "dangerous sexual offender".

The same principle was at play within the Legion of Christ; criticism was contained and silenced. Such an arrangement could perhaps be maintained when the Church authorities and religious orders controlled the infrastructure of religious media. With a new media landscape, where laypersons were (as encouraged by the Second Vatican Council) taking on new active roles—as Don and Michael had done when they founded *Nazareth Journal*—this was no longer feasible.

With the Internet and the World Wide Web, which were established in the early 1990s, and with the later explosion of social media, it became impossible. There is now an army of watchmen blogging, tweeting, and vlogging (that is, video blogging).

Michael could not resolve the tension between all the spiritual words, visions, and inspirations that he had received during the years and the admonition of his spiritual supervisor. He began to mistrust his own experiences.

> Perhaps all consolations are either emotional states self-induced or diabolical deceptions ... a non-verbal language? I no longer trust any words, not even my own various levels of the mind. If I am to accept my spiritual director's admonitions as God's will for me, then I have no foundation for believing anything that comes to me along the paths which I have come to believe over the years God speaks to me and guides. If Fr. [———] is right, then all I have discerned is self-delusion or diabolical delusion.[35]

He continued, "I wish to leave everything connected to writing and painting and editing."

On the vigil to the feast day of St. Thérèse of Lisieux (October 1, 1992), he could not sleep. At half past five, he had made an effort at conscious prayer, which was very difficult. He said to God that he was completely finished, that he had failed; he felt condemned by the religious community that was supposed to be his support, and weighed down with the economic situation of his family; he had no energy to paint in order to catch up with the economic deficit. In the midst of this existential dark night, there came a strong visual image of Catherine Doherty, who had been dead since 1985. It was a total surprise to him.

She said, "I ask you please to forgive me."

Michael was flooded by emotion; he still had not been able to heal completely from the brusque treatment that he had received from her fifteen years earlier. In this early hour of the day, he did not think that this was perhaps an illusion, a hallucination brought on by emotional strain and lack of sleep, or, more sinisterly, a diabolical delusion aimed at leading him astray. He had a very strong sense that it was a real presence conversing with him, something beyond his imagination. He, therefore, accepted the address as genuine and replied:

"I forgive you. Why did you do that to me?"

"I am asking you to forgive me. I have asked you many times but you do not forgive me."

"I have never heard you ask for forgiveness."

"I have asked many times but you do not hear."

"I forgive you."

"You see how you feel this day. That is how I felt on that day when I hurt you. I was in blackness; I was near despair. I struck out at you because I did not understand."

"Your priest,... he too is angry with me ... and now I do not understand."

"You must forgive him. If you do not forgive, there will be much suffering. If you forgive, much light will spread."

At this point, Michael began to wonder if he was not after all imagining the dialogue; perhaps his mind was beginning to disintegrate. Nevertheless, he replied, unsure if he was talking to himself or to a genuine spiritual communication.

"I do not know if this is real. I think maybe I am insane."

"You are not insane. You are hurt."

At this point, all the dammed-up frustration and feelings of being mistreated welled forth. He was not ready to forgive so easily. Though he was by nature a person who accepted correction of his faults and failings, to take correction humbly in the area that concerned his understanding of his own vocation, for which he had suffered so much, was an extreme test. He was hurt emotionally, but he had also been contradicted in the very core of his life's project—the sacrifice of his life in the manner of an apostolate.

Michael responded with some bitterness: "When a person speaks to another human being with such rudeness as he spoke, such as he has done three times to me, it is a pattern, not a meaningless accident. It communicates volumes of unspoken information. He tells me that he does not respect me, nor does he love me (except theoretically). And he dislikes me. He has judged me. Judgement—it is the main pastime of your community. I will not be going back to see him...."

"I ask you, DO NOT GIVE UP."

"Why?"

"Because he has much to learn from you and you have much to learn from him."

"I have already learned many important lessons from him. I am grateful for what he has taught me. But he is the kind of father who hands his son a loaf of bread in one hand and slaps him on the face at the same time with the other hand."

"You must forgive him. Do not give up on him. Please, I have asked you to forgive me."[36]

In his heart, Michael forgave both Catherine Doherty and his spiritual advisor, and then he felt peace and fell asleep. A stone that had weighed on his soul for fifteen years had been lifted. He would later come to understand that his spiritual director had his own emotional struggles, compounded by his fears for the security of his community and his worries over the condition of the Church in Canada. Michael's relationship with his spiritual director continued for many more years, and to this day the O'Briens have a close relationship with the Madonna House community.

Nazareth Resurrected

The first issue of *Nazareth* appeared toward the end of 1990; during 1991 and 1992, Don and Michael published four issues a year containing stories, witnessing from families, small theology pieces, baking recipes, extracts from the writings of Pope John Paul II, book reviews, and some reflections on faith and culture by Michael. It was a part of the Catholic revival during the John Paul II period and was beginning to build up some momentum. In 1992, the journal reached four thousand subscribers in eleven countries. The majority of subscribers were in Canada, and the next largest number was in the United States.

Its weak point was that it depended on volunteer work and very low part-time salaries for a few enthusiasts. Despite this, the income from subscriptions did not cover the publishing costs. In 1992, there appeared some advertisements for Catholic liberal arts colleges in the United States, but still it was not sufficient. The journal depended upon the larger context of Nazareth Family Apostolate, including the retreat centre. The crisis was thus serious when after the fall issue of 1992 had been finished, Don told Michael that he and Posie were moving to the United States. They were closing down the Nazareth

Retreat Centre, and in November, it seemed as if the journal would fold as well. The main reason for moving was concern for their own children, and hence a change of milieu was a chance to recollect themselves. Thus, for the sake of their family, Don and Posie had to close down the family apostolate.

First Michael felt relief, but then Sheila asked him, "Why don't we see if there is a way *we* could keep it going." When Michael asked Don, he replied that he might be able to transfer some of Nazareth Family Apostolate's resources to Michael and Sheila, if they decided to continue working with the journal. They would have to apply to be a nonprofit organization, since the apostolate could not legally dispose of its assets to anything other than a nonprofit organization.

In the beginning of December, Michael wrote in his diary, "The magazine is being resurrected." The arrangement was that Madonna House would fund it to a degree and guarantee a salary (one thousand dollars, then raised to two thousand dollars) for Michael during two years—that is, until 1994. This was in compensation for the work that Don and Posie had done on the house in which the Nazareth Retreat Centre had been housed and which now would be returned to Madonna House. Michael had a good meeting with his spiritual director in connection with settling the arrangement.

In January 1993, the offices of *Nazareth* were transferred to the old bedroom of Michael and Sheila in Brudenell; Michael was now both publisher and editor and had to learn new skills, which included design and layout, physical production and printing processes, and so forth.

At the same time, through Bethlehem Books in the USA, Michael was selling copies of *The Mysteries of the Most Holy Rosary*, the first publication of the White Horse Press. In the 1993 Advent issue of *Nazareth*, there was an advertisement for a second publication, *The Small Angel*, a children's book written and illustrated by Michael about the smallest angel in Paradise, Nehemiah, and his way to become a guardian angel. The printing of the book was funded as a gift by some friends.

A Landscape with Dragons

In his youth, Terry, Michael's brother, left the Catholic Church, but continued to argue with God, and during a crisis later in his life, he returned to the Christian faith, now as an Evangelical Protestant.

Despite this, Michael let him publish a story in *Nazareth Journal* about a childhood experience of racism. In the same issue, there was the second instalment of Michael's analysis of modern fantasy fiction, "A Landscape with Dragons". There had been a reversal of good and evil in modern fantasy writing, Michael argued, and this was connected to a general trend in modern literature.

> Something is happening in modern literature that is unprecedented in human history. The entire symbolical life of the Western world is being turned topsy-turvy.... On practically every level of culture, in numerous works of art, good is no longer presented as good, but rather as a prejudice held by a limited religious system (Judaeo-Christianity). Neither is evil any longer perceived as evil in the way we once understood it. Evil is increasingly depicted as a means to achieve good. In fact it is not uncommon to see the meaning of the two reversed.[37]

The most conspicuous makeover, according to Michael, as shown by his choice of title, was the attempt to domesticate the dragon, the biblical symbol of supreme evil. There appeared, therefore, in children stories the themes of the misunderstood dragon, the cute dragon, and the dragon as close friend. In Michael's understanding,

> The dragon has a vested interest in having us dismiss the account of the battle as make-believe. It is not to his benefit that we, imitating our Lord the King, should take up arms against him. He thinks it better that we do not consider him dangerous.[38]

Intrigued by Michael's argument, Terry photocopied the three parts and showed them to some of his friends and to his pastor. When he found that they were quite enthusiastic, he asked Michael if they should try to make a book of the articles; Terry offered to put up the money to get it printed. Touched by his generosity, Michael agreed that it was a good idea, and in February 1994, the book *A Landscape with Dragons* was printed by Northern River Press, Terry's own little publishing house, which only published this book. In the summer the same year, Ignatius Press picked it up and distributed it together with *The Mysteries of the Most Holy Rosary* and *The Small Angel*.[39]

With Ignatius Press distributing Michael's books, the period of self-publishing was coming to a close. None of these books was a best seller in the sense that Michael and Sheila could live by the income from the sales. Nevertheless, as Michael, from 1992 to 1994, had a small income from his double job as editor and publisher of *Nazareth Journal*, he was free to engage in a number of writing projects. He not only wrote pieces in *Nazareth* and in other journals, but also worked on his novel series, the biography of Kurelek, and some smaller books. The balance in Michael's creativity was shifting toward the written word.

The last publication from the White Horse Press was *The Family and the New Totalitarianism*, published in 1995. It was a collection of six of Michael's articles that had been published in various journals, among them *Nazareth Journal* and the *Chesterton Review*. In *A Landscape with Dragons*, Michael's Christian analysis of literature is wedded to his concerns for families, and the kinds of stories children and adolescents were reading. In *The Family and the New Totalitarianism*, the theme of the family continues as a central concern, but is now connected to a critique of modern Western society. The subthemes ranged from school education, catechesis, and the gospel of life as presented by John Paul II in his encyclical *Evangelium Vitae* in 1995, to the gradual transition in the West from democracy founded on absolute values to a form of soft totalitarianism, of state-controlled social engineering. Michael put forward an alternative Christian culture, built upon the family. It was the ideal of small-scale traditional life.

> We must also support a widespread rebirth of those small, diverse and beautiful works of man which retain their human dimensions and thereby foster the full meaning of the human person. There is need for a rediscovery of the family farm, cottage industries, new and old literature that is as vital as it is true, arts and crafts that are beautiful and made with love, schools small enough so that children can be known and nurtured as unique individuals, worker-owned co-operatives, small presses, libraries, community bees, works of mercy, discussion groups, etc.—these are only a beginning.
>
> We must learn and relearn that the only effective response to degeneracy, political, cultural or otherwise, is to create an alternative culture that is so good, so beautiful and true, that man is drawn back to his own true home.[40]

We need to insert a caveat here, as 1995 was also the year when the Internet took off in earnest. A new virtual world was being created, especially for young people. If earlier in the twentieth century an arts and crafts ideal, such as that put forward by Michael, was pitted against a dirty, industrial, and mechanized society—symbolized by factories, huge turning wheels, and the railroad—now a slick, cerebral, and clean world of instant social communication of texts, pictures, and sounds was born, challenging his traditional family ideal. Michael stood on the threshold of the digital revolution, but I am not sure that he really understood that. The new possibilities of instant communication would have implications also for the fate of *Nazareth Journal*; much of its production cost was due to printing on paper and distribution by post. Now a world was opening up in which the number of copies did not change the cost; on the same budget, one could reach a thousand or a million people. The question was how Michael's dream of small-scale village life could be transposed to the world of digital media and social communications—or, if this was the task of younger generations.

15. The Absentminded Apocalyptic

In 1994, Michael had been painting sacred art for eighteen years; he had written three novels and planned to write at least one more for his series, all still unpublished; he had been editor of *Nazareth* for three years, and publisher for a year; he had written a substantial number of articles on Catholic family life, art, and literature in various periodicals; he had his own little publishing house, which had released three volumes, and one more was to appear in the coming year. Living in a large rectory in the countryside, Michael and Sheila had six children, of whom they were now homeschooling four. It was by all accounts a full life.

The year 1994 was also the climax of the pontificate of John Paul II. By 1995, he had promulgated twelve of his fourteen encyclicals, and two years earlier the major publication of *The Catechism of the Catholic Church* had been released. Despite resistance among some bishops and cardinals and a serious attempt against his life, he had, according to Michael, done heroic work in presenting the teachings of the Church with vigour and joy. Nevertheless, Michael was concerned that the Church and Western society were sliding into neo-paganism, and he saw this as part of a larger end-time scenario. The pope had not been able to turn the Church around completely.

In February, Michael had a dream about the Book of Revelation, in which he saw a sphere representing the multidimensional vision of St. John. All the symbolic scenes, with angels, the rider on the white horse, signs in the sky, and evil beasts, happened at the same time. The actual Book of Revelation was, according to Michael, the rendering of that synchronic vision of overlapping tableaus into strings of letters on a page, or scroll. The linearity of the text could give the reader a wrong, simplistic impression of events neatly lined up, one leading to the other. Michael thought the sphere of vision instead provided a view into a period at the end of history as a spiritual condition, a state of climax. What emerges from repeated reading of it is a sense of the complexity of that climax.... In the literary form of the Book, we find not so much a single chronology of events, but a layering of symbols, as if one were looking deeply into a globe of glass or water, in which numerous dramas were taking place simultaneously.[1]

He had progressed from his earlier understanding of a clear chronology of end-time events to take place during the 1990s. Now he saw the Book of Revelation as representing a period of, "3½ years, 25 years, a century or a millennium, no man knows".[2] The multilayered, achronological nature of the visions in the last book of the New Testament made them applicable to all periods in human history, but Michael still believed that there was a general progression, with overlapping periods, that would lead to the ultimate crisis. For example, besides the many manifestations of the spirit of Antichrist, there would come a single powerful person identified as *the* Antichrist, unleashing the final persecution against Christians worldwide.

One day in March 1994, when he was alone in the house, Michael made an offering of his writing to God, while listening to the Polish composer Henryk Gorecki's "Symphony of Sorrowful Songs" on a tape recorder. It included a fifteenth-century lament of the Virgin Mary, a message written by a girl on the wall of a gestapo cell, and a mother's search for her dead son—all three sung by a single soprano. The music of the first movement slowly increased in intensity and then shortly faded into almost silence before the opening song, which, through the repetition of slow circular movements, worked itself toward a climax, and then faded with a solemn dignity. Michael prayed with uplifted arms and tears in his eyes during the almost one-hour-long symphony. He offered his work to God, and thought, "Such joy and sadness combined—equally intense. My novels are impossible to publish."[3] Yet he sensed that his prayer had been heard.

In a sense, the structure of the symphony corresponded to Michael's dream of the multilayered vision of the globe. Both were constituted by repeated circular patterns proceeding with gravitas and increasing in intensity toward a climactic end. Each repeated melodic cycle was similar yet different, like the series of tribulations brought by the angels in the Book of Revelation.

Through his increased focus on writing, his pondering of the apocalypse, and his understanding of the 1990s as a crucial time period,
Michael's fertile imagination was prepared for crystallizing all of this
into the tangible form of a narrative. The great jubilee of the year
2000 was approaching and, in 1994, John Paul II released the apostolic letter *Tertio Millennio Adveniente*, which outlined the preparation
up to the year 2000—dedicating 1997 to Jesus, 1998 to the Holy
Spirit, and 1999 to God the Father.

Father Elijah

One day in April 1994, while praying in Our Lady of the Angels parish church and sorrowing over the condition of the Church and the
world, Michael understood that God was bringing something good
out of the present problems. Suddenly, there came into his mind
the story of a priest living during the end-time; and before his inner
eye an apocalyptic tale unfolded itself. Later, when looking back, he
described it in the following manner:

> This experience was so unexpected, certainly without any prompting
> from my musings or imaginings, that I was stunned. I shook it off
> as a distraction. But it wouldn't go away; it just grew and grew in a
> moment of timelessness, peace, and consolation. I kept kneeling there
> in front of the Cross, watching the story unfold in my mind, as if
> watching a film. Yes, it was like that, as if I were merely an observer.
> With this came an inner sense that I was supposed to write it down,
> and that I must ask the Holy Spirit for an angel of inspiration.[4]

For the next eight months, he spent every spare moment writing the
story and went each morning to the Blessed Sacrament to ask for an
angel of inspiration and for that day's grace for writing. Still, the writing was not without its struggles, and in April, he wrote in his diary,

> The novel of Fr. Elijah is underway but endangered by my discour-
> agement. It is, in human terms, an exercise in folly! Who will even
> buy it, read it, understand it. Yet I hear these words while praying in
> front of the Blessed Sacrament: Work on, looking neither to the left
> nor the right.

One morning in June, during his eight-month writing of *Father Elijah*, when drowsily emerging from sleep, Michael saw in his imagination the clear picture of a balding middle-aged man seated at a desk. He was lean, even ascetic, and wore a black cassock upon which rested the pectoral cross of a bishop. He was, however, not a holy man. Michael's impression when looking into his dark eyes was that of cold dedication and intelligence, devoid of charity. He wondered if the bishop was morally corrupt, or if he was an idealist, an ideologue who had infiltrated the Church to demolish it and create a new one. Then it became clear to him that this was the image of the prophet of Antichrist—perhaps he was a tool in the hands of Antichrist, or a betrayer by choice, Michael wondered; he was unsettled by the uncanny realism of the picture and the power of his imagination.

> All of the above may be a product of my imagination, because I have been pondering the various scenarios of the apocalypse and one of them includes a cardinal who betrays the very nature of the Church by acclaiming the Antichrist as "The Christ of the New Age."[5]

In this we can see how visionary seeing, in which Michael's imagination surprised him with clear pictures, even dramas, was combined with study and reflection of religious themes. The story of *Father Elijah* and its characters, including the prophet of Antichrist, appeared to him with a veracity that made him wonder if this was more than simply imagination. On the other hand, in the article "Chesterton and Paganism", published in the *Chesterton Review* in 1990, he refers to the writings of John Henry Newman on the Antichrist and to the apocalyptic novel *Lord of the World* (1907) by Robert Hugh Benson and Vladimir Soloviev's tale of the Antichrist in *Three Conversations* (1900):

> All three were highly conscious of the dissolution of the old order of things. They said in literary forms, what a number of Catholic saints, mystics, and apparitions had already warned of: that the twentieth century would be the arena of an ultimate conflict with the powers of darkness.[6]

In this way, by reading and pondering the apocalypse, and the brutal manifestations of modernity during the twentieth century—the

First World War, Nazism, Communism, and hedonist liberalism—
the way had been paved for his imagination to see a fictive apocalyptic story. This dual process matched the combination of painting
(seeing) and writing of essays and the earlier unpublished novels
(thinking) that had been part of his creative labours since the 1970s.
To be able to paint with satisfaction, Michael had to "see" the theme,
not deduce it, which made him dependent upon inspiration for creating. At the same time as he tried to be open to inspirations, he was
reading and writing, all the while reflecting on his own artistic work
in the perspective of the crushing power of totalitarian modernity.

For him the concentration camp and the Gulag were the primary
visible manifestations of Antichrist—the raw power of mechanized
society unleashing its destructive potential. Liberalism still had a
benign mask, promising to open the way to never-ending progress
and self-realization—its spell had not been broken yet.

The protagonist of the *Father Elijah* novel, David Schäfer, had
been formed by his experiences as a young Jew in the Warsaw ghetto
during World War II. Later he became Christian and a Carmelite
friar, taking the religious name Elijah and living on Mount Carmel
in Israel. After *Father Elijah* was completed, *Sophia House*, the novel
that Michael began writing in 1992, was rewritten to incorporate the
young David Schäfer.

Michael's Antichrist is a cultured politician, the president of Europe,
who will unite the diverse religions into a neo-pagan, universal religion. He promotes a spiritual, diabolical form of modernity cloaked
in a shroud of well-meaning discourses. The ecclesial prophet of the
Antichrist is the incarnation of the heresy Modernism, and both of
them are powerful ambitious men, while the true prophet, Father
Elijah, opposing them both, is an obscure survivor of the Holocaust.

On March 19, 1995, Michael sent his manuscript of *Father Elijah* to
Ignatius Press. The writing of the novel seems to have imbued him
with new energy to work on his previous as-yet-unpublished books.
He began rewriting *Strangers and Sojourners* in a cabin a friend had lent
to him, a twenty-minute walk from Brudenell.

In April 1995, Father Joseph Fessio, the publisher of Ignatius Press,
phoned Michael and expressed his interest in publishing *Father Elijah*.
The proposed release date was in spring 1996. He said he could not
promise that it would sell many copies, but he believed it should be

"out there" in the world. Sheila and Michael were awestruck that finally one of his novels was going to be published. They had difficulty believing that it was real, but were grateful to Father Fessio for taking the risk in publishing a work that would probably be controversial and might not sell well.

Later that same month, another publisher, Wm. B. Eerdmans of Grand Rapids, Michigan, wrote to say they were interested in publishing some of Michael's works, but by then he had decided for Ignatius Press, and let Eerdmans know that he withdrew his submission to them.

In the Advent 1995 issue of *Nazareth Journal*, Michael wrote that the cost of producing the journal was twice the amount they received from subscriptions, a dire situation despite the supplement of some small and large donations. The arrangement with Madonna House, which had agreed to help support the magazine until 1994, had come to an end. The problem now facing the journal's board of directors was that if the subscription fee were raised by enough to cover the costs of publishing, it would become too expensive for the intended readers. It was a shaky business model, and in November the journal was on the verge of closing down. Michael thought that Lent 1996 might be the last issue, unless something extraordinary happened.

Our Lady of Guadalupe

While *Father Elijah* was at the printer, Michael and Sheila were invited by friends to accompany them on a pilgrimage to the shrine of Our Lady of Guadalupe in Mexico. This was something that Sheila very much longed to do. In their home, there had always been a large reproduction of the famous image; they saw her not only as the Mother of the Americas, but also as the Mother of their family. And importantly for Michael, she was the woman of the Book of Revelation who would crush the serpent with her heel. Unfortunately, they could not afford the trip, as their finances were, as always, strained. Michael thus had to decline the offer, but his decision was also due to his scruples about costly pilgrimages to countries where there was great material poverty. Sheila, however, saw this from a different perspective and conspired with their friends, who decided to buy the tickets as a gift (without telling Michael) and wisely did not include cancellation insurance. When looking back later, Michael wondered if his aversion to leaving was also due to "workaholism", as he believed that he had no time to spare. But Sheila had outwitted him, and he could not back out, so somewhat unhappily he sat in the southbound airplane not knowing what was waiting for him.

His first impression after landing was that of warmth and light: his northern body, made stiff by work, winter darkness, and cold, began to relax. Moreover, his soul thawed when he saw the liveliness of devotion on the plaza in front of the Basilica of Guadalupe at Tepeyac. There were young families and children everywhere: praying, laughing, and dancing. The combination of a warm climate and lively religious life spoke to his heart, and he reflected on the contrast with his homeland: "Canada is desolate, barren, and joyless. What do we do about it? I simply do not know." His own family life had a good measure of joy, but they often felt isolated, as if they were members of a shrinking, harassed minority.

When entering the cathedral displaying the cloak of Juan Diego, on which was the famous image of Virgin Mary, he passed a five- or six-year-old boy who held out his hand begging. Michael had nothing in his pockets to offer him, but said, "Gold and silver have I none, little boy, but I give you what I have," then ruffled his hair and made the sign of the cross on his forehead. Despite his empty palms, the boy looked up at Michael, and a kind of understanding was established between them, before the boy was shooed away by the plaza guards.

A few minutes later, while praying in front of the image of the Virgin, Michael felt an invisible hand come out of the picture, ruffle his hair, and make the sign of the cross on his forehead. He was startled, but did not really understand the meaning of it until he was back on the plaza, when it dawned upon him: "We are all small beggars in God's eyes; all our important projects and deadlines are mere trifles; we are the beloved beggars of God."[7]

They also went to the place of the first apparition of Our Lady of Guadalupe, and Michael heard interiorly when praying in the apparition chapel, "I am giving you many blessings here, but many more await you when you return home."[8] When some days later they arrived in Brudenell, there was a package in the mail with the just-published volume of *Father Elijah*. Michael took it to be the blessing referred to in Mexico.

In March 1996, Michael received a contract for *Strangers and Sojourners* from Ignatius Press, which was the next novel to be published (in 1997). He had been writing and rewriting it for eighteen years; and as it was already completed, he began to work on another novel, *Eclipse of the Sun*, which was the continuation of *Strangers and Sojourners*, mirroring the European apocalyptic plot with one taking place simultaneously in Canada.

Leaving *Nazareth*

With his first novel published, Michael wanted to move away from editing in order to focus on creative writing and art. He spoke with a priest friend who confirmed Michael in his decision to let *Nazareth Journal* go. But he was still dependent on the income from the editing; he had not yet received any royalties from the sales of *Father Elijah*, and he did not know how it would sell, so it was a risky decision to make. Nevertheless, at a board meeting in April 1996, he resigned from the journal. The members of the board were supportive of his decision. They expressed strong regret that the magazine would no longer have him as editor, but several of them had read *Father Elijah* at this point and encouraged him to continue with writing fiction.

Sheila also wanted to move soon, as the house was not good for Ben's asthma. It was a smoky, dusty place. Michael wondered if they should move to Ireland, as he had heard that artists there did not pay income tax. Their economic situation became more difficult without the income from *Nazareth*; and in May, Michael wrote a begging letter to Father Fessio, who offered them royalty advances to keep them afloat. Royalty payments were paid by the publisher once a year, and the sales of *Father Elijah* had not yet begun to gain momentum.

However, by December 1996, it was becoming clear that *Father Elijah* had found its readers and was a real success. Michael had finally achieved his breakthrough.

On the day before Christmas Eve, he completed *Eclipse of the Sun*, after nine months of work. It was published in two parts, as

Ignatius Press tried to reduce the size of each volume. The first part was released in 1998 as *Eclipse of the Sun* and the second in 1999 as *Plague Journal*.

Thus, all of Michael O'Brien's apocalyptic novels were written before 1997. After that, until the return of the figure Father Elijah in 2015, he turned to other themes.

Michael and Sheila made several resolutions for the New Year—among them one that Michael would withdraw from all public speaking. In this way, he would be able to focus on painting, taking commissions for a time before returning to writing. His plan was to alternate between the two creative gifts.

From then on, he would accept painting commissions at the same time as he was writing a novel, though these would have to wait until the novel was completed. Then he would dedicate some months to painting, and after that he would return to writing.

Readers and Critics

With the publication of *Father Elijah*, Michael was not only at last having one of his novels published; he was also putting before a larger audience and professional critics one of his creations. Previously, he had published mainly essays in different Catholic periodicals and collected some of them in book form and self-published them. The novel is a different genre, driven by drama and the description of "believable" characters. The teaching tone of the essays needed to be put aside, as the success of a novel is largely measured by its power to grip the reader and enable him to surrender to the world being presented. Nevertheless, for Michael the apocalypse was not only a dramatic story; he believed he had crucial truths to communicate, and yet he decidedly did not want to seduce the reader. His insistence on sincerity and spiritual purity became integral parts of his aesthetic approach. He was convinced that he had to be true to the story that he saw with his imagination, but also that he had to uphold the moral laws governing both reality and wholesome fiction. This latter principle he based on J. R. R. Tolkien's idea of sub-creation, which he had used in his earlier analyses of the fantasy genre.[9]

Father Elijah was published only a year after the apocalyptic Protestant Left Behind series of novels had been launched, which since has grown into a major franchise with computer games, movies, and so on. In comparison with the Left Behind novels, which have sold over sixty-five million copies, Michael O'Brien's Children of the Last Days series is a minor phenomenon, at least as concerns impact in the shorter perspective. The Left Behind novels were consciously written as fast-paced suspense thrillers, while Michael is by nature much more reflective and concerned about authenticity in his approach. He did not want, as I have said, to seduce the reader, and did not hesitate when his imagination invited him to add subplots and narrative excursions. The power of the images he saw carried with them a demand for inclusion. Not surprisingly, his preface is a kind of warning to the reader, ending in the following paragraph.

> The reader should be forewarned that this book is a novel of ideas. It does not proceed at the addictive pace of a television micro-drama, nor does it offer simplistic resolutions and false piety. It offers the Cross. It bears witness, I hope, to the ultimate victory of light.[10]

Despite this warning, the novel, a Catholic apocalyptic narrative with reference to conflicts in the Church and in society, harmonized with something in the air of the mid-1990s. The book quickly found readers who deeply connected to its message. When browsing reader comments on Amazon, I frequently found responses focusing on the religious aspects, as in the following:

> Reading this book has been a spiritual experience for me. Only a few times in my life have I found myself reading a book that slowly penetrated the self-protective layers of my soul, and that led me at times to put it aside and just sort of groan in prayer. I am a Protestant, but reading this book makes me wish I were a Catholic.[11]

The comments on Goodreads provide the same impression of personal religious readings. Besides such *Lectio Divina* (Divine Reading), the readers sometimes see the book as fulfilling a prophetic role, providing an interpretation of the present times, as in the following reader response:

This is probably my favourite novel.

Father Elijah is an apocalyptic novel, but is really entirely believable ... which is probably why I found it so gripping. It is, I think, the only novel I have reread ... several times.

As I see the world unfolding, *Father Elijah* almost takes on a prophetic sense.[12]

In the reader responses, the points of criticism mostly express a difficulty with the apocalyptic theme or with technical aspects of the story telling. *Father Elijah* is sometimes demanding reading, with much dialogue and less action. The latter was also not as convincing as the spiritual aspects for some readers, as one reader expressed:

The action portions of the story, the car chases and sinister plots, were definitely not the author's strength. But he excels at writing the quiet, crucial interior journey that Father Elijah is on throughout this story. Seeing Father Elijah's choices and transformation was amazing.[13]

The cliff-hanger ending of the novel was not appreciated by some, and criticism was also directed toward too drawn-out discursive passages that could have been edited to make the story tighter. This links to what some saw as a tendency toward a didactic tone at the expense of character development and action. However, these points of criticism were often part of a general positive evaluation of the book; most readers who have rated or written comments seemed to have been captivated by *Father Elijah*, with a few exceptions. The rating at Amazon in January 2016 was 4.7 stars out of 5 (with 82 percent giving it 5 stars) and 4.33 at Goodreads.

Reviews in journals and magazines were mixed in their evaluation of the book. In 1997, there appeared a glowing review by David Lyle Jeffrey in *Books and Culture*. He considered the plot development brilliant, the characterization even more impressive, and he clearly sympathized with the message. For him, as with many of the reader responses, *Father Elijah* took on a prophetic role:

At its deepest reach, however, *Father Elijah* is a wake-up call— perhaps even (let me venture it) a last days' wake-up call to the church. What O'Brien is asking his readers to do is evident from the novel's epigraph: "Awake, and strengthen what remains and is on the point of death" (*Revelation* 3:2).... His concern as a novelist-under-obligation is to call the church at the end of the Western era to repentance and self-sacrificing ministry to those cast in doubt or shaken by betrayal from within the church as well as by enmity and scorn from without.[14]

This theme of fiction and reality, of apocalypse and modern times, was earlier put forward in a sympathetic review by Helen Valois, which concluded in the following manner:

> Michael O'Brien has certainly given us an imaginative novel to help us conceive of our own times in a different way. Like the author, however, this reviewer will leave it up to the individual reader to decide for himself whether *Father Elijah*'s perspective on the apocalypse is literally true. That his many points are well worth pondering is beyond doubt.[15]

She was, however, like some of the readers, critical of certain manners of storytelling:

> On the literary level, *Father Elijah* is reasonably well-done. The interesting plot is presented at a good pace. If the presentation has one weakness, however, it is the author's tendency to tell us about the story rather than telling us the story itself. O'Brien is much more effective when he brings us into a scene and introduces the characters and situations directly, rather than simply describing them to us from a distance.[16]

After twenty years of writing and editing his novels, Michael had now become a sensation within Catholic literature. One cannot but wonder how that affected him and his family. My impression of their material standard of living is that very little has changed. However, over the coming years his influence broadened, spreading from Canada to the United States, to Europe, and to the Hispanic world. *Father Elijah* began to appear in translations, eventually even into Swedish. In one interview, Michael was asked: "With the publication of *Father Elijah*, you have become one of those 'overnight sensations' who toiled for years and years. How has the success of the book affected you?" Michael replied:

We work hard to protect the privacy of our family life. Strangely enough, I feel rather detached from the whole mystique of "success." The real success is to love the Lord and to do his will.

Because I am deeply involved in completing several more novels and also some painting projects, my mind is always directed toward the future. I tend not to dwell on the accolades of the present. Public images are always false.[17]

When I visited him in 2011 and during other visits up to the present, my impression was that Michael and Sheila's lifestyle remained one of simplicity, with a fondness for sacred art, nature, handicraft, and books.

The Real Elijah

A curious thing is that, unbeknownst to Michael, there actually was a Carmelite friar by the name of Father Elias Friedman living on Mount Carmel in the Stella Maris Monastery. Among other similarities, Friedman was a convert from Judaism. He had founded the Association of Hebrew Catholics, an apostolate based in part on St. Paul's prophecy in his Letter to the Romans (11:1–2, 25–32, and also his Letters to the Thessalonians) that the whole household of Israel, the Jewish race, would one day come to Christ after "the full number of Gentiles has come in". In this sense, like the fictional Father Elijah, the work of Father Elias has an apocalyptic dimension, preparing the way for a period during the end-time when converts from Judaism would need help finding their home in the Church.

After the publication of *Father Elijah*, Michael received letters from around the world, asking him if Father Friedman was the model for the central character of the novel. This was not the case, as Michael had never heard about him before. In 1997, a Canadian pilgrim returning from Israel wrote to Michael, telling him about his meeting with Father Friedman, and gave him the priest's address. Immediately, he sat down and composed a long letter in which he explained his novel and reassured the real Father Elijah:

Perhaps, you are somewhat concerned that my fictional character will be too much identified with you. I surely see some potential for confusion in this, because your work is very important, and my novel is only a minor note in Catholic literature. I hope you will feel free to share this letter with anyone who may be confused about this. I want to assure you that my "Fr. Elijah" is entirely imaginary, a character plunged into one of many possible scenarios that might develop in the actual unfolding of history. It is entirely a speculation. It merely asks the question: What if? What if it turns out this way?[18]

In August 1997, Michael received a postcard with a reply from the Stella Maris Monastery:

Moved by your communication of July 23, 1997, very much so. Reckon there is more to it than mere coincidence. The AHC needed the publicity.
    Still waiting for the Holy See to call me!
    I feel we are bonded!

In J & M, Elias Friedman O.C.D.[19]

Strangers and Sojourners

After the publication of *Father Elijah*, Michael promised Ignatius Press to write five more novels in his Children of the Last Days series. Fortunately, as he had written for many years without being published, he had a backlog of manuscripts. In the middle of March 1997, *Strangers and Sojourners*, on which he had worked on and off since the 1970s, was published. Despite being included in the series, its content was not explicitly apocalyptic. The story was quite different from *Father Elijah*. One reviewer put the contrast in the following way:

One is tempted to refer to *Father Elijah* as "a man's book" full of action, political and ecclesiastical intrigue, whereas *Strangers and Sojourners*, O'Brien's second published novel could be called a "women's book." But both designations would be limiting. In *Strangers and Sojourners*, O'Brien takes us deep into the inner life of a refined and cultured English woman, Anna Kingsley Ashton. He does so through narrative, her own diary entries and daydreams. From her childhood at the turn of the century to her death in 1976 O'Brien takes us through the experiences, dreams and tragedies that touch and set the course of her sojourn through life.[20]

The absence of a thrilling apocalyptic plot disappointed some read-ers, who found it slow and not very exciting reading.[21] However, the majority of reader responses seemed to be enthusiastic, and what deterred some readers—that is, a slow-moving plot, the focus on interiority, and use of letters within the narrative—drew them into the characters, their psychological and spiritual struggles. In the *Pem-broke Observer*, Peter Lapinskie noted in his review:

> O'Brien's ability to take you deep inside his characters, right to the essence of their very souls, is what sets him apart from most modern writers who barely scratch the surface of their protagonists. In *Strangers and Sojourners*, you will find yourself experiencing many of the emo-tions the Delaneys feel. There were times I chuckled out loud and others where I was reaching for a Kleenex.[22]

With *Strangers and Sojourners*, Michael took a risk with his readers, but avoided at the same time a significant danger. If he had cashed in on the success of the apocalyptic story line (as the authors of the Left Behind series did) and released a second suspense-filled book, he might have achieved higher sales. However, his desire to give energy to a Catholic vision of life would then probably have been compro-mised. The apocalyptic plot was, for Michael, one important way of understanding the present times, but only part of a larger sacramental understanding of life: building upon the progression from sin to grace and conversion.[23] For Michael, sincerity, being true to his inspira-tion, was always more important than success.

Strangers and Sojourners was conceived and written in the 1970s, though rewritten during the 1980s and 1990s. In 1998 and 1999, two more novels were published that continued where *Strangers and Sojourners* ended, forming a trilogy that recounted the history of the fictional Delaney family in the mountains of British Columbia. How-ever, the plot of the latter two novels now turned to end-time sce-narios. They had in essence already been written in 1996. In 1998 Michael's literary imagination turned to other themes, that of father-hood and the role of Russia, which would lead him to make research trips to Russia in 1999 and 2000.

Since the beginning of 1998, Michael suffered two bouts of bron-chitis and a spell of pneumonia, but at the same time, as he wrote in his diary, he received many graces. He was happy with the beauty of his children and their faith; a large crowd had come to his talk and exhibit at the Church of St. Barnabas in Ottawa; and, it was the finale event of his time as guest lecturer at Augustine College, a small ecumenical college devoted to the liberal arts. For the time being, the royalties from his books were now so high that they could almost live on them; *Eclipse of the Sun* would be published in two weeks, and he had learned that a person had been converted after reading *Father Elijah*. He was also looking forward to going to Rome during Pentecost to give a talk at a Marian conference.

Rome

One of the persons who attended a Nazareth retreat in the early 1990s was Dr. Mark Miravalle, a professor at Franciscan University of Steubenville in Ohio, where he had been teaching since 1986. He was and is prominent among American theologians in his work for the pope to proclaim a fifth Marian dogma—the Virgin Mary as Co-Redemptrix, Mediatrix of All Graces, and Advocate for the People of God.[24] Moreover, Miravalle had a strong interest in contemporary Marian private revelations. In 1985, he defended his doctoral thesis at the Angelicum in Rome (the Pontifical University of Saint Thomas Aquinas), on the messages of the Međugorje apparitions in Bosnia-Hercegovina.[25] After the Nazareth retreat, Michael and Miravalle kept in touch, discussing things mostly over the phone. Sometimes it was personal matters, but they also talked about issues and concerns relating to the Church.[26]

In 1997, after Michael visited him in Steubenville, Miravalle invited him to give a talk at the international conference in Rome regarding Vox Populi Mariae Mediatrici (Voice of the People for Mary Mediatrix), the organization that worked for the proclamation of the fifth Marian dogma and of which Miravalle was president.[27] The conference took place during Pentecost 1998, and Michael's talk was titled "The Hidden Face: Our Lady Reveals the Father".[28] Michael, who began by apologizing for not being a theologian, mainly used pictures and stories to make his points. He described his awe when, before the talk, he had looked at one of the many large pinecones littering the street outside the conference centre. Suddenly, for the first time, he had seen the incredible design of the pinecone, with its many seeds each containing the code of a potential, unique, individual tree. The point was how we need to see ordinary things with new eyes if we want to perceive the Father through His works; otherwise, the pinecone is merely one of many marvels we either ignore or blindly crush beneath our feet.

To illustrate the mediating role of Mary, he told the story of how every night he went to the beds of each of his children, prayed with them, and blessed them with holy water. When coming to the last bed, he was sometimes very tired after a long day. One evening, exhausted, he lay his head on the pillow of the child last in line for blessings, and she said, "Papa, can I say a prayer for you and can I bless you?" Surprised, Michael answered, "Oh, yes, Angela, I would love that very much." The little child closed her eyes, put her hands on her father's forehead, and began to whisper prayers to God the Father. This developed into a habit, and every evening for some months afterwards, Michael was both blessing and being blessed. One day, he said to her, "You know, I am very grateful for your prayers for me." She looked deep into his eyes, put her hand on his shoulder, and answered compassionately, "Yes, Papa, I have noticed a great improvement."[29]

When he told this story, the audience roared with laughter.

Part of the plot of *Father Elijah* takes place in Rome, but Michael had never visited the Eternal City before. For him it was thrilling to walk through its streets and to visit places that he had included in the novel. He sometimes stopped and imagined himself witnessing scenes from the story being enacted before his own eyes.

On Sunday morning, he attended the Pentecost Mass in St. Peter's Square and found the pope's homily clear and strong: "a holy old lion of God invoking over and over, *Veni Creator Spiritus*".[30]

16. A New Beginning

A Home

Ever since they sold their house in Blue River in 1982, Michael and Sheila had not had a home of their own. They rented various houses in Valemount, Mission, and Brudenell, sometimes being caretakers of a church, but they were always dependent upon finding something with a very low rent to make ends meet. It was the result of choosing the painting of sacred art—a life with limited economic resources, balancing on the social margins. Lacking a stable place on earth, a place to call their own, they had constantly wondered where they were supposed to live, always feeling that the present situation was temporary, not really the place where they belonged. Like many families, their dream was to find a piece of land where they could grow things, create art, and build a family culture, without being plagued with the knowledge that soon they had to uproot and leave again. Their restlessness was also caused by the longing for a community of likeminded people, in which they would feel at home and be part of something larger.

They knew that Brudenell was not a long-term solution, and in May 1997, Michael wondered where they should go: San Francisco, the home of Ignatius Press; or Steubenville, Ohio, where there was a dynamic Catholic university; or Combermere, thus drawing even closer to Madonna House? The choice was whether they were to leave Canada altogether in search of a community, or if they should deepen what they already had. The following year, with the increasing revenue from the sale of Michael's novels, they were in a position actually to buy a house: not an expensive one, and it would be largely owned by the bank, as Michael said, but a home of their own nevertheless.

After prayer and much discussion, they decided to move closer to Madonna House and the community of Catholic families living in and around Combermere. Within their income bracket, there was little to rent or buy in the Combermere area, but they kept searching and finally found an old refurbished farmhouse on 14 Maplewood Road, available for purchase at a low cost, and about a ten-minute drive from the village. They were required to offer a large down payment, which ate deep into their income from the sales of *Father Elijah*, but with this the bank hesitantly agreed to give them a mortgage.

The move was in June 1998, and several local families came to help, resulting in a veritable fleet of cars, including a memorable pickup truck that crashed enroute, when it was making the half-hour drive from the old rectory in Brudenell to Maplewood Road. The O'Brien family was happy to move from relative isolation to a thriving community of strong believers.

Their new home was a T-shaped, single-storey house with typical North American, pale grey, horizontal boards; large windows with shutters; and a roof consisting of black shingles. In the wing to the left was the kitchen, with an impressive centrally placed iron cookstove, and further on were three small bedrooms. Michael built a studio room onto the end of the house, where he both wrote and painted. Some years later, when his aged mother, Elaine, came to live with them, she moved into the studio, and he built a separate studio building, a one-room cabin heated by an iron woodstove.

The great living room with its massive fireplace was not insulated, and the Canadian winters in Combermere were long and cold. As countermeasures, they covered the walls with bookshelves and installed an airtight wood-burning heater. In the corner stood their old upright piano, which Sheila and the children all played. Elizabeth and Ben were especially musical, learning fiddle and accordion as well—the accordion once belonging to William Kurelek and given to Michael by Kurelek's widow.

On the wall facing the forest, beside a large picture window, they hung two of Michael's paintings, one on each side of a wooden crucifix. They were painted in clear hues of blue and red. One of them was of the Sacred Heart of Jesus, and the other was of the Immaculate Heart of Mary; both Jesus and His mother were looking straight at the beholder, intensively and compassionately. Beneath the two paintings, on the home altar, was a statue of St. Joseph holding the Christ Child. It was here that the family prayed their Rosary in the evenings and the Divine Mercy Chaplet at three o'clock in the afternoon. Most mornings, they attended Mass at the local parish, Canadian Martyrs.

My impression when visiting in 2011 was of a home that focused on art and letters, gardening, and handicraft; it was, however, not a hip installation showcasing a calculated rustic identity. The lack of economic resources was palpable; nothing was new and shiny, but rather, old and weather-beaten. There was no designed uniformity; still, the structure of things was simple and orderly. The deep saturated red of the kitchen cabinet doors, together with the herbs being dried on a grate above the wood-burning stove, and the tomatoes and pumpkins ripening on the windowsill, radiated a homely, organic atmosphere. The one thing that broke this atmosphere was the Apple computer in Michael's studio with its sleek, silvery design. But for the first three years, Michael did not have an Internet connection in his studio. Besides the old car parked in the driveway, this was their one major concession to modernity. However, Sheila refused to come near the computer or to use any cell phone, whether smart or not. To this day, she refuses to become "cyberliterate". She has a rich correspondence by regular post and loves to make home-crafted greeting cards for friends and family. Michael is her "scribe" on the Internet, and, as he says humorously, "She's one of the few free women on the planet."

Behind the house was a grassy area sloping toward the forest edge, against which the silhouette of a large wooden Celtic cross stood as a landmark. Close to the house, Sheila had her kitchen garden, where she grew vegetables and herbs. In the middle of the seedbed stood a statue of St. Francis, the saint with a special love of God's nature.

They also had a chicken coop, and a grey board henhouse with a bright red door, which Michael named the "Palazzo Poletti". To this refuge, their small band of chickens retreated during the nights. They had a particularly close relationship to Michael; at times, he was the only one who could calm them down when they were threatened by predators such as raccoons and foxes; they would stop shrieking and instead begin clucking softly when they heard his voice—something they did not do for anyone else.

From the O'Brien house, one could not see the house of any neighbour, surrounded by trees as it was in all directions, but Madonna

House was a ten-minute drive away, and a few kilometres down the road were close friends with a large family of children the ages of the O'Brien's children. There were more homeschooling families in the Combermere area than was the case in Brudenell, which was great for the children. Sheila and Michael also had what one of the children described as an open-door policy. In addition to friends, neighbours, teachers, and students, various people visited in connection with Michael's work—so it was a very busy household. The challenge was always how to balance hospitality with the developmental and educational needs of the children, plus the solitude required for Michael's creative work.

The two older girls were now in their teens: Mary was seventeen and Elizabeth fifteen years old, while Ben was eleven and Angela eight. For them the move to Combermere was a definite change for the better. They could now see their friends almost every day, and they were intensely involved in the local parish only a few minutes' drive away in the village of Combermere.

The outdoor life that had begun in Brudenell continued with hikes and adventures. There was a small lake not far from the house where they did some canoeing and swimming all summer. Sometimes Ben would get together with friends who brought their homemade swords and shields, and together they would stage mock battles in the O'Brien backyard, inspired by scenes from *The Lord of the Rings*. Though on occasion the garden would be trampled by the warriors, for the most part their battles took place in the surrounding woods.

Sheila was open-minded when it came to the tricky question of pets, which for most families is an area where parental control is necessary—that is, if the home is not to turn into a zoo. Besides the chickens, Elizabeth raised two baby raccoons, while Ben had a flock of pigeons in the garage loft. As if this was not enough, they had a wild turtle and a mongrel dog named Sam, who loved to throw his head back and howl "musically" beside the piano whenever the children played. Unfortunately, Sam had a Dr. Jekyll and Mr. Hyde temperament, being the model dog when at home; but, now and then, he would slip away on a tour of destruction and death. They began to receive phone calls from angry neighbours complaining about killed chickens and destroyed gardens. This meant that Sam had to be put down to preserve the peace of Combermere. The children were, of course, sad, but, not long after, John was given a white collie dog, which he brought home. Chester (short for Chesterton) lived with the O'Briens for many years until his death from old age and disease.

With the publication of his novels, Michael was becoming increasingly well known, but he tried to keep that out of the local context, and on principle he did not often speak about his work in front of the children. When on occasion they had a family discussion about Michael's work, he deliberately downplayed his personal importance. It was only when Ben joined him on a trip to Ottawa or Toronto for one of his talks that he caught a glimpse of his father's public role. For the children, Michael was more a painter than a writer, as the novel-writing phase came later in his life, and he never made much fuss about it. Writing is also a more abstract art, while for a child, painting is immediately accessible. As the children grew older, Michael let them read pre-publication manuscripts and asked them to offer suggestions. But his first and foremost editor was Sheila, who read all his manuscripts with a sharp and unsentimental eye.

More Novels

With the success of *Father Elijah* and the publishing pace of one novel a year, Michael's life was reaching a climax of intense activity. In September 1998, just three months after moving, he felt burnout symptoms and could not work creatively. This lasted for a month; he just went to the studio every day and prayed, read Scripture, and waited in silence for God to relight the fires of creativity.

Plague Journal was published in 1999—but it had been written already two years earlier together with the *Eclipse of the Sun*—and concluded the Canadian part of the Children of the Last Days series. After that, there was a gap until 2003 when *A Cry of Stone* was published, but this was written even earlier; in fact, it was his first novel that he had written in 1977, though he later revised it in a major way. Then *Sophia House*, the prequel to *Father Elijah*, was published in 2005, though it had been more or less written before his breakthrough.

It was with *Island of the World* in 2007, and the following *Theophilos* in 2010, *The Father's Tale* in 2011, and *Voyage to Alpha Centauri* in 2013, that we can discern a new creative phase with completely new stories and themes that did not form part of the previous series of novels. It was as if the end-time had been put on hold.

Island of the World is set in Croatia and Bosnia-Herzegovina in the middle of the twentieth century and is a historical novel—which is also true of *Theophilos*, an imaginative background story to the Gospel of Luke and the Acts of the Apostles, written in diary form— while *The Father's Tale* is set in contemporary Russia. Finally, with *Voyage to Alpha Centauri*, Michael made a daring incursion into the science-fiction genre, despite his discomfort with technology. All of these were voluminous novels thematically unconnected to each other. It was as if a new wave of creative energy had been unleashed in Michael's imagination. My impression is that all the unpublished novels, written before *Father Elijah* and closely after it, first had to be released, and that only then could the author begin anew. The pause between these two phases was also due to the extensive research demanded by the new novels. The story of *The Father's Tale* was largely set in Russia, and Michael made two research journeys to Russia (in 1999 and 2000).[1] It signified an increasing shift of interest on his part toward Central and Eastern Europe, which of course for a long time had been a natural part of his spirituality through his icon painting and connection to Madonna House. But now it surfaced also in his novels.

Another reason may be that it was in the Czech Republic and then in Croatia that his novels were first published in translations. The warm reception of his storytelling and religious message was an overwhelming experience for him, especially in the case of Croatia, to which we will return later. Something in Michael's creative sensibility spoke to Christians who had experienced Communist oppression; perhaps the crucial part was his understanding of (and the literary form he gave to) experiences of suffering under totalitarianism, as seen through the perspective of a strong inner religious conviction.

The cultural climate of the West in the beginning of the twenty-first century was still firmly anchored in the belief of consumerist hedonism as a viable lifestyle. However, the terrorist attacks in New York on September 11, 2001, and the subsequent global war on Islamist terrorism, slowly eroded the self-confidence of both the neo-conservative and liberal camps. The stillborn Arab Spring of 2011 and the rise of the Islamic State in Syria and Iraq destabilized Europe through a massive wave of immigrants, and interestingly also laid bare a cultural divide between Eastern and Western Europe.

In 2014, Michael returned to writing the conclusion of the story of *Father Elijah*, which had been left dangling since 1996. In the sequel, most of the thriller elements are gone. The widespread apocalyptic expectations of the great jubilee of 2000 had faded, but Michael continued to be concerned by the way apocalyptic elements in the emerging third millennium were growing stronger—particularly the seemingly unstoppable apostasy from traditional Christian faith. At the same time, the savage nature of Islamist terrorism now not only upset the whole of the Muslim world from Afghanistan to Morocco; it also struck in the metropolises of both Europe and North America. The sense was of, if not the end of times, then at least a premonition of the end of civilization. Michael's final instalment of the Children of the Last Days series was appropriately titled *Elijah in Jerusalem*. The antagonist, that is the Antichrist, was still the personification of Western modernity, the president of Europe, the cultured peacemaker, and religious syncretist. However, he is not present in the narrative until the end, and then only briefly. The story focuses almost entirely on the interior drama of Father Elijah's mission, and his effect on a variety of characters—an exploration of human spiritual conditions and psychology during a time of ultimate testing.

In the preface to the novel, Michael warns the reader against treating his fiction as a prophecy that provides a roadmap for the coming end-time. But how should one then read it? "What, then, is the role of Christian fiction in this regard? If it is to be an authentic contribution to faith, its primary mission must be to awaken the reader's imagination in such a way that he is recalled to the basic principles of life in Christ. It does not attempt to predict the future, but rather, in the sense of Tolkien's concept of 'sub-creation', it offers an imaginative possibility for the purpose of stimulating reflection."[2]

Justin Press

In 2009, Michael began to collaborate with a small, newly established Catholic publisher in Ottawa, Justin Press. With them, he published some older texts, including the biography of Kurelek and anthologies

of his articles and short stories, as well as his correspondence with
Mate Krajina, a Croatian Catholic publisher.

Dr. John Gay, one of the founders of Justin Press and presently
president of the board of directors, acknowledged that it was with
some diffidence he approached Michael after a Sunday Mass. His
mission was to ask Michael if he would be willing to publish something with them. His worries were unfounded.

> His [Michael's] response was immediate; he had, he said, six manu-
> scripts already prepared or nearly so, and was delighted with the pro-
> posal. I remember him saying that Justin Press sounded like "just what
> we need in Canada." This was, in fact, just what Justin Press needed:
> a Canadian Catholic author with an established reputation, and not
> only in Canada.[3]

Michael was under contract with Ignatius Press for his novels, but
not for nonfiction or short stories, which opened up a possibility
for cooperation with Justin Press. With this new outlet for his writings, Michael's backlog of unpublished nonfiction manuscripts more
or less emptied out.[4] The first volume, *Remembrance of the Future*, a
collection of his essays, was beset with some technical difficulties as
the new publisher was learning the trade, so to speak. Nevertheless,
despite expressing some concerns, Michael continued to publish with
Justin Press, and he also allowed them free access to his paintings as
cover images for his books and those by other authors.

John Gay believes it is unlikely that Justin Press would exist today
if it had not been for his support. The initiative spoke to the pioneer
spirit of Michael, which has been a recurrent pattern throughout his
life. He could not help but support projects that worked toward a
rejuvenation of Catholicism, even when they lacked the prospect
of anything resembling great success. We saw it earlier in his work
with *Nazareth Journal* and in his unflinching adherence to a Catholic
perspective in his paintings and novels, even though he knew it kept
him decisively outside the mainstream of Western culture and society. The lack of resources and the impossible and humble nature of
the task appealed to his spiritual instincts.

In my conversation with John Gay, he confessed that he was
somewhat surprised that Michael seemed to be more known in the

United States than in Canada. As an example, he told me about an episode when attending a parish supper in Barry's Bay, not far from Combermere. He had begun to talk politely with the woman beside him, and remarked on the good fortune at having so distinguished a Catholic author as Michael O'Brien in their midst—upon which she replied: "Michael who?" It seems that Michael had succeeded not only in keeping his children largely unaware of how widely known he was, but also the local parishes.

17. Our Lady Seat of Wisdom

Since the late 1980s, Sheila had undertaken the hard work of home-schooling their six children. She had been prepared by her teacher training, and by her pioneer experience in British Columbia, but homeschooling is possible only up to grade twelve. Then it is time for college, but where should their children study? This question was important for Sheila as she was convinced that the age between eighteen and twenty was the period when young people were especially open to existential, and thus religious, questions. This was reinforced when she received a postcard from her niece, Theresa Ulmer, whose family had embarked on the ultimate adventure of crossing the Pacific Ocean in a small sailboat, their only home. Theresa had always been a devout girl, and while on watch one starry night, she wrote a postcard to Sheila saying, "It isn't that I don't believe in God anymore, Auntie. It's just that I have such Big Questions."

A few weeks later, their son John brought home an Irish student from Franciscan University of Steubenville, who underlined the message on the postcard, by telling Sheila that he planned to go back to Ireland, "to teach seventeen to twenty-three-year-olds because that is the time of the big questions".[1]

As one can see in the advertisements in *Nazareth Journal*, it was the new Catholic colleges in the United States (with their explicit faithfulness to the teachings of the Church) that were the natural destination for children within the Canadian Catholic revivalist subculture. However, Michael and Sheila were not happy with how this had played out for John and Joseph, who had left home for high school. Now Mary was of college age, ready to tackle the Big Questions, but they did not consider her ready yet to engage the cultural revolution reigning at secular universities.

Furthermore, there was not much possibility of sending the children to college in the United States, due to the high tuition fees and the weak Canadian dollar. And, according to Michael and Sheila,

Canadian Catholic colleges had become mixtures of "liberal theology, moral relativism, syncretistic philosophies, and generally rudderless concepts of education".[2]

It was this sorry state of affairs that compelled Sheila to make an eight-kilometre prayer walk to the pilgrimage statue of Our Lady of Combermere and ask for guidance. She was pondering the idea of a postsecondary institution in the Madawaska Valley. Not long after, on the steps of the Canadian Martyrs Catholic Church, a small group of mothers were sharing the same concerns. They were joined in the discussion by a young student who had just graduated from Franciscan University, George Dienesch, who enthusiastically agreed to participate in a novena to Our Lady of Combermere for direction. Within that first novena, they decided to establish the Mater Ecclesia Study Centre for six young students who were willing to spend a year studying a nonaccredited, postsecondary curriculum. It would be based on Cardinal Newman's seminal book *The Idea of a University* and the Catholic Church's teachings on the role of higher education.[3] They realized that there was no time to seek the sponsorship of ecclesial leadership because the young people's need was so immediate. In the beginning, it had to be a lay initiative, but before long the local bishop (and his successors) encouraged them to continue.

George persuaded another graduate from Steubenville, Luc Dauvin, to join him as a teacher, and, without receiving a salary, these young men launched the inaugural year. Within the first semester, they were joined by a third professor, John-Paul Meenan, who held a master's degree in science and who had also recently completed his theology studies at the Toronto Oratory of St. Philip Neri. He agreed to teach and further define the initial curriculum. With almost no funds or salaries, and existing on savings and stipends given by parents, the three stalwarts began to teach their faith-oriented liberal arts program.

The group met in the O'Brien living room and in a neighbour's barn, eating lunch with the families or packing their own. Every Wednesday, they either went for a hike in the magnificent scenery of the valley, or for a pilgrimage, or a visit to Ottawa museums or cultural events. When the weather was good, they had classes outside.

One of the students remembers the adventurous feeling of being involved in something unique and completely outside of the beaten track. For example, they would carry a few volumes of Plato, Aristotle, and St. Thomas Aquinas in their backpacks and drive to a remote location in pickup trucks, and, then, seated around a campfire, spend the morning debating and discussing ethical questions against a backdrop of the colourful spectacle of the Canadian autumn hardwood forests.[4]

Behind the scenes, more parents became involved, and, led by the work of a dynamic mother, Helen Fritz, the original charter was registered, tax exemption status obtained, and during the winter of 1999, the name Our Lady Seat of Wisdom Academy (OLSWA) was chosen. At this time, the vacant St. Joseph's convent in the nearby town of Barry's Bay was offered to the academy in exchange for sharing the upkeep with the diocese. Also, they received a library of thirty thousand volumes from a Cistercian monastery outside Orangeville, Ontario, which was closing. Now they had a building, a library, and more teachers, including Scott Nicholson, another graduate from the Oratory, and some support staff, all working for a small stipend.

OLSWA's inaugural year had nine students signed up for a one-year program that now included philosophy, history, magisterial thought, biblical studies, and Latin. As one of the teachers expressed it, "What was lacking in salary for faculty and staff was more than made up for by the students' zeal for knowledge, and the adventure of starting a vibrant, orthodox Catholic college fully faithful to the Magisterium."[5] This first one-year program functioned as a bridge between high school and university. During the following years, two more years were added to the program, and some universities began to accept their credits for transfer, so that students could complete an undergraduate degree. Now, only nineteen years later, there exists in Barry's Bay a thriving college with well over a hundred students annually. Most of the students have gone on to professional careers, and more than fifty marriages have been formed between students, as well as many religious vocations that began during studies at OLSWA. The alumni include ordained priests, seminarians, and active and contemplative religious. To Sheila and Michael this was part of the new springtime of faith that John Paul II had encouraged. On May 1, 2017, the government conferred upon OSLW full degree-granting status as a university-level college.

In the early years of the academy, a number of alumni had the opportunity to study with Michael, who taught an art history course, with lectures and slide shows. Then as the demands of his writing and travels increased, he had to leave teaching aside. In 2007, the then president of the academy, the late Dr. David Warner, asked him to become artist and writer in residence. This involved occasional lectures on faith and culture, as well as some promotional work, as the academy continued to grow. In 2011, the succeeding president, Dr. Keith Cassidy, asked Michael to resume teaching, this time with a more developed course, Introduction to Fine Arts, which he taught until Spring 2018.[6] He continues to teach there as a guest lecturer, and is permanent artist and writer in residence.

18. On and Off the Grid

The Virtual World

After the publication of *Father Elijah* in 1996, Michael's life became increasingly public, and he had to respond to a continual influx of invitations to travel and speak all over the world. In order to be able to continue with his creative life, he decided to decline most invitations—95 percent, he said when I asked him in 2013, which was up 5 percent since 2011, when he had declared the level to be at 90 percent. He declined these offers with a heavy heart, as there were so many pressing issues of faith and culture on which he would like to speak.

During the first years in his studio in Combermere, he only used his large Mac LC (low cost) computer as a word processor. The texts he wrote had to be distributed by a publisher, and the paintings he created were accessible only where they were physically present—in churches, monasteries, and private homes. With the rise of the Internet and the World Wide Web during the 1990s, this situation changed. If he wanted, Michael could now send his texts directly to readers and display his paintings online so that millions could access them. Some years later it became possible to record talks and make them available in video format. In this way, he could make up for all the declined invitations and, in a way, multiply his presence.

The Internet became not only a means to communicate more efficiently. Increasingly this electronically created space—including interactive games, chat forums, and burgeoning social media—came to constitute multiple worlds of its own. In the twenty-first century, many young people live large parts of their lives online; for them these electronically processed machine environments are mediated worlds, as real as the ordinary world—perhaps even more real.

A cultural phenomenon that captured this perceptual shift in what constitutes a "living space" was the film *The Matrix*, released in 1999.

Its main theme is that the Western world of the 1990s is actually a computer-generated virtual reality, an elaborate illusion manufactured by intelligent, malevolent machines. The main protagonist, Neo, is offered the crucial choice: to wake up and face reality, symbolized by a red pill, or to remain within the comfortable illusory world, a choice symbolized by a blue pill. He chooses the red pill and wakes up to a harsh world in which the machines harvest bioenergy from humans plugged into the Matrix, the virtual reality of the 1990s.[1]

The question facing Michael was whether the growing cyberworld had to be taken seriously as a mission field, requiring a new form of evangelization. On the other hand, if it was a powerful gnostic deception, an overwhelming new "psychological cosmos", as suggested by *The Matrix*, how was one then to interact with it? And if it was both, what then?

In the late 1990s, Michael's visceral dislike for the artificial nature of computer technology prevented him from wholeheartedly venturing into such a project of cyberevangelization. Like his friend Peter Kreeft, a philosopher and Catholic apologist at Boston College and author of more than fifty books, he saw something potentially corrupting in the disembodied nature of computer-generated communication and virtual worlds.

The physical book, on the other hand, has a reassuring materiality, with texture, weight, and even smell. It adorns the walls of your home and has a long, distinguished tradition, closely connected to several thousand years of written scriptures. Electronic communications, on the other hand, bind humans to screens, which when switched off retain nothing of their information imprint. The electronic worlds are ominously evanescent, and volatile.

For Michael the computer, like television, was a *palantir*, one of the crystal globes in *The Lord of the Rings* that show those who look into them things far away, but which can selectively induce deceptions and despair in the viewer. According to Michael, the gaze mediated by the screen was dangerously seductive and addictive. He doubted that the cyberworld was just a neutral arena, and, for some time, he resisted building an online presence. Still, Michael's visceral *non possumus* to electronic communications was to change through a serendipitous accident in the Great Jubilee Year 2000.

An Accident

In 1997, when living in Brudenell, Michael had received a telephone call from a young man, Anton (Tony) Časta, who was finishing his second master's degree in environmental science at the University of Waterloo. At that time, Tony was trying to persuade the board of directors of *Nazareth Journal* to take the step from a printed magazine to an online presence. He argued that they then could multiply the outreach without increased cost—but they hesitated. During the telephone conversation, Tony presented his case to Michael, who had resigned a year earlier as editor of the magazine. He remembers Michael as being very kind and understanding,[2] but he was no longer involved in the *Nazareth* apostolate. Michael thought the idea was good, but did not see how it could be done, considering the apostolate's dwindling resources, so he left it to the board to decide.

In 1995, Tony and his wife, Monique, had participated in a Nazareth retreat in Bancroft, Ontario, where former members of the Nazareth circle continued the program of family retreats that Don and Posie McPhee had built up in the early 1990s. This had sown a seed in the Častas' minds of trying out an alternative way of life with a spiritual focus in the woods of Combermere. They were one of the families drawn out of the cities into the countryside in this way, first by the attraction of Madonna House, and then by the sheer critical mass of families clustering around it. This had been the case for Michael and Sheila, but Tony and Monique did not yet know that there was an established Catholic family network in the area.

At the time, they had three children and thought, "Why not try it out for a year." Said and done; in January 2000, they put all their belongings into a large moving truck and waved goodbye to their friends, who, unsurprisingly, thought they were insane. "What are you going to do in the wilderness?" they asked. Tony had achieved some momentum in his work, as he had created the first website for LifeSite, the Internet news and information site initiated by the Canadian pro-life organization Campaign Life Coalition (CLC) in 1997.[3] Moreover, he would be able to continue to work over the Internet as he now mainly designed websites as part of the evangelization of new media.

The decision to become a media missionary was as bold as the move away from the city, and in a sense parallel to Michael's decision for sacred art. Tony worked with security encryption technology, when he, together with Monique, chose the materially much more insecure way of life of a media apostolate.[4]

On April 2, 2000—that is, on Michael's fifty-second birthday—Tony and Monique had a car accident on the highway just below the hill of the O'Brien home. Michael was one of the first to assist them after the accident, and in that way a friendship began that would lead him, despite protests, onto the Internet. In the ensuing months, he and Tony began to discuss many issues regarding the new evangelization, and Tony argued forcefully for the need to engage with new media as "roads" of evangelization.

As I said, Michael entered the Internet by an accident—or perhaps one should say because of his willingness to help. He could not help himself.

LifeSite

The story of John-Henry Westen, one of the founders of LifeSite and its present editor in chief, and his wife, Dianne, is similar to that of Tony and Monique. They were of the same generation, born when Michael was in his twenties. Despite living in Toronto, they agreed that a big city was not the ideal place to raise their children. Therefore in 1994, they moved to Bancroft, a small town of four thousand inhabitants fifty kilometres south of Combermere, the same place where Tony and Monique a year later attended a Nazareth retreat. After a while, they felt restless again and began to search for a place with a stronger Catholic community—one in which they could fit with their growing family and their habit of attending daily Mass.

During their discernment process, they heard about the vibrant Catholic homeschooling community in Combermere, only a forty-five-minute drive from Bancroft. One Sunday in 1999, they drove out and attended Mass in the Church of the Holy Canadian Martyrs to see what it was like. They loved the warm friendliness of the parishioners, including the O'Briens; and shortly after the visit, Michael invited them to his and Sheila's home in Combermere.

When there, the two couples immediately fell into an engrossing conversation centred on faith and family. For John-Henry it was like meeting a long lost older brother, not a stranger whom he had only just met.

Having found what they had been looking for, John-Henry and Dianne tried to sell their house in Bancroft; they finally succeeded in 2001 and moved to Combermere. At the time, they had four children and one on the way, and they became part of the larger, loosely connected network of Catholic homeschoolers.

In 2013, Michael joined John-Henry on the board of directors of LifeSite, but Michael had already been a regular speaker at the organization's annual meetings for some years. His main role had been that of providing spiritual inspiration for the employees. With a more formal role on the board in 2013, he also had to vote on decisions affecting the growth and direction of the Internet apostolate. It is an important function, as the website is the largest Catholic pro-life news service in the world, with millions of visitors each month.[5] Somewhat ironically, despite his reservations about electronic communications, Michael in this way became drawn into one of the largest Catholic Internet apostolates. His openness to a younger generation, especially through ties of friendship, overcame his deep cyberscepticism. But he was never completely converted, and there is still an undercurrent in his mind dreaming of a simple life, more organic than technological.

Personality

The personality of Michael is a particular combination of sometimes conflicting traits: unassuming manners, dressing simply and not putting himself forward, being almost shy, and perhaps overly worried about the dangers of pride. At the same time, he is direct and sincere when it concerns religion, art, and the Church; he does not hesitate to state his mind in private and public, and face the resulting rejection or calumny. He sees himself as having a mission.

This is combined with a warm sense of humour tinged by a melancholic trait, which makes him wish for solitude, or at least a peaceful place, away from the hustle and bustle of human affairs.

Underlying all of these traits is a rich interior, emotional, and spiritual life, which is intimately fused with his artistic imagination. This conjunction of diverse tendencies and interests is reflected in his novels where the discursive, narrative, and poetic languages are joined together to form a whole, while at some points there are tensions when they pull in different directions.

When Michael finds people who resonate with the streams of his inner life, there often grow strong bonds of friendship. Sometimes these affinities bridge quite radical distances of age, culture, and even language—and, as we have seen, attitudes toward cyberreality.

Second Thoughts

After Tony had persuaded Michael that the Internet was a world worthwhile to inhabit, he began to build an online gallery of Michael's paintings. It was launched in October 2001, and besides paintings, it contained some essays (for example, one on the recent September 11 attacks), information about Michael's novels, and a discussion forum. A new version was launched in 2004, after they had to close down the online forum due to too much spam, and, as Michael told me, to recode the site after repeated attacks by Islamist hackers based in Turkey. A redesigned and more secure site now sent out a monthly newsletter containing Michael's reflections and studio news to those who registered on the homepage (www.studiobrien.com).

Despite the phenomenal outreach of his writings and paintings achieved in this way (his website had five hundred thousand visitors the first year), Michael continued to be concerned about aspects of the new media. In 2005, he wrote an essay called "Musing on the Internet", which was sent out with his newsletter.

> Ironically, as you can see, I am using the media to critique the media. Such is our world. Such is its potential for good fruit and its potential for bad fruit. Untold millions of stunning images are available on the Internet, most of them for free, most of them produced by cameras, most of them made not so much by art as by mechanism, of course with a human being controlling the mechanism. It begs the questions: Does the controller shape the work of the mechanism, or

does the mechanism shape the controller? Or both? And is the near-totality of mechanistic culture altering everyone's consciousness? If so, in what way?[6]

His concern was whether our consciousness was reshaped without our realizing the depth and radicality of the change; in a sense, it seemed as if we were gradually entering into the Matrix, where our consciousness lost contact with the real world, being instead satisfied with an artificial construct.

He believed that the very qualities (structures) of the medium were changing our mind in an unhealthy direction; media are not neutral in that sense—they shape our views and relation to nature and human relationships. "In other words, are we mistaking an increase of communication for an increase of communion? Is basic human loneliness driving us ever deeper into a culture of dislocated virtual relationships that temporarily relieve symptoms but worsen the disease?"[7]

Michael's concern was that this new form of communication was transforming us into something we should not be. I would like to add that this was also the case in the transition from a predominantly oral to a literate society.[8] And, one might ask, does not the same argument apply to the telephone and newspapers? Even the quill leaving its black marks on the vellum changed our consciousness.

Michael realized this, but emphasized that the new electronic tools had unprecedented power to reshape the human mind.

In the essay, Michael mentions how a philosopher friend of his had decided not to be sucked into the cyberworld. Instead, they corresponded mostly through handwritten letters, but lapsing now and then to typing.

When one of his letters arrives, I sit down and slip peacefully into a curious sense of—well, how to express this—a sense of timelessness is the only word I can think of. Timelessness and attention. I expect that one day he will tell me he has finally done what he has so often threatened to do: he will progress to the next level of communication by destroying his computer with an axe (he presently compromises for email essential to his work). He is at this moment sharpening the point of a quill, and looking for a reliable supplier of vellum letter-paper—and honing his axe.[9]

This anonymous philosopher was Peter Kreeft, who in his letters, besides commenting on Michael's manuscripts, the state of the world, and expressing cybercriticism, continually invited Michael to come to his small summerhouse on Martha's Vineyard, an island south of Cape Cod, Massachusetts, so that they could surf together. For Kreeft this was no small thing, as he sees the sea and to surf on it as powerful analogies of the human relationship with God. In his essay "Surfing and Spirituality", Kreeft elaborates on surfing as an extended symbol for spiritual life. "The key elements in the symbolism are pretty clear: I, the surfer, am—myself. The body with which I surf in the sea symbolizes the soul, with which I 'surf' in God. The sea is God. The beach is the approach to God. Surfing is the experience of God, or the spiritual life."[10]

In a sense, the focus on personal presence in their joint criticism of impersonal computer mediation exists in a tension with the nature of their friendship, which is mainly mediated through the written word, as they have only met on a few occasions. It is a relationship of words between two writers in which they mainly comment on each other's textual creations. The oscillation between the use of handwritten letters and printed computer files, then, perhaps even more than in a relation mainly based on personal interaction, comes to signify shades and levels of personal presence, as in 2011, when Kreeft acknowledges:

> As you see, I've been corrupted by computers to the extent of writing on a keyboard rather than by hand. I can't compose by hand any more. It used to be that I wrote better by hand. The change has been imperceptible, like the tide, and I suspect it was as dangerous as the tide.[11]

The metaphor of the tide brings us back to the sea and to the incarnated symbol of surfing, which, contrary to its cyber meaning of mindless browsing of websites, points to the nonverbal, profoundly corporal and sensual. To this day, Michael has not answered the call of the Atlantic waves, despite writing jokingly in a letter in 2015, "P.S. I do not own a surfboard. Would a slab of blue Styrofoam insulation board be okay? Can I bring it?" Delighted at the prospect of Michael coming at last, Kreeft replied, "Bring nothing; I have six bodyboards. And no, Styrofoam is not a bodyboard, but a sponge."

I can very well imagine that one day Michael will actually show up at the ocean, carrying his Styrofoam board in spite of its absorbent nature, and that the two old writers will stand side by side, silently looking at the large waves breaking on the beach. This form of immediacy and presence is the symbol of the ultimately spiritual goal of direct seeing, of no mediation (not even that of handwritten letters), as Kreeft writes:

> No amount of words or verbal explanations can substitute for seeing. You only *believe* the truth of the words in a travel folder. But you see the sea when you arrive there, and that sight strikes a chord in the heart, a chord of joy and homecoming—and at the same time of further longing. It's a mysterious mingling of deep satisfaction and dissatisfaction, a divine discontent. For the restless heart that God has made for himself is not only restless until it *gets* to God; it's restless until it rests *in* God.[12]

Michael was clearly worried that the new electronic form of communication was distorting our humanity, our capacity for genuine communion. And, at the same time, he was self-consciously communicating his doubts through the very medium that he was so worried about. Was the logical conclusion, then, to "go off the grid"? To delete his website? Was it an experiment that had proved to be a failure, because it did not provide a new real world worth inhabiting? He wrestled with the question for years, wondering whether he should put his axe to the infernal machine or not.

For him personally, the question was also how to manage the massive amount of emails he was receiving; he was after all now a public person. After a while, he realized that he could not answer all of the incoming requests for dialogues and for involvement with other apostolates, regardless of how deserving the cause was. The problem was similar to the numerous invitations he received to travel and give talks. He needed to focus on his creative work, he believed, and yet find a way to meet the demands of the medium. He could not relate to all these persons on a one-to-one basis; there could never be a personal communion with millions of people. Or could there?

Toward the end of 2011, all of these concerns made Michael and Sheila wonder if they should choose greater electronic simplicity.

In 2012, they made the decision to go off the grid; that is, Michael would quit email and Internet altogether—Sheila had never been on the grid—though the website would remain up and running.

After a few weeks, Michael partly relented and began to use email again, but then only within the inner circle of the family and with his publisher. Despite this restriction, he gradually slipped back into replying to a portion of the unsolicited messages he received. He found it very difficult to unplug.

Barry's Bay

In 2014, Michael and Sheila decided to sell their home in Combermere and move to the nearby town of Barry's Bay, where many of their friends lived and where they did their shopping. It was the home of the college, and of St. Hedwig's parish, where they frequently attended Mass, and it was also the place where Michael's mother now lived in a nursing home. The reduction of driving would take some of the stress off their finances, and free up a good deal of time, they thought.

In May of that year, their house in Combermere was sold to a Catholic family with seven children, who needed to move in as soon as possible. The O'Briens, therefore, had to find a new home for themselves within the space of a few weeks. As they searched in the Barry's Bay area, they could find nothing available within their price range. Increasingly desperate, they prayed earnestly for an answer.

One day, Sheila took her young grandsons to a cemetery where her old friend Father Joseph Murray was buried. An Oblates of Mary Immaculate (O.M.I.) missionary in British Columbia for more than four decades, Father Joseph had been a close friend of the Mercer family, and he was one of the priests who had concelebrated Michael and Sheila's marriage. When he died, his body was shipped for burial to Barry's Bay, where he had been born and raised. After Sheila and the boys prayed for his intercession—"Help us find a home, Father Joe!"—they returned to Combermere and hoped for the best.

A day or so later, Michael and Sheila happened to drive by a house in downtown Barry's Bay with a "For Sale" sign on it. It seemed too large and imposing for them to buy, but they contacted the real estate agent anyway, just to have a look through the house. They discovered that it had been empty for more than a year, and a bank was selling it at a very low price. They put in an offer, and it was accepted.

For nearly forty years, the O'Briens had lived in the semiwilderness, or on its fringes, and now they were to become "urban", they thought, with all the attendant noise, artificial lights, and loss of privacy. It was a quiet, small town, but there would be a good deal of adjustment, they feared, though the benefits of the move were also significant.

An army of friends helped with the move: transporting furniture, paintings, and a mountain of books, in cars and pickup trucks and vans.

Not long after they had moved in, a neighbour dropped in to welcome them, and said out of the blue, "Oh, by the way, did you know that this is the house Father Joseph Murray was born and raised in?" It seemed the prayer to Father Joe had reached its intended receiver.

The new home had a Wi-Fi service, and for a time it looked like the Internet had won again; it was an indispensable medium, a tool as necessary as the refrigerator, perhaps even more so, since Michael needed it to communicate with the outer world and to sell his paintings. However, he fought back, and a few months after the move, in October 2014, once again unplugged the Internet at home. Since then, Michael has walked to the college to access his email and manage his website.

As Michael puts it, "Sheila and I have chosen to be minimalists in this regard, to write paper letters and live in a different cosmic time zone. We do it for our own good, but we also see that there is a sign value in the way we live—yes, there is life, there is happiness, without the Internet."[13]

Michael, California, 1956

Patti, Terry, Danny, Michael, desert east of Los Angeles, 1957

Michael, Cambridge Bay, 1962

Wedding, Blue River, British Columbia, August 2, 1975

Michael and Sheila,
Mission, British Columbia, 1984

Michael and daughter Mary,
Mission, British Columbia, 1984

O'Brien family, Okanagan Valley, British Columbia, 1991

Examples of Michael's Artwork

Barren, ink drawing, 1971

The Assumption, 1992

Examples of Michael's Artwork

The Rescuer, 2003

The Crucifixion, 2008

Michael in studio, Combermere, 2011

Michael and *Nazareth* painting, St. Joseph's parish,
Mission, British Columbia, 2014

19. Speaking in Tongues

The success of *Father Elijah* in North America naturally began to spill over into other linguistic areas. The first request to do a translation of the novel came from the Czech Republic, where it was published in 1998, only two years after the English edition.[1] The pattern is that the translation of *Father Elijah* opens up the market of a language area, and then other titles follow when the publisher thinks the interest is high enough. So far in the Czech Republic only *Father Elijah* has been translated, but in the next country, Croatia, this would prove to be very different.

Through the process of translation, to date into thirteen languages, Michael's writings entered the globalized streams of culture and religion. Nevertheless, his books are without exception published by Catholic publishers. In this way, he travels with the help of translations within the Catholic world; he rarely manages to reach outside of the Catholic "ghetto". This subculture is, of course, of different size depending on the population and condition of the Catholic Church in the respective country.

Michael's outreach through translations highlights the limited nature of Catholic cosmopolitanism. The majority of, for example, Croatian or Polish Catholic publications do not appear outside of their linguistic boundaries. English, of course, has a special place as the new lingua franca of global communications; still, Michael's books have to be translated if they are to be read widely in a specific country. And I would like to emphasize that more is involved in this than a mere linguistic transmutation of his works—Michael himself is changed, gains new experiences, insights, and inspirations.

Croatian

In 2002 *Father Elijah* was released by the Croatian publisher Verbum as *Posljednja vremena* (*The End Times*), and it became an instant best seller. When I looked on the Verbum website in March 2016, I saw that the sequel *Elijah in Jerusalem* was listed as their eighth best-selling book. In an interview in 2005, Michael claimed that his books had sold more copies in Croatia than in Canada. Somehow, Michael's storytelling touched the hearts of Croatian Catholics.

One explanation is that at the beginning of the novel, Elijah meets the tall and massive Croatian friar Jakov in Assisi. Jakov came to the Franciscan monastery after his family had been brutally massacred in the Yugoslav wars. In the figure of the Croatian friar, the moral dilemma of giving up hatred, to be able to forgive after a traumatic experience, is personified.

During one of their last meetings, Elijah puts his hands on Jakov's head and prays for the healing of his memories. Through Elijah's intercession, Jakov manages to take the first steps away from hatred and the thought of revenge; it was as if Michael, through the main character of his novel, had stretched out his hands and offered to the Croatian people healing from the recent war. There were many psychological and social wounds still open and terrible memories to handle—and more concretely a country to rebuild.[2]

Already in 2003, Michael was invited by Verbum and the Catholic lay apostolate Militia Immaculata (MI) to come to Croatia.[3] After a long journey with a change of flights in Prague, Sheila and Michael collected their luggage at Zagreb International Airport. At the same time, Mate Krajina, an editor, journalist, novelist, and manager of a small publishing house (Treći Dan), was waiting to receive them. With him was the translator Vesna Borović, as Mate spoke no English, and Michael no Croatian.

Mate, who like the fictional friar Jakov was tall and imposing, did not have the friar's melancholic temper. In his youth, he had been like a fired-up racehorse bubbling with energy: a truth teller and passionate Christian. This combination of traits naturally brought him into trouble with the Communist Party. For example, during his first year at university, in an obligatory Marxist class, he could not help himself when the lecturer made derogatory remarks about the Immaculate Conception. Riveted by indignation, Mate stood up and said, "Please, professor, kindly stop this lecture!" and continued, "These are sheer lies and calumnies!" The crowd began to cheer, "Mate, Mate!" Nevertheless, he was in trouble with the security service, and it took him seven years to pass that Marxist exam, which took place before a hostile board of examiners. Only then was he allowed to graduate.[4]

Like Michael, Mate was an idealist, one who does not think first of personal material gain, but of the righteousness of the cause. And, like Michael, he had to suffer the fate of living on the margins of society with a chronic shortage of resources—which is difficult when raising a family, being constantly torn between the idealism of the new evangelization and the running of one's own minisociety, the family. Where is the line to be drawn? When must apostolic work cede ground to the family, and vice versa? These two men, similar in position, mission, and in zeal, were destined, it seemed, to recognize themselves in each other—like seeing oneself in the mirror of a different culture and society.

However, Mate was worried and restless as he stood waiting for the Canadian writer's arrival. "Is this O'Brien a madman, a nutcase; is the money that [the lay apostolate] *MI* has put into inviting this famous author a waste for which I am responsible?" he complained. Vesna assured him, "You'll see, Mate, he's a great and most humble soul." At that moment, Michael waved at them through the thick glass wall. He looked humble indeed, even scruffy in his weather-beaten brown suit jacket; he even resembled a figure from Mate's childhood in the mountains of Herzegovina in the 1970s. And, they were scheduled to go immediately to a luxurious restaurant where among others the mayor of Zagreb was waiting.

Michael and Sheila were very tired, as they had not slept for thirty-six hours. In this dazed condition, Michael's first impression of Mate was that of an extremely polite giant, "with a facial expression of ferocious gravity".[5] Mate had prepared a small speech and delivered it on the spot in the airport reception hall. Michael was astonished by this old-world formality and courteousness; and he thought of how manners and respect had all but faded in North America, replaced by a strange mixture of niceness and rudeness.

Later at the banquet with the mayor, Michael felt that his jacket was indeed shabby, not to speak of his shoes; and his brain felt completely exhausted by the lack of sleep. At one point during the dinner conversation, he threw his arms wide open to make a point in a story, with the unfortunate consequence of hitting a glass full of red wine. It fell over the table with a crash, spraying the dresses of Sheila and several other ladies. Michael thought of Prince Myshkin in Dostoyevsky's novel *The Idiot*, who had thrown his arms wide in a similar gesture and broken an expensive vase even as he discoursed on beauty. But everyone in the restaurant was kind and took it with good humour. Nevertheless, Michael felt chastened; perhaps he was somewhat of a madman after all.

This was the beginning of a three-week trip that took Michael and Sheila from Zagreb to Pula in Istria, then along the Dalmatian coast south to the city of Split. Michael could not help falling in love with the country. Croatia has a stunningly beautiful coast, with sand and stone beaches and archipelagos of islands, walled off from the interior of the country by the mountains of the Dinaric Alps. Moreover, Michael met a deeply Catholic people who gave him a warm welcome that took him completely by surprise. The experience was similar to that in Mexico seven years earlier—a combination of strong southern light and the human warmth of unpretentious, sincerely believing Christians; so dissimilar, he thought, compared to the cold of the North and its cultural condition of late modern ennui.

When coming to Croatia in 2003, Michael was at a low point in his inner battle with discouragement. It was the old struggle of maintaining hope when confronted by a social development that seemed to go inexorably in the wrong direction. Despite the fact that his novels were now being published and read by many (which he saw as more or less a miracle), their income was still low and they struggled to keep afloat. And his new outreach was foremost a phenomenon within the North American subculture of "orthodox" Catholicism. When coming to Croatia, this understanding of his role changed: a Catholic nation was taking his novels to its heart. He was received as a celebrity by a people who were more or less unknown to him. It was an overwhelming experience, and it was happening in a beautiful Mediterranean setting, Croatia in springtime.

Michael gave four major talks, two lesser ones, one radio interview, and three magazine and newspaper interviews. Sheila was not present during his talks, as her habit is to pray for him in front of the Blessed Sacrament whenever he is speaking before an audience, in this way offering him spiritual support. And as she said to me in 2014, after one of Michael's talks at the island city of Krk, in northern Croatia, "I know already what he is saying."

In 2003, they also went to the pilgrimage site of Međugorje in Bosnia-Herzegovina. Sheila walked barefoot on the sharp rocks up the mountain called Križevac (Cross Mountain). On the top, she received an insight into her and Michael's relationship, which unlocked some things that she had hid in her heart. A similar illumination happened to Michael. On the plane home, they compared notes from the trip and found a new openness about their failings and shortcomings during their twenty-seven years of marriage.

During that first journey to Croatia, a friendship between Mate and Michael began, and it developed over the years. At the same time, they had no common language with which to communicate: all their words had to be translated, back and forth between Croatian and English. Basically, it was a communication on the level of heart and soul, and of shared deeds.

In 2005, Michael was invited once again to Croatia, this time as part of the new Days of Christian Culture in Split (March 12–22), an event initiated by his publisher Verbum in conjunction with the Catholic Church in Croatia. It included talks by authors, concerts, theatre plays, and displays of contemporary Christian art and other cultural creations, all with the purpose of illuminating the Christian roots of European culture.

During a ceremony in Split, the first Andrija Buvina Award was awarded to an individual who, according to the jury, had made a highly significant contribution to Christian culture. That year it was given to Michael, who was astonished. At the time, none of his books had been published in his native land, and yet, he said, "Here they were being read and reviewed widely with enthusiasm by a highly educated, culturally sophisticated Catholic people."[6]

Michael continued to return to Croatia; to date he has made five trips there, and Sheila has accompanied him three times. His imagination was deeply influenced by the unexpected reception of his work in Croatia, and by the personal stories that Mate told him, while liberally offering rakija (brandy) and wine. In this way, a seed for a novel was planted, which bore fruit two years later, when Michael wrote the massive, eight-hundred-page novel *Island of the World*.[7]

Island of the World is, on one level, a historical novel told through the perspective of one man, Josip Lasta, who was born in a little mountain village in Hercegovina in the 1930s. Josip has to bear the sufferings of the Croatian people, first those of the Second World

War, when as a child he witnesses the massacre of his village, then as a newly married young man, when he is incarcerated by the Communist Yugoslavian authorities on the infamous prison island of Goli Otok. He manages to escape by swimming the long way to the shore, only to learn that his wife is dead. After escaping the prison island, emotionally and physically exhausted, he flees to Italy, but becomes psychologically ill and slowly has to regain his sanity at an Italian asylum. By a circuitous route, he ends up in New York, working as a janitor, and follows from a distance the war in the Balkans in the 1990s and the establishment of the state of Croatia.

This was the first of Michael's new novels, after the initial inspiration for the Children of the Last Days series. Still, it is a typical O'Brien story: at the centre is personal suffering at the hands of twentieth-century totalitarianism, balanced and challenged by an intense interior spiritual life. The recurrent story of his novels is that of a person setting out on a journey alone, leaving behind his social context, material possessions, and self-esteem. After the departure from home, the plot mostly involves a series of misfortunes and sufferings that gradually destroys the little that the protagonist carried with him or had managed to gain on the journey. It is as if Michael wants to remove layer after layer from the individual to see if he can finally reach an essence, a nucleus of real personality. This is, of course, the Christian Way of the Cross, the process of self-emptying, kenosis, but it is also compatible with a modern secular search for the true individual beneath the surface of social roles and masks. The authentic person is purified by trials and intense suffering, and at the end of the novel, reconciliation is offered. But it is not in the form of exaltation and success; mostly, the protagonist achieves peace of mind before death and leaves this life with the expectation of eternal beatitude. It is not as in the story of Job, who regained everything he had lost and died full of years. In Michael's stories, the hero dies poor, but with a smile on his lips.

In *Island of the World*, this basic spiritual story is connected to the history of a nation—a contentious and sensitive history, where it is easy to fall into controversy. In one Croatian review, the novel was praised as providing a testimony, which accurately informs readers about what actually happened.[8] The reviewer even suggested that it should be required reading in Croatian schools. In March 2016, the

English version of the novel had received five stars from 95 percent of the readers on Amazon.com. The common theme of the reader responses was the emotional and spiritual engagement with the main character, and not with Croatian history, with some exceptions.

In the book, Michael's tone of address is—despite the sufferings of the hero and the tense political context—lyrical and visionary. Typically, his prose has an almost dreamlike quality; it is seldom prosaic. Things, nature, and persons are imbued with a glow of transcendent meaning. For example, in *Island of the World*, the swallows are, of course, birds, but they point to something more, to something beyond this world, and at the same time to Josip's family name, Lasta, which means "swallow" in Croatian (a synonym is *lastavica*).

It was not Verbum that published *Island of the World* in Croatian (as *Otok Svijeta* in 2012), but Mate's publishing house, Treći Dan. Initially, Verbum, the largest Catholic publisher in Croatia, hesitated over publishing it, possibly because the novel dug deep into the most painful memories of the country under the Tito regime and was written by a non-Croatian. After Mate's Treći Dan published it, the much larger Verbum, nevertheless, offered to distribute the novel and from then on has distributed all of Treći Dan's books.[9]

In 2015, Treći Dan published the correspondence between Mate and Michael from 2012 to 2014 as *Razgovor očeva (Magareći dijalog)*. It had been published one year earlier by Justin Press as *The Donkey Dialogues*. The cover features a painting by William Kurelek of a donkey with a tabernacle on its back, in which there is a Host in a shining chalice, spreading a strong light on the road in front of the animal. In their letters (or more correctly emails), Michael and Mate tell their life stories and share their struggles as husbands, fathers, and lay apostles. One main theme is how to provide materially for the family and to sustain the theological virtue of hope, in the face of lack of success and trials on so many levels. It is as if the two Catholic fathers, like the Kurelekian donkey, had decided to carry Christ on their backs; and in old age, they feel weighed down toward the earth, their heads so bent by the load that at times they do not see the light that their burden sheds on the path ahead.

This intercultural testimony of two Men of Emails is, in a sense, together with *Island of the World*, the first obvious sign of the globalization of Michael's work. Through the translations of his novels, his homepage, and his travels, threads were cast out into new countries, cultures, and languages, establishing a network of like-minded people within the larger Catholic world. One recurrent pattern is that Michael encounters persons and groups that have, as he had tried to do in Canada since the 1970s, resurrected a Catholic way of life, despite fierce internal and external resistance. It was not only a Canadian or North American experience, Michael discovered, but also, for example, a Croatian one. Globalization made it possible for different pockets of Catholic resistance to modernity to connect and exchange stories.

Nevertheless, in the second decade of the twenty-first century, the translations of Michael's novels were restricted to European languages, which despite their global presence, leaves Africa and most of Asia still largely outside of his reach.[10]

Italian

As a young man, Michael dreamt of going to Italy to study the old masters and to paint in the sun-drenched landscapes of Tuscany and Umbria; in the 1980s, he longed to bring his whole family on such a trip. This dream did not come true, but *Father Elijah* had been published in Italy as *Il Nemico* (*The Enemy*) by Edizioni San Paolo in 2006, and, two years later, *Sophia House* was released as *Il Libraio* (*The Bookseller*). The same year in August, Michael was invited as one of the main guests to the annual Rimini "Meeting for Friendship among Peoples", organized by the Catholic, predominately lay, organization Communion and Liberation (Comunione e Liberazione). They had chosen *Il Nemico* as their monthly reading, which had contributed to making it a best seller in Italy. At the event, in front of six thousand listeners, Michael spoke about fatherhood under the title "The Quest for the Father". The audience gave his talk a wholehearted and attentive reception. According to his translator, the Italian Catholic reading audience was thrilled to get to know this new and unusual literary voice.

The day after the talk, one of the participants, a sixteen-year-old Italian boy, wrote a letter to Michael, saying he had found the courage to write to him as he wanted to thank Michael for everything he had said yesterday; and, the boy continued, he wanted to be like Michael, but he did not know how yet. The sixty-year-old Canadian painter and author had made a deep impression on this young Italian, and on numerous other young people who also wrote to him. In the same way, the young people in Rimini had deeply impressed Michael. As in Croatia, he was overwhelmed by the positive response he received from so many young people.

Despite this welcome, one must acknowledge that Catholicism in Italy is in serious decline. Italy is nominally Catholic and within its borders is the seat of the pope, the Holy See, and the Vatican City State. However, secularization has gradually drained the vitality of Italian Catholicism. For example, in a recent poll (March 2016), only around 50 percent of Italians identified themselves as Catholics, while 20 percent said they were atheists.[11] On the other hand, 25 percent believed in reincarnation and 17 percent in astrology.[12] There is thus a strong presence of what one can call a neo-pagan atmosphere.

If in the newly established Croatian state Catholicism is closely connected with national identity, Italy, like most Western European countries, is a post-Christian nation. Memories and traces of the Christian past remain in the national psyche, anchored by mediaeval and baroque churches, artwork, and music. These come to the fore in life-passage rites such as weddings and burials, but religious practice and belief, despite Church membership, is largely a personal choice and is in steady decline.[13]

To the trend of decreasing support for Christian values and churches, one needs to add the demographic decline in Europe: the total fertility rate for Italian mothers in 2014 was a mere 1.31 (the mean number of births per woman), close to what is called the "lowest-low fertility" (below 1.3), which leads to a halving of the population in less than forty-five years.[14] The number of children required for the population to remain stable is 2.1.

It is, therefore, clear that Michael's novels and essays speak mainly to the approximately 5 to 10 percent of Western Catholics who in polls answer that they support Church doctrine on faith and morals. His voice harmonizes with their sense of living through the twilight of Western civilization, if not the end of the world.

In November of the following year, Michael returned to Italy, this time to promote the *Island of the World*. In Centro Culturale Di

Milano, he took part in a panel discussion with his translator Edoardo Rialti and Carlo Bajetta, associate professor of English literature. Michael remarked what a miracle it was that his novels were translated into Italian; he still had trouble understanding that his work appealed to people outside of his native country, where he had been marginalized for such a long time. How was this sympathy that crossed cultural divides possible? he wondered. Then he told a story about something that had happened to him and Edoardo on the train from Florence to Milan, to illustrate his point, or perhaps merely because it was such a good story.

Gandalf on the Train

When boarding the train in Florence, Michael had already given talks in Rome, Florence, and Genoa, plus numerous interviews. Being by nature not an extrovert, he was somewhat exhausted after all this publicity and looked forward to being anonymous during the three-hour journey, although the train carriage was packed with people. He and Edoardo discussed everything under the sun, including faith and literature, and they joked continuously, laughing a lot. No one in the carriage paid them the least attention.

As the train drew into Milano station, Michael confessed to Edoardo that he was somewhat exhausted from the past weeks' unceasing encounters and had, as a result, thoroughly enjoyed being "the invisible man". With these words, he stepped out of the carriage onto the platform in Milan, and immediately a young man and woman ran up to him with paper and pens in their hands.

"Oh, sir," they said enthusiastically in Italian, "could we please have your autograph?" As so many times previously on the trip, Edoardo translated this into English for Michael.

"Of course, I would be happy to," he replied with a smile and began signing their papers. As he did so, it struck him as amazing that anyone in Italy had recognized him, a visiting Canadian writer.

"How did you recognize me?" he asked them.

"Oh, sir," the young woman answered warmly, "*everyone* in Italy knows your face!"

A wave of pleasure washed over Michael. In his mind, he silently attributed this "fame" to the fact that four of his books had been translated into Italian by then, with his photo on the back covers. And in recent weeks there had been several interviews in media and major newspapers.

"Yes," exclaimed the young man enthusiastically. "*You* are the actor who played Gandalf in *The Lord of the Rings!*"

Both Edoardo and Michael bent over double, loudly guffawing. The two young people looked puzzled. Edoardo then explained that it was a case of mistaken identity, that Michael was a Canadian writer, among other things. The couple blushed, said they would try to find his books, and hastened away.

The event was both humbling and hilarious. At the same time, it illustrates nicely the interconnection between fiction and reality: a Canadian author was mistaken for an actor playing a fictive wizard, who was the creation of another Catholic author.

Eugenio Corti

Earlier on the trip, when Michael and Edoardo stayed in Genoa, their hosts arranged a meeting with the well-known writer Eugenio Corti in his home in Besana Brianza, Lombardy, not far from Milan. At the time, Corti was eighty-eight years old, and his major work was the massive, one-thousand-page historical novel *The Red Horse* (*Il cavallo rosso*). Michael had written the back-cover endorsement for the English edition, published by Ignatius Press in 2000.

As a young man, Corti fought on the Russian front and was one of the few in his regiment who managed to return home in 1943, after the total collapse of the Italian army. Back in Italy, he went south and joined the Allies in their fight against the Nazis until Italy was liberated in 1945.

After the war, Corti together with a friend wrote the book *Few Returned* (*I più non ritornano*) on their experiences on the Eastern Front in 1943.[15] The same year it was published, he finished his law studies, but continued to nurture the dream of being an author, which had been born when in sixth grade he read the *Iliad* and the *Odyssey*.

One of Corti's motives for signing up for the Eastern Front in 1942 was to "feel first-hand the results of the gigantic effort to build a new world, completely free from God, indeed, against God, governed by the Communists".[16] His studies led him to write the play

The Trial and Death of Stalin (*Processo e morte di Stalin*) in 1962. His anti–Communist stance made him suspect in the eyes of the Italian mainstream press and world of culture, which were increasingly leaning to the left.

In 1972, he left the family firm and began to work on his definitive novel, which took him eleven years of full-time work to complete. The gargantuan *The Red Horse* was published by a small publishing house, but it became a great success in Italy and has since appeared in numerous editions and translations.[17] The novel portrays the Italian experience of the Second World War and its aftermath. Although it was a work of fiction, Corti was determined to be absolutely true to the historical details. This of course made the writing a very laborious process.

One can compare his literary approach with that of the Russian author Aleksandr Solzhenitsyn, who exposed Soviet Communism with similar attention to historical detail. It is an intriguing thought that Solzhenitsyn and Corti both fought on the Eastern Front, but on opposing sides. And both turned against their own governments: Corti by joining the Allies, while Solzhenitsyn spent time in the Gulag. Both began their literary careers with stories based on their wartime experiences, and both were sincere Christians, offering a critique of the modern godlessness and its totalitarian consequences.

Corti's worldview was foundationally Christian, and he was very critical of the compromises with modernity underway in the Catholic Church. His voice was part of the minority, because the same year as he published his critique of Communism in the form of a tragedy, the Second Vatican Council began. To his dismay, the bishops gathered in Rome decided not to condemn Communism explicitly. In 1995, he, therefore, collected his published and unpublished articles on the decay of the Church in the volume *The Smoke in the Temple* (*Il fumo nel tempio*).[18]

The Meeting of Two Wise Men

When Michael and Edoardo arrived in Besana, they were met by Corti, who looked like the quintessential North Italian gentleman—smartly dressed, supported by a cane, he retained something of the taut posture of the soldier. He was courteous and at the same time quiet, looking at them with eyes set behind sharply inclining eyebrows, which together with a thick white goatee and carefully combed white hair gave his gaze a piercing quality—a witness of his sense and attention to details.

He led them from the spacious park into a large, three-story, ochre stone villa with pale blue window shutters. After lunch, the dialogue between the two seasoned writers began. Edoardo was fully occupied in translating back and forth from English to Italian and from Italian to English. Despite the language barrier, the meeting had a deep emotional undercurrent, and at times there was a glimpse of tears in the eyes of some of the people present. They understood that this was a onetime event—two old writers, who had fought a similar fight for the Christian faith, met briefly to exchange thoughts before death.

Corti began by saying that he had not read any of Michael's novels, but he hoped to, because his secretary was constantly urging him to read them. He went on, "Now as I am getting older, I struggle between two worthy causes; on the one hand, I would like to devote my time to writing. On the other hand, I receive so many manuscripts from young writers—and I feel the urge to read them and give them advice." Corti used to put the manuscripts he received on his bedside table and read them in the evenings. Later he would send his comments to the aspiring authors, adding that it was up to them to rewrite. He also used to receive groups of students in his house, and he confessed that he could only answer half of the thousands of letters arriving on his desk.

Michael had the same problem, but said that the primary task, even duty, was to write. "Though we must help the young generation in any way we can," he said, "our primary calling is to create, and this is what will be most fruitful for souls, and for the times in which we live."

Finally, after a long conversation ranging over the themes of art and faith, Corti said to Michael, "I want to give you a word of advice.... Hold on to Jesus in all that is about to happen. We are at war." Once again, it was the quiet determination of the soldier-poet that shone forth.

Corti walked side by side with Michael back down the long laneway to the visitors' car, moving very slowly with his cane, both men saying little. At the end, they shook hands warmly, and as the car drove away, Corti kept looking at Michael with a warm smile, until they rounded a curve and disappeared from sight.

The meeting was similar to that between Michael and Mate in Croatia: two cultural warriors sharing experiences and comparing notes. Once again, Michael had been able to reach outside his linguistic and cultural context through the medium of literature and Christian faith.

French

In connection with the publication of *Theophilos* in French translation, Michael was invited by the Parisian publisher Éditions Salvator for a promotion tour. He was to arrive on Sunday, September 23, in 2012, for a first day of acclimatization, but the flight was delayed due to technical problems and that day was instead spent in Montreal. When Michael arrived on the following day, he had not slept for twenty-four hours, but was immediately rushed to Radio Notre Dame for a recording on the book-discussion program *Vox Libri*. Carine Rabier-Poutous, the translator of his novels and a novelist herself, met him and served as interpreter.[19] She thought that this was an extraordinary, but tired, man. The first words he said to her, after an exchange of courtesies, were that his French friends who had read her translations had told him that they were not only faithful to the substance, but also true to the spirit of his writings. For her it was a nice recognition (and a relief too).

Then there were interviews with journalists from magazines and journals: *Famille Chrétienne*, *Le Figaro Littéraire*, *France Catholique*, *L'Homme Nouveau*, and *La Vie*. In the evening, the Jesuit centre Sèvres, which offers courses in theology and philosophy, organized an event with Michael speaking on the assigned topic "Can We Find God in a Novel?" Sixty people attended, and Michael spent a long time afterwards signing his books. Readers seemed eager to meet and talk with him, and some even asked him to pray for them.

Later that night, after the day's intense schedule, Michael went to the studio of the television channel KTO, and there, at last, after more than forty-eight hours awake, he fell asleep in the middle of the interview. A metallic voice kept buzzing in his translation earphone,

"Are you sleeping, Michael? Wake up! Wake up, Michael!" He jerked awake to find the interviewer, cameramen, and all the studio staff laughing heartily. Fortunately, it was a recorded, not a live, interview. Being a well-known author is not always *la vie en rose*.

The next day, after a train journey to Bordeaux, the string of interviews and conferences continued once again on the theme of finding God through a novel. Carine found great joy in the conversation with Michael on the train, which continued the next day when they proceeded to Lourdes. They frequently went from serious topics to laughter. When they spoke about their lives and vocations, she appreciated that Michael was sensitive to the fact that she was herself a novelist, and not only a translator. Carine had come to faith through a protracted process of conversion beginning when she was working for L'Oréal in Tokyo, through travel to India, the practice of Buddhist meditation, and an Ignatian retreat. After three years with Mother Teresa's sisters, she finally discerned her vocation to be a writer and a wife.[20]

In Lourdes, Michael was mainly a pilgrim and managed to reduce his sleep deprivation somewhat. The next stop, on the following day, was Toulouse, which meant more newspaper and radio interviews, book signings, and a conference at a Dominican convent, not surprisingly on the theme "Can the novel open the way for spirituality?" At a similar stop in Lyon, he spoke on, "Are we living in apocalyptic times?"

After returning to Paris, they drove out to Chartres and had a picnic in the hills above the city. Michael managed to get a quick tour of the famous cathedral. Upon this followed the usual: a talk, book signing, and interviews, followed by another talk in the evening. On Sunday morning, he flew back to Canada, after an intense week, considering that he only had some free time during the day in Lourdes. Even a twenty-year-old author hungry for publicity would have been worn out after such a schedule.

A Prophet from Canada

Éditions Salvator has continued to publish Michael's novels in French translations, and, according to Carine Poutous, they have found an extremely loyal and fervent public, which is probably predominantly

Catholic. As a comment on this, there appeared in *Le Figaro*, the larger of the two main daily newspapers in France, on November 15, 2012, a highly appreciative article on Michael and his novels, by the columnist Astrid De Larminat. It was titled "Michael D. O'Brien, *un prophète venu du Canada*" (Michael D. O'Brien, a Prophet from Canada). She concluded her article with the following assessment of Michael's religious stance:

> O'Brien disarms prejudices. He is not an excited Catholic, loudly pro-testing, on the defensive or preachy. His face is formed, as if hollowed out, by struggles. It is full of gravity and sweetness, radiating a quiet inner strength that does not impose itself, but invites to dialogue. He is certainly not fanatical, perhaps prophetic; in any case, here is a writer whose novels make an intelligent appeal to your best self and invite you to see beyond the tip of your nose.[21]

For a moment, it seemed as if Michael had managed to escape the ghetto; his voice was at last reaching readers who did not share his religious convictions. Moreover, he had not immediately been rejected as a religious fanatic. Anyone who has heard Michael speak can bear witness to the fact that he has a very deep voice, and he talks with a slow, gentle seriousness. Add to this his above-average height, white curly hair, and short beard (the Gandalf look), and the impression is, as De Larminat writes, that of a prophet, despite the lack of flowing garments and a staff. Therefore, even if his person and works should reach out into the secular sphere in a more substantial and per-manent manner, I am convinced it will not be as merely a literary and artistic phenomenon. Michael O'Brien is at heart a religious person, and from that core flow his novels, essays, paintings, family life, and opinions on politics, morals, and art.

His message, whether prophetic or not, is countercultural in the present social and ideological climate of the Western world, and I have little doubt that it will remain so if these societies do not change in a radical way. Still, I believe that even for those who do not share his worldview, an understanding of what he tries to articulate is worth a hearing. It is as if the Catholic tradition, which combines visionary baroque exuberance, ascetic world renunciation and clarity of mind, abstruse theology, and rustic piety, had been reformulated in rural

Canada for a last exhortation before the complete modernization of global society. Is he a prophet or a madman? I suppose many readers share the doubt that afflicted Mate Krajina at Zagreb International Airport. My suggestion is that you take some time to get know him by his creations before judging.

EPILOGUE

A challenge when writing the biography of a living author and artist, or for that matter of any person, is where to end. Since I began my studies of Michael O'Brien's life and work in 2011, the horizon of possibility has been moving steadily in front of me. As he is still furiously active, interesting material and developments are added each year, or even month. These new pieces change "the whole" of his life. A biography of a living person is hence a work in progress; as life is until death draws the curtain—then the story has both a natural beginning and end.

The final four chapters, therefore, explore different themes of the period after 1997, and finish in an open-ended way with the translation of Michael's novels into new cultures and languages. To tie these developments together in relation to the new era of Catholicism inaugurated by Pope Francis is, I think, premature and will have to wait.

Nevertheless, what we now can see, as remarked by Ross Douthat in January 2016, is that the conservative centre established by John Paul II and his successor, Benedict XVI, seems to falter.[1]

The proponents of a hermeneutic of continuity consider that they occupy the middle between the extremes of radical progressivism and rigid traditionalism. Where they see signs of reform, those on the "fringes" see evidence of a revolution, perceived either as something good or as something pernicious and dangerous.

One of the most prominent voices for this position in North America is George Weigel, who in his programmatic 2013 book *Evangelical Catholicism: Deep Reform in the 21st-Century Church* writes:

> Evangelical Catholicism is not the Catholicism of the future as imagined by either "progressive" Catholics or "traditionalist" Catholics, although Evangelical Catholicism does take from the former the imperative of development and from the latter the imperative of a development—a reform—that follows the essential form of the Church given to it by Christ.[2]

In the 1990s, Michael clearly adhered to this centrist position. He never was a liberal progressivist, nor a traditionalist in the narrow sense, but neither was he a neoconservative. He combined the ideas of continuity and reform with mystical religious experiences, a strong eucharistic and Marian devotion, attention to modern Christian prophecy, and an apocalyptic understanding of twentieth-century modernity. He saw, experienced, and lamented the decline of faith and morals, but still believed that lay apostolates inspired by the documents of Vatican II, as interpreted by John Paul II and Benedict XVI, showed the way forward.

Still, he was also convinced that the health of the Church greatly depended upon the evangelical vitality of her bishops and priests, something which, however, introduced a question mark to the project of a lay new evangelization. The John Paul II revivalism built, as I have written earlier, upon a particularly close relationship between laypersons and the pope, and it often bypassed the bishops and bishops' conferences, which in many places did not want to confront the modern world, but instead chose the path of compromise. With Pope Francis, this situation is changing. The tendency or intention is to give more power to bishops' conferences, and to open up discussions on moral topics that seemed already to have been decided. This has led to increased polarization in which religious conservatives either drift toward a more traditionalist understanding of the Council and its legacy or welcome the new "nonjudgmental openness" to the world championed by the pope. The centre is clearly weakened.

The crucial question for a program of reform is where the exact line between, on the one hand, essence and infallible teachings, and, on the other hand, accidental and fallible teachings, actually runs. What precisely cannot be changed, and what can be left behind or transformed in the process of reform? The main argument of traditionalists is not that there should be no change at all, but that this line, in a simplistic enthusiasm over modern lifestyles and ideologies, has been drawn at all the wrong places.

Moreover, the present strong emphasis on a chasm between "pure" doctrine and practical applications, including moral rules and customs, seems to retire "the essential form of the Church" to a state of impotence. Even Pope Francis in his apostolic exhortation *Evangelii Gaudium* proposes a criterion of usefulness in contrast to beauty and "deep historical roots".[3]

However, such a utilitarian criterion casts doubt over the principal questions of the culture wars, including those of sexual morality. How about contraceptives? Perhaps the ban issued in *Humanae Vitae* was fallible; perhaps this is a mere rule, no longer useful to transmit the centre of the joyful gospel. The majority of Catholics in the affluent secularized West seem to think so, and a large contingent of theologians as well. For the "conservative" Catholic position that has embraced deep reform as a principle, the outcome of that question will be decisive on the level of fundamental principle. If the changes become too drastic and too deep, reform becomes revolution.

I have made the question of teaching authority and the limits of reform central in this epilogue, as through it the life project of Michael O'Brien (together with all of those who since the Council have struggled to revitalize a traditional Catholicism) is facing a decisive crisis.

I do not know how Michael will handle this new situation, and what it will mean for his creative work. (Probably, he does not know that himself either.) Still in his article "The Family and Totalitarianism" in *Inside the Vatican* magazine, December 2015, we can see that he continues to build his argument on the texts and teachings of John Paul II. The article recapitulates the content of Michael's earlier publications, but it is important, in the light of the two synods on the family, that he continues to direct the reader to the legacy of John Paul II.

He ends the article with a reflection on the present situation, pointing to Benedict XVI's use of the notion of Creative Minorities, but he leaves in doubt the actual ability of such a minority to influence the larger culture and society.

> Synods may come and go, alternatively edifying or inconclusive, but the Bride of Christ will remain, continuing in a state of ongoing preparation to meet her Bridegroom. We must never allow ourselves to be dismayed when confusion and ambiguity are manifested within her, either in the particular churches or in the seat of authority at its highest levels.
>
> Will the Church go on to convert the world, or will she, as Pope Benedict XVI suggested, become much smaller, a remnant of believers purified by global persecution? Christ alone knows the answer. But of this we can be sure: despite the sufferings we will face in the future, the family will remain what it is—an oak flourishing in winter.[4]

At the same time, Michael is moving toward that stage of life when most of his work is completed. Maybe the present struggle in the Catholic Church on the nature of her reform will be decided without his playing an active role—or, perhaps, his greatest task is yet before him.

Still, with a strong faith the gaze increasingly becomes directed toward eternity, while the joys and sorrows of the earth fade away, and become as it were transparent. As Michael experienced in 2001:

> After Communion, an inner vision of the Christ Child. He is smiling at me and takes my hand. We run together hand in hand. I am an old man, very weak, stumbling. But with a look of encouragement he shows me I can do it, get up, press on. As I run with him, I grow younger and younger and my strength increases.[5]

APPENDIX 1

Writings by Michael O'Brien

Published Fiction Books

The Small Angel. Brudenell, Ontario: White Horse Press, 1993.
Father Elijah: An Apocalypse. San Francisco, CA: Ignatius Press, 1996.
Strangers and Sojourners. San Francisco, CA: Ignatius Press, 1997.
Eclipse of the Sun. San Francisco, CA: Ignatius Press, 1998.
Plague Journal. San Francisco, CA: Ignatius Press, 1999.
A Cry of Stone. San Francisco, CA: Ignatius Press, 2003.
Sophia House. San Francisco, CA: Ignatius Press, 2005.
Island of the World. San Francisco, CA: Ignatius Press, 2007.
Theophilos. San Francisco, CA: Ignatius Press, 2010.
The Father's Tale. San Francisco, CA: Ignatius Press, 2011.
Winter Tales. Ottawa, Ontario: Justin Press, 2011.
Voyage to Alpha Centauri. San Francisco, CA: Ignatius Press, 2013.
Elijah in Jerusalem. San Francisco, CA: Ignatius Press, 2015.
The Fool of New York City. San Francisco, CA: Ignatius Press, 2016.

Published Nonfiction Books

The Mysteries of the Most Holy Rosary [text and illustrations]. Brudenell,
   Ontario: White Horse Press, 1992.
*A Landscape with Dragons: Christian and Pagan Imagination in Children's
   Literature.* Quebec: Northern River Press, 1994.
The Family and the New Totalitarianism. Killaloe, Ontario: White
   Horse Press, 1995.

A Landscape with Dragons: The Battle for Your Child's Mind. Revised, expanded edition. San Francisco, CA: Ignatius Press, 1998.

Friendly Dragons, Moral Nightmares. Mount Morris, NY: Lamplighter Press, 2009.

John Paul II's Biblical Way of the Cross [illustrations]. Notre Dame, IN: Ave Maria Press, 2009.

Remembrance of the Future: Reflections on Our Times. Ottawa, Ontario: Justin Press, 2009.

Harry Potter and the Paganization of Culture. Rzeszow, Poland: Fides et Traditio Press, 2010.

Waiting: Stories for Advent. Ottawa, Ontario: Justin Press, 2010.

Father at Night. Ottawa, Ontario: Justin Press, 2011.

Arriving Where We Started: Faith and Culture in the Postmodernist Age. Ottawa, Ontario: Justin Press, 2012.

William Kurelek: Painter and Prophet. Ottawa, Ontario: Justin Press, 2013.

The Donkey Dialogues. Ottawa, Ontario: Justin Press, 2014. [O'Brien coauthored the book with Mate Krajina.]

The Stations of the Cross. Ottawa, Ontario: Justin Press, 2018.

The Apocalypse: Warning, Hope, and Consolation. Belmont, NC: Wise Blood Books, 2018.

Chapters in Anthologies

"Historical Imagination and the Renewal of Culture". In *Eternity in Time: Christopher Dawson and the Catholic Idea of History*, edited by Stratford Caldecott and John Morrill, 151–91. Edinburgh: T&T Clark, 1997.

"Catechesis and Evangelization". In *The Wisdom of Nazareth: Stories of Catholic Family Life*, edited by Michael D. O'Brien and Crucis Beards, 146–51. Oxford: Family Publications, 2008.

"Disaster, Rage, Repentance". In *The Wisdom of Nazareth: Stories of Catholic Family Life*, edited by Michael D. O'Brien and Crucis Beards, 63–73. Oxford: Family Publications, 2008.

"In Search of the Father". In *Either Protagonists or Nobodies*, edited by Alberto Savorana, chap. 16. Milan: Mondadori, 2009.

"Subsidiary in Art: The Flow of Celestial Language". In *Logos et Musica: In Honorem Summi Romani Pontificis Benedicti XVI*, edited by Elzbieta Szcurko, Tadeusz Guz, and Horst Seidl, 425–36. Frankfurt am Main: Peter Lang Internationaler Verlag der Wissenschaften, 2012.

Selected Essays and Articles

"Fire in Our Darkness: The Artist as Minister and Prophet". *Canadian Catholic Review*, November 1984, 10–18.

"The Hidden Face: Sacred and Profane in Canadian Painting". *Canadian Catholic Review*, February 1986, 11–18.

"An Original Theology: Creation and Matthew Fox". *Canadian Catholic Review*, April 1988, 125–31.

"Chesterton and Paganism". *Chesterton Review* 16, nos. 3–4 (August–November 1990): 181–201.

"The Flight into Egypt". *Nazareth Journal*, Advent 1990, 10–16.

"Barometer Falling: Landscapes of Unreality in Art and Society". *Canadian Catholic Review*, February 1990, 44–54.

"A Little Splinter in the Soul". *Nazareth Journal* 1, no. 4 (1991): 8–9.

"Landscape with Dragons Part I". *Nazareth Journal* 2, no. 2 (1992): 17–22.

"Landscape with Dragons Part II". *Nazareth Journal* 2, no. 3 (1992): 14–19.

"The Decline and Renewal of Christian Art". *Second Spring*, August/September 1994, 30–35.

"The Passion of William Kurelek". *Image*, no. 9 (Spring 1995): 75–93.

"Victims, Scandals, Truth, Compassion". *Catholic World Report*, June 2002. http://www.studiobrien.com/victims-scandals-truth -compassion/.

"The Potter Controversy". *StAR*, July/August 2003, 16–23.

"The Return of the Eternal King". *Catholic World Report*, February 2004. http://www.studiobrien.com/the-return-of-the-eternal -king-a-film-review-of-the-passion-of-the-christ/.

"Musings on the Internet". StudioOBrien.com, February 17, 2006. http://www.studiobrien.com/musings-on-the-internet/.

"The Family and Totalitarianism". *Inside the Vatican*, November 2015, 27–29.

Unpublished Writings

"Diary". 1971–2006. Handwritten manuscript.
"The Icon and the Role of the Contemporary Religious Artist: An Address Given by Michael O'Brien in the Loyola College Chapel of Concordia University, Montreal, November 6, 1979". Typewritten document.
"The Spirituality of the Artist: A Transcript of a Conference Given to the Poor Clares at Mission, British Columbia, Pentecost Week 1982, by Michael O'Brien, during the Painting of the Icon of St. Francis of Assisi". Typewritten manuscript.
"The Hidden Face: Our Lady Reveals the Father: A Talk Given at the International Vox Populi Mariae Mediatrici Conference, Rome, May 1, 199[8]". Unpublished printed Microsoft Word file. The printout says 1997, which is the wrong year.
"The Hidden Face: Some Reflections on the Vocation of an Icon Painter". Undated. Typewritten manuscript.
"The Sacred Arts: Ministry and Prophecy; A Transcript of a Lecture Given at Newman Theological College, March 7, 1983, by Michael O'Brien, Artist". Typewritten manuscript.
"Diary of Trip to Russia". July 14–23, 2000. Handwritten manuscript.
"Inner Locutions". September 28, 2006. Microsoft Word file.
"The Cooney Files". Undated, but after 2000. Microsoft Word file.
"A Stone in the Heart". Undated. Printed Microsoft Word file.

APPENDIX 2

Chronology of Michael D. O'Brien's Life

1948	Born in Ottawa, Ontario
1961–1963	Coppermine, Northwest Territories
1969	Conversion experience
1971	Show at Robertson Galleries, Ottawa
1972	Moves to Valemount, British Columbia
1973	Moves to Blue River, British Columbia; works as a weather observer
1975	Marriage: Michael O'Brien and Sheila Mercer
1976	Death of David O'Brien, Michael's father, and birth of John David O'Brien; decision for sacred art and move to Ottawa
1978	Birth of Joseph O'Brien; writing of first novel, *A Cry of Stone*
1979	Moves back to Blue River
1981	Birth of Mary Theresa O'Brien; writing of second novel, *The Sojourners*
1982	Moves to Valemount; first artists' retreat at Mount Angel Abbey, Oregon, USA
1983	Birth of Elizabeth O'Brien
1984	Moves to Mission, British Columbia
1985	First try at homeschooling
1987	Birth of Benjamin O'Brien
1988	Moves to Brudenell, Ontario
1990	Birth of Angela O'Brien
1990–1996	Editor of *Nazareth Journal*
1992–1995	White Horse Press
1994	Writing of *Father Elijah*
1995	Trip to Mexico

1996	Publication of *Father Elijah*
1997	Conference in Rome
1998	Moves to Combermere; publication of *Father Elijah* in Czech translation
1999	Founding of Mater Ecclesia Study Centre (later renamed Our Lady Seat of Wisdom Academy and then Our Lady Seat of Wisdom College) in O'Brien home
1999–2000	Fieldtrips to Russia
2001	Website StudiOBrien.com is launched
2002	Publication of *Father Elijah* in Croatian translation
2003	First trip to Croatia
2005	Andrija Buvina Award, Split, Croatia
2006	Trip to Italy
2012	Trip to France
2014	Moves to Barry's Bay
2016	The Aquinas Award, for the novel *Elijah in Jerusalem*, from Aquinas College, Nashville, Tennessee.
2017	The Feniks Award (Phoenix Award), for the novel *Elijah in Jerusalem*, from the Association of Catholic Publishers, Warsaw.

NOTES

Prologue

[1] Michael D. O'Brien, *William Kurelek: Painter and Prophet* (Ottawa, Ontario: Justin Press, 2013), 1.
[2] Nigel Hamilton, *How to Do Biography: A Primer* (Cambridge, MA: Harvard University Press, 2012), 110.

1. Dire Straits

[1] According to Kenneth McNaught, the recession lasted from 1957 to 1961, and it was preceded by a phenomenal expansion, the postwar boom, both of population and economy after the Second World War. Kenneth McNaught, *The History of Canada* (New York: Praeger Publishers), 293.
[2] As I have few sources for the prehistory and childhood of Michael, the chapter is mainly based on the interviews with Michael and his siblings.
[3] For a description of how things might have been for David in the Royal Canadian Air Force during World War II, see Lloyd Francis, *Ottawa Boy* (Burnstone: General Store Publishing House, 2000), 22–31.
[4] Stephen O'Brien's war experiences are described in a document that he wrote after the war. Stephen O'Brien, "Original Story of Experiences while a Prisoner of War, during the First World War 1914–1918, of Stephen O'Brien" (unpublished manuscript), typewritten, 52 pages.
[5] Terry O'Brien, interview by Clemens Cavallin, Barry's Bay, Canada, October 23, 2015.
[6] Michael D. O'Brien, email message to author, January 18, 2014, attachment Microsoft Word file, 5.

2. The Arctic

[1] Michael D. O'Brien, email message to author, November 8, 2013, attachment Microsoft Word file, 7.
[2] Terry O'Brien, *The Boy Who Fell to Earth: A Modern Pilgrim's Progress* (Terry O'Brien, 2001), 29.
[3] Michael D. O'Brien, interview by Clemens Cavallin, October 15, 2011, recorded and transcribed.
[4] T. O'Brien, *Boy Who Fell to Earth*, 39.

[5] For information see "Grollier Hall & 'The Devil of Grollier Hall' ", *Sylvia's Site* (blog), accessed June 20, 2018, https://www.theinquiry.ca/wordpress/accused /charged/houston-father-martin-houston; and Andrew Raven, "Grollier Hall Supervisor Sentenced", *Northern News Services*, last modified August 20, 2004, accessed August 15, 2016, www.nnsl.com/frames/newspapers/2004-08/aug20_04crt.html.

[6] Michael D. O'Brien, "Victims, Scandals, Truth, Compassion", StudiOBrien .com, accessed June 20, 2018, www.studiobrien.com/victims-scandals-truth -compassion. Previously published in *Catholic World Report*, June 2002.

[7] Ibid.

[8] Ibid.

[9] When new victims stepped forward in the late 1990s during a trial of two other hostel supervisors, Houston had to resign from his position at the Catholic parish in Carman, Manitoba. He was himself put on trial for the second time in 2004 and pleaded guilty; however, he was given a suspended sentence. Houston died in 2010. (Raven, "Grollier Hall Supervisor Sentenced".) Regarding Michael O'Brien's public witness, see a report from a panel at Saint Paul University in Ottawa in 2011: Fr. Raymond J. De Souza, "Openness to Grace Makes Reconciliation Possible", *Catholic Register*, March 30, 2011, http://www.catholicregister.org /columns/item/5287-openness-to-grace-makes-reconciliation-possible.

[10] See the official homepage of the Truth and Reconciliation Commission of Canada, www.trc.ca. The closing ceremony of the commission was held in the beginning of June 2015; as of December 18, 2015, the commission's offices are closed. See also Truth and Reconciliation Commission of Canada, *Canada's Residential Schools: The Inuit and Northern Experience; The Final Report of the Truth and Reconciliation Commission of Canada*, vol. 2 (Montreal & Kingston: McGill-Queen's University Press, 2015), 141–44.

[11] "Northern National Event, Highlights", Truth and Reconciliation Commission of Canada, accessed August 15, 2016, http://www.myrobust.com/websites /Northern/index. php? p=238#.

[12] However, abuse was widespread. In *Canada's Residential Schools* it is reported that "four of the Grollier Hall staff were convicted of abusing students." And consequently, "for a twenty-year period from 1959 to 1979, there was at least one sexual predator on staff at Grollier Hall at all times." Truth and Reconciliation Commission, *Canada's Residential Schools*, 141.

[13] T. O'Brien, *Boy Who Fell to Earth*, 45.

[14] Ibid., 49.

3. Back to Civilization

[1] This growth was combined with a conscious restructuring of the city according to the Greber Plan approved by Parliament in 1951. See Shirley Woods Jr., *Ottawa: The Capital of Canada* (Toronto: Doubleday, 1980), chap. 22; Wilfrid Eggleston, *The Queen's Choice* (Ottawa, Ontario: National Capital Commission, 1961), chaps. 10 and 11.

² Fr. Joseph Hattie, interview by Clemens Cavallin, Barry's Bay, Canada, September 17, 2014, recorded.

³ For an overview, see, e.g., Alex Owen, *The Place of Enchantment: British Occultism and the Culture of the Modern* (Chicago: University of Chicago Press, 2004).

⁴ I have not been able to ascertain what Rosicrucian group this was, but a number of such groups and associations were formed during the late nineteenth and early twentieth centuries, finding inspiration in the Rosicrucian manifestos written in the early seventeenth century. These groups were part of a larger loose conglomerate of movements and ideas (for example, the Theosophical Society founded in 1875 and the later diverse phenomenon of New Age) reaching back to late antiquity and labelled by scholars "Western Esotericism". See Antoine Faivre, *Access to Western Esotericism* (New York: Suny Press, 1994); Nicholas Goodrick-Clarke, *The Western Esoteric Traditions: A Historical Introduction* (Oxford: Oxford University Press, 2008).

⁵ Robert A. Orsi, *Between Heaven and Earth* (Princeton and Oxford: Princeton University Press, 2005), 56.

⁶ Michael D. O'Brien, email message to author, January 18, 2014, attachment Microsoft Word file.

⁷ They lived there for three years, but after some time they found commuting to be time-consuming, so in 1969 they moved back to the city, into a small house on Argyle Avenue, opposite the Victoria Memorial Museum Building.

⁸ Michael D. O'Brien, email message to author, October 16, 2013, attachment Microsoft Word file.

⁹ M. O'Brien, interview by Cavallin, Combermere, Canada, October 15, 2011, recorded and transcribed.

¹⁰ For a discussion, see the chapter "Teilhard de Chardin: 'Patron Saint' of 'New Age' Catholicism?", in *The Phenomenon of Teilhard: Prophet for a New Age*, by David H. Lane (Macon, GA: Mercer University Press, 1996), 71–88.

¹¹ Wouter Hanegraaf delimits the New Age movement chronologically as emerging in the latter half of the 1970s and reaching maturity in the 1980s, in order to differentiate between it and the counterculture of the 1960s. Wouter Hanegraaf, *New Age Religion and Western Culture* (Leiden: E.J. Brill, 1996), 12.

¹² The account of Michael's loss and regaining of his faith is based on interviews with him by the author in October 15, 2011, and October 20, 2015.

¹³ M. O'Brien, interview by Cavallin, October 15, 2011.

¹⁴ In an email to me regarding this experience (September 17, 2016), Michael wrote that the near-overpowering spiritual malevolence returned to attack him three more times during the following years. Each time, he repelled it with prayer and the name of Jesus, at which it always withdrew.

¹⁵ Gregory Bourassa, email message to author, August 29, 2016.

¹⁶ This story is recounted in Michael D. O'Brien and Mate Krajina, *The Donkey Dialogues* (Ottawa, Ontario: Justin Press, 2014), 87–90.

¹⁷ Michael D. O'Brien, "Diary", February 18, 1971 (unpublished manuscript, 1971–2006), handwritten. In the original, "above all else are the roots" says "above all else are the words" (i.e., "words" is here exchanged for "roots"), as Michael

thinks this is a mistake that obscures his intended meaning. (Unless otherwise indicated, all subsequent diary entries are from this diary and will be cited as "Diary" along with the date of entry.)

[18] Ibid., April 25, 1971.

[19] Ibid., March 25, 1971.

[20] The gallery was founded by Mary and John Robertson in 1953, who pioneered the showing and promoting of Inuit art. "Mary Robertson, Obituary", *Ottawa Citizen*, January 3–4, 2014, http://www.legacy.com/obituaries/ottawacitizen/obituary.aspx?n=mary-robertson&pid=168877608. For five years, John Robertson was a member of the Canadian Eskimo Arts Council, and it was probably this interest that put him in touch with David O'Brien. See "Lot 289, Unidentified, Arctic Bay Mother and Child", Inuit Art Auction, June 2, 2014, accessed June 20, 2016, http://inuitart.waddingtons.ca/64901/unidentified.

[21] "Diary", November 19, 1971.

[22] Jenny Bergin, "Delicate Pen Drawings Depict Natural Things", *Ottawa Citizen*, November 23, 1971.

[23] "Diary", November 19, 1971.

[24] Ibid., November 22, 1971.

4. Blue River

[1] Sheila O'Brien, interview by Clemens Cavallin, Krk, Croatia, April 5, 2014, recorded.

[2] The breakthrough was the construction of the Yellowhead Highway 16 through McBride in 1968. See "McBride", Travel British Columbia, accessed June 20, 2018, www.travel-british-columbia.com/north-bc/yellowhead-highway/mcbride.

[3] Nowadays, they are only renting cabins and running a campground. See the website for Mount Robson Heritage Cabins at www.mountrobsonranch.com.

[4] "Crossroads, 1960–1969", University of British Columbia, accessed June 20, 2018, www.ubc.ca/stories/2015-fall/100-years-of-discovery/1960-1969.

[5] Regarding the rebellious changes in Quebec, see, e.g., Brian D. Palmer, "Quebec: Revolution Now!", in *Canada's 1960s: The Ironies of Identity in a Rebellious Era* (Toronto: University of Toronto Press, 2009), 311.

[6] "Diary", March 22, 1975.

[7] Ibid., February 16, 1976.

5. Sacred Art

[1] Michael D. O'Brien, interview by Clemens Cavallin, October 15, 2011

[2] Ibid.

[3] "Diary", June 1, 1976.

6. Iconography

[1] Catherine Doherty, *Fragments of My Life: A Memoir* (1979; repr., Combermere, Ontario: Madonna House Publications, 2007).

² See their homepage, www.madonnahouse.org.

³ Catherine de Hueck Doherty, *Poustinia: Christian Spirituality of the East for Western Man* (Notre Dame, IN: Ave Maria Press, 1975).

⁴ This was the time when laws on security belts were just coming into place and children were mostly not required to travel in safety seats. A law on mandatory security belts for adults was introduced in British Columbia in 1977, while Ontario since January 1976 actually had such a law. "Seatbelts Saving Lives in Ontario for 35 Years", *News Ontario*, December 29, 2010, https://news.ontario.ca/mto/en/2010/12/seatbelts-saving-lives-in-ontario-for-35-years.html.

⁵ "Obituary of Joan Mary Bryant (1934–2011)", Your Life Moments, accessed August 17, 2016, http://yourlifemoments.ca/sitepages/obituary.asp?oid=466507.

⁶ For biographies narrating William Kurelek's life story, see Michael D. O'Brien, *William Kurelek: Painter and Prophet* (Ottawa, Ontario: Justin Press, 2013), and Patricia Morley, *Kurelek: A Biography* (Toronto: Macmillan of Canada, 1986), and the two versions of his autobiography, *Someone with Me: An Autobiography* (Ithaca, NY: Centre for Improvement of Undergraduate Education, Cornell University, 1973) and *Someone with Me: An Autobiography* (Toronto: McClelland and Stewart, 1980).

⁷ "Diary", April 18, 1977.

⁸ Ibid., May 2, 1977.

⁹ Iryna Yehorova, "'Angel in Flight' Lviv Luminaries Attend Unveiling of Mykola Bidniak's Gravestone", *Day*, December 12, 2006, http://day.kyiv.ua/en/article/culture/angel-flight.

¹⁰ "Diary", June 19, 1977.

¹¹ Ibid., June 20, 1977.

¹² John of the Cross, *Dark Night of the Soul*, trans. and ed. E. Allison Peers, 3rd ed. (New York: Image Books, 1959).

¹³ The description of the meeting between Michael O'Brien and Catherine Doherty is based on the account in Michael's diary in 1977.

¹⁴ Of course, in the Greek Catholic churches, which are Catholic with an Eastern rite, this has been the case before Vatican II.

¹⁵ This was followed up in the 1990s by the incredibly successful Left Behind series written by Tim LaHaye and Jerry B. Jenkins. See Amy Johnson Frykholm, *Rapture Culture: Left Behind in Evangelical America* (New York: Oxford University Press, 2004).

¹⁶ One such topic is a technological understanding of the mark of the beast (mentioned in Revelation 13:16–17) as a microchip implant or some other form of technology; for example, on the website of the Jeremiah Project, a number of candidates are listed, including iriscans, thermograms, and subcutaneous implants ("Signs of the Last Days: Mark of the Beast", accessed June 20, 2018, www.jeremiahproject.com/prophecy/markofthebeast.html). The basic problem is, of course, that computer technology evolves with amazing speed and more specific prophesies quickly become outdated. The basic point here is that the apocalypse is interpreted through the lens of technology: premodern symbols are translated into a technological language. See Glenn W. Shuck, *Marks of the Beast: The Left Behind Novels and the Struggle for Evangelical Identity* (New York: New York University Press, 2005), 2, 109, 114–21.

[17] An example is his talk "Are We Living in Apocalyptic Times?", given September 20, 2005, in St. Patrick's Basilica in Ottawa and printed in Michael D. O'Brien, *Remembrance of the Future: Reflections on Our Times* (Ottawa, Ontario: Justin Press, 2009), 376–428.

[18] Michael W. Cuneo, *Catholics against the Church: Anti-Abortion Protest in Toronto 1969–1985* (Toronto: University of Toronto Press, 1989), 5–25.

[19] Ibid., 7–8, 26–39.

[20] Paul VI, encyclical letter *Humanae vitae* (July 25, 1968), no. 14, http://w2 .vatican.va/content/paul-vi/en/encyclicals/documents/hf_p-vi_enc_25071968 _humanae-vitae.html.

[21] Canadian Press, "Birth-Control Pill Turns 50", CBC.CA, May 7, 2010, last updated May 10, 2010, http://www.cbc.ca/news/birth-control-pill-turns-50-1.908892.

[22] For example, in 2015, a poll by Pew Research Center reported that 66 percent of American Catholics do not consider it a sin to use contraceptives. Pew Research Center: Religion and Public Life, "U.S. Catholics Open to Non-Traditional Families", last modified September 2, 2015, http://www.pewforum.org/2015/09/02/u -s-catholics-open-to-non-traditional-families/. A poll in February 2014 claimed that 79 percent of Catholics in the United States support the use of contraceptives. "Voice of the People", *Univision*, accessed August 18, 2016, www.univision.com /noticias/la-huella-digital/la-voz-del-pueblo/matrix. In Reginald Bibby's *Fragmented Gods: The Poverty and Potential of Religion in Canada* (Toronto: Irwin Publishing, 1987), 156, it is reported that "the majority of Roman Catholics defy the Vatican's position: approximately 80% of all Catholics and 70% of those who say they are committed Catholics do not disapprove of premarital sex." And 88 percent think that birth-control information should be available to teenagers (ibid., 159). See also Reginald W. Bibby and Angus Reid, *Canada's Catholics: Vitality and Hope in a New Era* (Toronto: Novalis, 2016), 68, which despite its upbeat subtitle reports that while only 15 percent of Canada's Catholics say table grace, 19 percent read their horoscopes.

[23] See Michael W. Cuneo, "The Catholic Bishops and the Abortion Issue", chap. 2 in *Catholics against the Church*; moreover, see Vincent Foy, *Did Pope Paul VI Approve the Winnipeg Statement? A Search for the Truth* (Toronto: Life Ethics Information Centre, 1997).

[24] "Pro-Life Leader Charges Gov't Abusing Power", *Ottawa Journal*, May 7, 1977.

[25] William Kurelek, *A Prairie Boy's Summer* (Boston: Houghton Mifflin, 1975); William Kurelek, *A Northern Nativity* (Montreal: Tundra Books, 1976).

[26] "Diary", November 28, 1977.

[27] Martha Scott, "Icon Show Not for the Cynical", *Ottawa Citizen*, November 2, 1977.

[28] Tom Hill, "Painter Risks All to Develop Religious Art", *Ottawa Citizen*, November 5, 1977.

[29] Patricia Morley, *Korolek: A Biography* (Toronto: Macmillan of Canada, 1986).

[30] For an overview of Tillard's life and work, see "Nécrologie: F. Jean-Marie Roger Tillard, O.P., 1927–2000", Institut de Pastorale des Dominicains, accessed October 6, 2016, www.ipastorale.ca/ressources/partnr/varia/Jean-Marie%20Roger %20Tillard,%200.p.%20(1927-2000).pdf.

[31] "Diary", February 28, 1977.

[32] For an overview of Dewan's life and work, see Steven Baldner, "In Memoriam: Fr. Lawrence Dewan O.P. (1932–2015)", *Review of Metaphysics* 68, no. 4 (2015): 915.

[33] Jacques Maritain, *Art and Scholasticism, and the Frontiers of Poetry*, trans. Joseph W. Evans (New York: Charles's Scribner's Sons, 1962), 66.

[34] Duart Snow, "Icon Painting—An Ancient Art", *Ottawa Journal*, August 1978.

[35] Michael D. O'Brien, "The Spirituality of the Artist: A Transcript of a Conference Given to the Poor Clare's at Mission, British Columbia, Pentecost Week 1982, by Michael O'Brien, during the Painting of the Icon of St. Francis of Assisi" (unpublished manuscript), typewritten, 15.

[36] For a thorough historical analysis of the Council guided by a hermeneutics of continuity (although not shying away from actual discontinuities and crisis), see Roberto Mattei, *The Second Vatican Council: An Unwritten Story*, trans. Patrick T. Brannan, S.J.; Michael J. Miller; and Kenneth D. Whitehead (Fitzwilliam, NH: Loreto Publications, 2012). For an example of understanding it as merely the beginning of a new form of Catholicism, see Richard R. Gaillardetz, *An Unfinished Council: Vatican II, Pope Francis, and the Renewal of Catholicism* (Collegeville, MN: Liturgical Press, 2015).

[37] Alex McGegor, "The Icon & the Sublime", *Lambda*, November 1, 1978, 6.

[38] M. O'Brien, "Spirituality of the Artist", 15.

7. Logos

[1] The following fictional narrative of a day in Michael's life and the presentation in the chapter of Michael's view on icon painting in the late 1970s are based on the following sources: the brochure published by the rector Rev. Canon James A. Winters, *High Altar Triptych: Canon Cornish Memorial*; "The Icon and the Role of the Contemporary Religious Artist: An Address Given by Michael O'Brien in the Loyola College Chapel of Concordia University, Montreal, November 6, 1979"(unpublished manuscript), typewritten. And also the unpublished manuscript of a larger treatise (61 pages) on icon painting by Michael D. O'Brien, "The Hidden Face: Some Reflections on the Vocation of Icon Painter". And, finally, comments by Michael and Sheila to the author of what such an average day was like.

[2] O'Brien, "Hidden Face", 22.

[3] "Bilde, Künstler! Rede nicht!" E.g., in Klaus von Beyme, *Das Zeitalter der Avantgarden: Kunst und Gesellschaft 1905–1955* (München: C. H. Beck, 2005), 222.

[4] M. O'Brien, "Hidden Face", 29–30.

[5] "Diary", November 4–6, 1978.

8. Purification

[1] "Diary", May 11, 1981.

[2] The version of Terry differs somewhat from Michael's version. The main difference is who of the two brothers actually killed the bear.

[3] Terry O'Brien, *The Boy Who Fell to Earth: A Modern Pilgrim's Progress* (Terry O'Brien, 2001), 108.

[4] See webpage about Igor Khazanov, accessed June 21, 2018, www.igork hazanovart.com/about.html.

[5] Ibid.

[6] "Diary", November 20, 1981.

[7] Isaac Bashevis Singer, *The Power of Light: Eight Stories for Hanukkah* (New York: Farrar Straus Giroux, 1980).

9. The Winter of Our Discontent

[1] "Diary", November 22, 1981.

[2] Ibid., late January 1982.

[3] Ibid., February 1982.

[4] Ibid., February 28, 1982.

[5] Michael D. O'Brien, interview by Clemens Cavallin, October 20, 2015.

[6] "Diary", April 12, 1982.

[7] "History", Saint Luke Productions, accessed June 21, 2018, http://www .stlukeproductions.com/about/history.

[8] Leonardo Defilippis, email message to author, September 16, 2016.

[9] "Prayer at Hatzic Monastery: The Poor Clares; At Work in Mission", *Fraser Valley Record*, June 30, 1982, A7.

[10] Michael D. O'Brien, "The Spirituality of the Artist: A Transcript of a Conference Given to the Poor Clare's at Mission, British Columbia, Pentecost Week 1982, by Michael O'Brien, during the Painting of the Icon of St. Francis of Assisi" (unpublished manuscript), typewritten.

[11] Michael D. O'Brien, email to author, September 11, 2016.

10. Valemount

[1] "Diary", November 1, 1982.

[2] Ibid., December 5, 1982.

[3] Ibid., January 19, 1983.

[4] Ibid.

[5] Ibid., March 7, 1983.

[6] Michael D. O'Brien, "The Sacred Arts: Ministry and Prophecy; A Transcript of a Lecture Given at Newman Theological College, March 7, 1983, by Michael O'Brien, Artist" (unpublished manuscript), typewritten, 21 pages.

[7] Address of Pope VI to Artists (December 8, 1965), https://w2.vatican.va /content/paul-vi/en/speeches/1965/documents/hf_p-vi_spe_19651208_epilogo -concilio-artisti.html.

[8] Glen Argan, "Icon Painter Dislikes Holy Card Art", *Western Catholic Reporter*, March 14, 1983, 8.

[9] Adam Exner, previously bishop of Kamloops, had become archbishop of Winnipeg in 1982.

[10] Beatrice Fines, "B.C. Artist Brings 'The Message of the Cross'", *Catholic Register*, April 9, 1983, 11.

[11] I have changed the quotation from third person to first person.

[12] Andrea Lang, "Artist Serves God through Paintings", *Prairie Messenger*, April 3, 1983, 11.

[13] "Diary", July 26, 1983.

[14] Ibid., May 12 1983.

[15] Michael O'Brien, "Art—The Cry of a People", *Our Family Magazine*, April 1983, 32–36.

[16] CNA/EWTN News, "EWTN Forms New Publishing Group with Sophia Institute Press", *National Catholic Register*, August 19, 2015, http://www.ncregister.com/daily-news/ewtn-forms-new-publishing-group-with-sophia-institute-press. Update: Currently, EWTN broadcasts to over 268 million households in more than 145 countries ("About EWTN", EWTN, accessed June 23, 2018, http://www.ewtn.com/general/index.asp).

[17] "The History of Ignatius Press", *Ignatius Insight*, accessed June 21, 2018, http://www.ignatiusinsight.com/info/history_ip.asp.

[18] "The Purpose, Mission, and Vision of Christendom College", Christendom College, accessed September 5, 2015, www.christendom.edu/about/mission.php. (The current website can be accessed at https://www.christendom.edu/about/.)

[19] Daniel Williams, *God's Own Party: The Making of the Christian Right* (Oxford, NY: Oxford University Press, 2010).

[20] "Diary", October 7, 1983.

[21] Ibid., October 15, 1983.

[22] Ibid., September 8, 1983.

[23] Ibid.

[24] Ibid., June 14, 1983.

[25] Ibid., November 17, 1983.

11. Mission

[1] See the webpage about Mission, accessed June 21, 2018, www.mission.ca/about.

[2] Fr. Augustine Kalberer, O.S.B., "Our History: The Full Story", Seminary of Christ the King, accessed June 21, 2018, http://sck.ca/about-sck/history/the-full-story. In 1940, the monks relocated even closer to Vancouver, while in 1954 they moved to the new site in Mission. The priory was then recognized as an abbey, marking an increased independence from the abbey in Oregon.

[3] "The 'Star Light' of Clare Shines in Vancouver", Poor Clares: Contemplative Franciscan Women, Mission, British Columbia, accessed June 21, 2018, http://poorclaresosc.org/our-monasteries/mission-british-columbia.

[4] Jose Ramos Ruba, "The Canadian Pro–Life Movement in the 21st Century: A Statistical Analysis", LifeIssues.net, reprint with permission, accessed June 21, 2018, http://www.lifeissues.net/writers/rub/ca1.html.

[5] For example, Seton Home Study School, established in 1980; see their webpage "Helping Parents Since 1980", accessed June 21, 2018, http://www.setonhome.org/seton-home-study-school/about.

[6] Wendy Priesnitz, "Life Learning: Canadian Home-Based Learning Resources; A History of the Modern Canadian Home Education Movement", Life Learning, accessed June 21, 2018, http://www.lifelearning.ca/articles/history_of_Canadian _homeschooling_movement.htm.

[7] Michael D. O'Brien, email to author, October 6, 2016.

[8] George Weigel, Witness to Hope: The Biography of Pope John Paul II (New York: HarperCollins, 1999), 479.

[9] Laureen McMahon, "Memories Shine from Sunny Papal Visit", B.C. Catholic, May 10, 2011.

[10] Ibid.

[11] "Ernest Hemingway's Typewriter—Ultra Rare Relic for Sale", YouTube video, 1:24, posted by University Archives, November 4, 2009, https://www.you tube.com/watch?v=7NVioC4pHRM.

[12] Michael D. O'Brien, "Fire in Our Darkness: The Artist as Minister and Prophet", Canadian Catholic Review, November 1984, 10–18.

[13] Ibid., 15. In later essays, Michael clarifies his remarks about beauty saving the world. According to Michael, Dostoyevsky's novel dramatizes the truth that, contrary to public sentiment, beauty cannot save the world—only the profound spiritual beauty of sacrifice united to the Cross of Christ can assist in the redemption of man. Michael D. O'Brien, "Will Beauty Save the World?", in Remembrance of the Future: Reflections on Our Times (Ottawa, Ontario: Justin Press, 2009), 12–17.

12. The Enchanted Garden

[1] Mario O. D'Souza, "Some Reflections on Contemporary Canadian Catholic Education", Interchange 34, no. 4 (2003): 363–81.

[2] John O'Brien, email to author, October 23, 2015.

[3] This story actually took place June 6, 1984, but was put here as part of a fictive, but representative, day of life in Mission. The characterization builds upon interviews with the children of Michael and Sheila, and also on the extensive article "Profile 87: Michael O'Brien; Light on the Hill Top", in the magazine Our Family in July/August 1987, 14–21.

[4] "Diary", July 2, 1985.

[5] Ibid., September 18, 1985.

[6] Ibid., October 9, 1985.

[7] The story is in Michael's diary, but also in Michael O'Brien, "A Little Splinter in the Soul", Nazareth Journal 1, no. 4 (1991): 8–9.

[8] "Diary", January 21, 1986.

[9] Ibid., June 15, 1987.

[10] See Chesterton's book on Shaw, George Bernhard Shaw (London: Lane, 1914); Matthew Yde, Bernard Shaw and Totalitarianism: Longing for Utopia (New York: Palgrave Macmillan, 2013); and Stanley Weintraub, "GBS and the Despots", Times Literary Supplement, August 22, 2011.

[11] Michael D. O'Brien, "An Original Theology: Creation and Matthew Fox", Canadian Catholic Review, April 1988, 125–31.

[12] See e.g., Richard E. Kuykendall, *Even Witches Have Names* (Bloomington, IN: Trafford, 2012), x–xi, and Ed Hird, "An Analysis of Starhawk and the Witch-craft Revival", *Incourage Magazine* 2, no. 4 (October–December 1988), http://www3.telus.net/st_simons/arm15.html. For the connection to David Spangler see O'Brien, "Original Theology", 131.

[13] Raymond A. Scrotch, "Former Dominican Takes on the 'Inquisitor'", *National Catholic Reporter*, January 11, 2012, https://www.ncronline.org/books/2017/08/former-dominican-takes-inquisitor.

[14] Molly O'Neill, "At Supper with—Matthew Fox; Roman Catholic Rebel Becomes a Cause Celebre", *New York Times*, March 17, 1993, https://www.nytimes.com/1993/03/17/garden/at-supper-with-matthew-fox-roman-catholic-rebel-becomes-a-cause-celebre.html?scp=1&sq=&st=nyt.

[15] See his self-presentation at www.matthewfox.org/matthew-fox.

[16] "Diary", October 1988.

[17] "Brudenell: History", Ontario Ghost Towns, accessed June 21, 2018, www.ghosttownpix.com/ontario/towns/brudenel.html.

[18] Ibid.

13. Angels and Divine Humour

[1] Mark McGowan, "A Short History of Catholic Schools in Ontario" (Toronto: Ontario Catholic School Trustee's Association, 2013).

[2] See, e.g., the story recounted in Michael D. O'Brien and Mate Krajina, *The Donkey Dialogues* (Ottawa, Ontario: Justin Press, 2014), 87–90.

[3] The consecration was to be performed a year later, but Michael and Sheila did not go through with it, as they did not want to become formal members of the movement Opus Sanctorum Angelorum, which had been founded in Austria in 1949, based on the private revelations of Gabriele Bitterlich (1896–1978). She claimed to have had many visions of angels in which they revealed their names and functions. After her death, an investigation was carried out by the Congregation for the Doctrine of the Faith, which in 1983 issued some rules and regulations. Nine years later, they followed up these with a decree, making it clear that the organization was not to use the private revelations of Bitterlich and the consecration to the angels. However, in the year 2000, a revised form of the consecration was approved, and some years later (2008) the Opus Sanctorum Angelorum was recognized as a public association of the faithful. See "Brief History of the Opus Angelorum and Its Development within the Church", Opus Sanctorum Angelorum: Work of the Holy Angels, accessed June 21, 2018, www.opusangelorum.org/about-us/brief_history.html.

[4] The biography would eventually be published several years later: Michael D. O'Brien, *William Kurelek: Painter and Prophet* (Ottawa, Ontario: Justin Press, 2013).

[5] Michael D. O'Brien, "Disaster, Rage, and Repentance", in *Father at Night* (Ottawa, Ontario: Justin Press, 2011), 16–31.

[6] "Diary", October 21, 1989.

14. Family Matters

[1] Don McPhee, "The Road to Nazareth", *Nazareth Journal*, Advent 1990, 24.

[2] "Cana Colony: Family Retreat", under the heading "Beginnings of Cana", Madonna House, accessed June 21, 2018, www.madonnahouse.org/programs/cana .html.

[3] Don McPhee, "Nazareth: A Proposal to Establish a Catholic Family Life Centre in Combermere, Ontario" (unpublished document, May 13, 1982), typewritten.

[4] John Paul II, apostolic exhortation *Familiaris Consortio* (November 22, 1981), nos. 29, 31, 34, 58, http://w2.vatican.va/content/john-paul-ii/en/apost_exhortations /documents/hf_jp-ii_exh_19811122_familiaris-consortio.pdf.

[5] Michael W. Cuneo, *Catholics against the Church: Anti-Abortion Protest in Toronto 1969–1985* (Toronto: University of Toronto Press, 1989), 196–97. This situation changed with the election of Pope Francis in 2013, and the difference between the Synod on the Family in 1980 and that in 2015 is radical. One could say that revivalist Catholicism is presently living through a crisis of authority and confusion, which is shown by the very critical reception of *Amoris Laetitia* in comparison with the role of *Familiaris Consortio*. This reference to the present situation is illuminating for an understanding of "conservative" Catholicism in the 1980s and 1990s, in that it clearly shows how the pontificate of John Paul II was a unique period of late twentieth-century Catholicism. Cuneo in a later book, *The Smoke of Satan: Conservative and Traditionalist Dissent in Contemporary American Catholicism* (New York: Oxford University Press, 1997), seems to incline toward fundamentalism as an umbrella notion for Catholic discontent with modernism, which he divides into Catholic conservatism, Catholic separatists, mystical marianists, and apocalypticists.

[6] Posie McPhee, interview by Clemens Cavallin, Combermere, October 2015.

[7] "Diary", April 5, 1984.

[8] See the official website about Međugorje at http://www.medjugorje.hr/en/; and for an overview in the context of modern Marian apparitions, see Sandra L. Zimdars-Schwartz, *Encountering Mary: From La Salette to Medjugorje* (Princeton: Princeton University Press, 2014).

[9] Clemens Cavallin, "A Pilgrimage Within", *Journal of Contemporary Religion* 22, no. 2 (2007): 235–51, and Clemens Cavallin, "Globalized Apparitions", *Bandue*, no. 3 (2009): 81–97.

[10] For the website of the Marian Movement of Priests, the movement based on the messages allegedly received by Fr. Stefano Gobbi from the Virgin Mary, see http://www.mmp-usa.net/.

[11] The Chesterton Society in Ottawa was one more example of an institution within post–Vatican II Catholic revivalism in Canada. It was formed in 1989 by a group of Catholic men, and the meetings were held in the National Press Club, on Wellington Avenue, directly opposite the Houses of Parliament. The format was dinner, followed by a talk on the works or life of Chesterton, or of his circle of friends. Michael was a speaker on several occasions, and he had actually not been familiar with Chesterton until his contact with the society. However, it folded in 1998, according to its first president, John Gay, because of the cost of dining out at

each meeting and as it was an exclusively male society. John Gay, email message to author, November 5, 2015.

[12] See the official report of the Holy See in 2010 regarding the Legionaries of Christ: "Communiqué of the Holy See regarding the Apostolic Visitation of the Congregation of the Legionaries of Christ", May 1, 2010, http://www.vatican.va /resources/resources_comunicato-legionari-cristo-2010_en.html.

[13] See, e.g., Joseph Bottum, "The Cost of Father Maciel", *First Things*, May 12, 2010, https://www.firstthings.com/web-exclusives/2010/05/the-cost-of-father -maciel .

[14] See *Betrayal: The Crisis in the Catholic Church* by the Investigate Staff of the *Boston Globe* (Boston: Little, Brown & Company, 2015).

[15] The article was also later published in his *Remembrance of the Future: Reflections on Our Times* (Ottawa, Ontario: Justin Press, 2009).

[16] Monica DeBruyn, "Cat Trauma", *Nazareth Journal*, Advent 1990, 6.

[17] Michael D. O'Brien, "The Flight into Egypt", *Nazareth Journal*, Advent 1990, 16.

[18] Francis Fukuyama, "The End of History?", *National Interest* 16 (1989): 3.

[19] Ibid., 4.

[20] Ibid., 14.

[21] Ibid., 275.

[22] Ibid., 18.

[23] "Diary", October 16, 1990.

[24] Adding to the blow, in 1978 another spiritual father, the Benedictine monk Fr. Damasus Payne, had fallen to his death while mountain climbing in the Rockies, on the very day that John Paul II was elected to the papacy.

[25] "Diary", November 3, 1990.

[26] Ibid., April 9, 1991.

[27] Michael D. O'Brien, *William Kurelek: Painter and Prophet* (Ottawa, Ontario: Justin Press, 2013).

[28] "Diary", April 5 1992.

[29] Michael D. O'Brien, "Landscape with Dragons Part I", *Nazareth Journal* 2, no. 2 (1992): 2.

[30] "Diary", May 1992.

[31] Ibid., October 1, 1992.

[32] See "About *Fully Alive*", Assembly of Catholic Bishops of Ontario, accessed June 21, 2018, http://acbo.on.ca/englishdocs/Brief%20History%20Fully%20Alive .pdf. The first version of *Fully Alive* was published between 1988 and 1992, and later revised in 2006.

[33] "Diary", October 1, 1992.

[34] Ibid.

[35] Ibid., September 12, 1992.

[36] Ibid., October 1, 1992.

[37] Michael D. O'Brien, "Landscape with Dragons Part II", *Nazareth Journal* 2, no. 3 (1992): 17.

[38] Ibid., 15.

[39] In 1998, Ignatius Press published an expanded version of *A Landscape with Dragons*.

[40] Michael D. O'Brien, *The Family and the New Totalitarianism* (Killaloe, Ontario: White Horse Press, 1995), 67.

15. The Absentminded Apocalyptic

[1] "Diary", February 25, 1994.

[2] Ibid.

[3] Ibid., March 21, 1994.

[4] "Novelist of the Last Days: An Interview with Michael O'Brien", *Ignatius Insight*, April 30, 2005, www.ignatiusinsight.com/features2005/mobrien_intvw1_apro5.asp.

[5] "Diary", June 26, 1995.

[6] Michael D. O'Brien, "Chesterton and Paganism", *Chesterton Review* 16, nos. 3–4 (August–November 1990): 194.

[7] The story is told in "Our Lady and a Little Beggar", in Michael D. O'Brien, *Father at Night* (Ottawa, Ontario: Justin Press, 2011), 64–71.

[8] "Diary", February 6–12, 1996.

[9] J. R. R. Tolkien, "On Fairy-Stories", in *Essays Presented to Charles Williams*, ed. C. S. Lewis (1947; repr., Grand Rapids, MI: Wm. B Eerdmans, 1966).

[10] Michael D. O'Brien, *Father Elijah: An Apocalypse* (San Francisco: Ignatius Press, 1996), 13.

[11] Daniel C. Harlow, "Man of Sorrows", November 25, 2010, customer review of *Father Elijah* on Amazon.com. The book had on January 4, 2016, 232 customer reviews with an average rating of 4.7 of 5.

[12] Jaye Procure, "Review of *Father Elijah*", Goodreads.com, April 10, 2009. See another review of *Father Elijah* written by the same reader: "Book Review: Father Elijah", *Catholicanuck* (blog), May 16, 2014, http://catholicanuck.blogspot.se/2014/05/httpwww.html. The average rating of *Father Elijah* on Goodreads was 4.33 of 5; in January 4, 2016, it had 1,369 ratings and 148 reviews.

[13] Miss Clark, "Review of Michael D. O'Brien, *Father Elijah*", Goodreads.com, March 23, 2015.

[14] See the review of *Father Elijah* by David Lyle Jeffrey, "Do You Believe the World Is Coming to an End?", *Books and Culture*, March/April 1997, 18–20.

[15] Helen Valois, "*Father Elijah: An Apocalypse* by Michael O'Brien reviewed by Helen M. Valois", *Lay Witness*, December 1996, 21.

[16] Ibid. In 1996, Philip Jenkins wrote a review in the *Chesterton Review* that struck a more critical tone: "Naming the Beast: Contemporary Apocalyptic Novels", *Chesterton Review* 22, no. 4 (November 1996): 486–97, doi: 10.5840/Chesterton 1996224116. The misinterpretation of the cover painting of the novel made Michael write a response to Jenkins that was published a year later: "A Reply to Philip Jenkins", *Chesterton Review* 23, no. 4 (November 1997): 549–52, doi: 10.5840/chesterton1997234108.

[17] Tracy Moran, "We No Longer Think with the Mind of Christ", *National Catholic Register* 73, no. 48 (November 30, 1997): 11.

[18] Michael D. O'Brien, letter to Fr. Elias Friedman, July 23, 1997.

[19] Fr. Elias Friedman, postcard to Michael O'Brien, August 1, 1997. Fr. Friedman died two years later. See "Elias Friedman, OCD", Association of Hebrew Catholics, accessed June 21, 2018, www.hebrewcatholic.net/elias-friedman-ocd.

[20] John Mallon, "Book Review: Strangers and Sojourners", *Catholic Online*, accessed June 21, 2018, https://www.catholic.org/featured/headline.php?ID=2271.

[21] The rating at Amazon.com was in January 5, 2016, 4.4 stars, with 67 percent awarding it 5 stars and 13 percent 4. It was lower when compared with *Father Elijah* that had 4.7. On Goodreads *Strangers and Sojourners* had 4.06 stars. As of April 8, 2014, it had sold approximately one-fifth of what *Father Elijah* had achieved. Fr. Fessio, S.J., email to author, April 8, 2014.

[22] Peter Lapinskie, "Combermere Author a 'Jewel in our Midst. O'Brien's New Book an Epic'", *Pembroke Observer*, April 11, 1997, 11.

[23] For a comparative analysis of *Father Elijah* and *Strangers and Sojourners*, see Dominic Manganiello, "Restoring the Imago Dei: Transcendental Realism in the Fiction of Michael D. O'Brien", in *Between Human and Divine: The Catholic Vision in Contemporary Literature*, ed. Mary Reichardt (Washington, DC: Catholic University of America Press, 2010), 242–61; and Clemens Cavallin on the same subject, "Deep Realism: A Discussion of Christian Literary Realism with an Analysis of Passages from Michael O'Brien's Children of the Last Days Novel Series", *Logos: A Journal of Catholic Thought and Culture* 18, no. 2 (2015): 104–20.

[24] "Why a New Marian Dogma?" FifthMarianDogma.com, accessed June 21, 2018, www.fifthmariandogma.com.

[25] "Bio-reference for Dr. Mark I. Miravalle, S.T.D.", MarkMiravalle.com, accessed June 21, 2018, www.markmiravalle.com/biography_mark_miravalle.

[26] Mark Miravalle, telephone interview by Clemens Cavallin, September 24, 2014 (recorded).

[27] Michael also designed a medal for the movement: the Triumph of the Immaculate Heart of Mary Medal. On one side is the picture associated with the private revelation of Our Lady of All Nations, which had been approved by the bishop of Amsterdam. For more information, see the website of the Lady of All Nations at http://www.de-vrouwe.info/en. In front of a large cross, the Virgin Mary stands on the globe of the earth with outstretched arms, from which rays are pouring forth. Surrounding the globe are innumerable sheep, and the text around the rim of the medal is "Mother of All Peoples". This image is also associated with the apparitions in Akita in Japan, where a wooden statue of the Our Lady of All Nations was reported to have wept real tears. On the other side of the medal is a design with God the Father on the top with both arms outstretched; beneath Him are the hearts of Jesus and Mary beside each other, and below them is the Holy Spirit in the form of a dove.

[28] Michael D. O'Brien, "The Hidden Face: Our Lady Reveals the Father; A Talk Given at the International Vox Populi Mariae Mediatrici Conference, Rome, May 31, 199[8]" (unpublished printed Microsoft Word file). (The printout says 1997, which is the wrong year.)

[29] Michael D. O'Brien, "The Father and the Lowly Pinecone", in *Father at Night* (Ottawa, Ontario: Justin Press, 2011), 49–57.

[30] "Diary", May 1998. For the homily, see the Vatican's website at http://w2
.vatican.va/content/john-paul-ii/en/homilies/1998/documents/hf_jp-ii_hom
_31051998.

16. A New Beginning

[1] Michael D. O'Brien, "Diary of Trip to Russia", July 14–23, 2000 (unpublished
handwritten manuscript).

[2] Michael D. O'Brien, *Elijah in Jerusalem* (San Francisco: Ignatius Press, 2015), 10.

[3] John Gay, email to author, November 5, 2015.

[4] There remains, however, the humorous work "The Cooney Files" (undated
[but after 2000]), printed Microsoft Word file, 37 pages.

17. Our Lady Seat of Wisdom

[1] Sheila O'Brien (through Michael O'Brien), email message to author, July 3,
2016.

[2] Michael D. O'Brien, email to author, July 3, 2016.

[3] John Henry Newman, *The Idea of a University* (1852; New Haven, CT: Yale
University Press, 1996)

[4] Email to author, March 7, 2016.

[5] Email to author, November 23, 2015, attachment Microsoft Word file.

[6] Sheila O'Brien (through Michael D. O'Brien), email message to author, July 3,
2016.

18. On and Off the Grid

[1] See, e.g., Glenn Yeffeth, ed., *Taking the Red Pill: Science, Philosophy and Religion
in the Matrix* (Chichester, UK: Summersdale, 2003).

[2] Tony Časta, interview by Clemens Cavallin, September 25, 2014.

[3] See the LifeSiteNews website at www.lifesitenews.com. See also the website for
the Campaign Life Coalition at www.campaignlifecoalition.com.

[4] Tony Časta, email message to author, August 21, 2016, attachment PDF file.

[5] See the analysis at SimilarWeb, www.similarweb.com/website/lifesitenews
.com, accessed June 21, 2018. According to SimilarWeb, 56 percent of the readers
of LifeSite are from the United States and only 8 percent from Canada, followed by
6 percent from the United Kingdom.

[6] Michael D. O'Brien, "Musings on the Internet", studioObrien, February 17,
2006, www.studiobrien.com/musings-on-the-internet.

[7] Ibid.

[8] For a discussion of the transition from oral to literary culture and its influence
on human consciousness, see Walter J. Ong, *Orality and Literacy: The Technologizing
of the Word* (London: Routledge, 1982).

[9] Michael D. O'Brien, "Musings on the Internet", studiObrien, December 2005,
http://www.studiobrien.com/musings-on-the-internet/.

[10] Peter Kreeft, "Surfing and Spirituality", accessed June 21, 2018, www.peterkreeft.com/topics/surfing.htm.

[11] Peter Kreeft, letter to Michael O'Brien, March 16, 2011. He continued defiantly to write with pen and paper, but confessed in July 5, 2015, "I am so corrupted by technology that it is much harder for me to handwrite a letter than to type it, and I can no longer compose books by hand. Something in the brain, it seems, dries up when something else is continually watered."

[12] Peter Kreeft, "Surfing and Spirituality".

[13] Michael O'Brien, email to author, July 3, 2016.

19. Speaking in Tongues

[1] Ignatius Press both owns and handles the right to translations of Michael's novels.

[2] "Interview with Glas Koncila, 2006, April 14", StudioOBrien.com, captured by Internet Archive Wayback Machine, accessed March 11, 2016, https://archive.org/web.

[3] "Hrvatski katolički zbor MI", *Porečka i Pulska Biskupija*, accessed June 21, 2018, www.biskupija-porecko-pulska.hr/ud-ruge-i-pokreti/frama.html?id=42:odrana-konferencija-za-novina re-prigodom-boi&catid=1:basic.

[4] Ibid., 39–40.

[5] Ibid., 20.

[6] "Diary", July 1, 2016.

[7] Michael D. O'Brien, *Island of the World* (San Francisco: Ignatius Press, 2007); the Croatian translation was published in 2012.

[8] Damir Borovčak, "Osvrt na knjigu: Michael D. O'Brien—Otok svijeta", *Portal Hrvatskoga Kulturnog Vijeća*, last updated August 26, 2008, www.hkv.hr/kultura/osvrti-kultura/3073-osvrt-na-knjigu-michael-d-obrien-otok-svijeta.html.

[9] Treći Dan has continued to translate Michael's nonfiction work, mainly collections of his essays and smaller stories, originally published by Justin Press in Ottawa. They have also published his novel *Theophilos*.

[10] In 2006, *Father Elijah* was published in Spanish and Italian; in 2008, in French, German, and Swedish; in 2009, in Polish; and in 2012, in Hungarian and Slovenian. A translation is also set to appear in Portuguese. However, Michael O'Brien has received reader correspondence from parts of Asia and Africa; the letters are from English readers on those continents.

[11] Catholic World News, "Italy Now Only Half-Catholic, Poll Says", CatholicCulture.org, April 1, 2016, www.catholicculture.org/news/headlines/index.cfm?storyid=27955.

[12] "Solo la Metà Degli Italiani Si Dichiara Cattolica", *Giornale.it*, last updated March 30, 2016, www.giornale.it/2016/03/30/solo-la-meta-degli-italiani-si-dichiara-cattolica.

[13] There is a large scholarly debate on secularization, which for three decades now has tried to come to terms with signs of religious revitalization; but for a forceful articulation of the classical secularization thesis, see Steve Bruce, *Secularization: In Defence of an Unfashionable Theory* (Oxford: Oxford University Press, 2011).

[14] "Demographic Indicators", Italian National Institute of Statistics, February 12, 2015, http://www.istat.it/en/archive/149007. Francesco C. Billari, "Lowest-Low Fertility in Europe: Exploring the Causes and Finding Some Surprises", *Japanese Journal of Population* 6, no. 1 (March 2008): 2–18.

[15] Eugenio Corti and Peter Edward Levy, *Few Returned: Twenty-Eight Days on the Russian Front, Winter 1942–1943*, trans. Carlo W. D'Este (Columbia, MO: University of Missouri, 1997).

[16] "Eugenio Corti", *Cathopedia*, last updated December 31, 2014, http://it.cathopedia.org/wiki/Eugenio_Corti.

[17] In English as *The Red Horse* (San Francisco: Ignatius Press, 2011).

[18] Eugenio Corti, *Il fumo nel tempio* (Milano: Ares, 1996).

[19] The address of her website is http://carine.poutous.free.fr.

[20] Carine Rabier-Poutous' biography was published as *Une Soif de Plénitude, D'HEC à Mère Teresa* (Paris: MédiasPaul, 2015).

[21] Astrid De Larminat, "Michael D. O'Brien, un prophète venu du Canada", *Le Figaro*, November 15, 2012: "O'Brien désarme les préjugés. Il n'est pas un catholique excité, revendicatif, sur la défensive ou moralisateur. Son visage est comme évidé par les combats. Il est empreint de gravité et de douceur, d'une force intérieure paisible qui ne s'impose pas, mais invite au dialogue. Certainement pas fanatique, peut-être prophétique, voilà en tout cas un écrivain dont les romans rendent intelligent, font appel au meilleur de soi et invitent à voir plus loin que le bout de son nez."

Epilogue

[1] Ross Douthat, "A Crisis of Conservative Catholicism", *First Things*, January 2016, www.firstthings.com/article/2016/01/a-crisis-of-conservative-catholicism.

[2] George Weigel, *Evangelical Catholicism: Deep Reform in the 21st-Century Church* (New York: Basic Books, 2013), 3.

[3] Pope Francis, apostolic exhortation *Evangelii Gaudium* (November 24, 2013), no. 43, http://w2.vatican.va/content/francesco/en/apost_exhortations/documents/papa-francesco_esortazione-ap_20131124_evangelii-gaudium.html.

[4] Michael D. O'Brien, "The Family and Totalitarianism", *Inside the Vatican*, December 2015.

[5] Michael D. O'Brien, "Inner Locutions" (unpublished manuscript describing mystical experiences from 1976 to 2006, written September 28, 2006), Microsoft Word file.